Canada and the New World Order

Facing the New Millennium

Edited by

MICHAEL J. TUCKER
RAYMOND B. BLAKE
P.E. BRYDEN

Centre for Canadian Studies
Mount Allison University

 IRWIN
PUBLISHING

Canadian Cataloguing in Publication Data

Main entry under title:

Canada and the new world order : facing the new millennium

Includes some text in French.
ISBN: 0-7725-2827-6

1. Canada — Foreign relations — 1945-   . I. Bryden, P.E. II. Blake, Raymond B. (Raymond Benjamin).   III. Tucker, Michael, J. 1943-   .

FC635.C35 2000   327.71   C00-930429.0
F1034.2.C283 2000

Design by: Linda Mackey
Cover photo: AP/Wide World Photos

Published by
Irwin Publishing Ltd.,
325 Humber College Blvd.,
Toronto, Ontario
M9W 7C3

1 2 3 4 5   04 03 02 01 00

Printed and bound in Canada.

COVER PHOTO: A Canadian soldier from the Pioneer Platoon of the Royal Regiment stands near the bridge dividing the Kosovo city of Kosovska Mitrovica.

Contents

Introduction

There is probably nothing magical about the arrival of new millennia. No wand was waved at midnight, January 1, 2000, to dramatically transform the behaviour of nations, Canada included. This does not preclude the possibility of very nasty surprises come the new millennium, amongst which prophets of doom might include global economic depression or, currently less likely, nuclear war. International cataclysms, while seldom of such magnitude, have habitually caught even the most perceptive of foreign policy planners well off guard. Still, come the new millennium, the likelihood is that continuity will prevail over dramatic change in Canada's approaches to world order.

Given this, it follows that the importance of the approaching new millennium must be seen to lie not so much in what it portends but in what it demands. For students of foreign policy, Canadians included, the impending millennium should compel a stocktaking of past practices in the statecraft of their respective polities. For a world in which the past is often prologue, this is a minimum prerequisite for trying to understand the future, much less hoping to cope with it. Appropriately then, this study in "Canada and the New World Order: Facing the New Millennium" is less an exercise in predicting the future than in critically analyzing the past.

Essentially this was the challenge that the editors of this volume set for its contributors when they met at a conference at the Centre for Canadian Studies at Mount Allison University in Sackville, New Brunswick in, April, 1998. Theirs was not an enviable task because the past is at best only marginally more knowable than the future. Drawn as the contributors were from the sometimes disparate disciplines of economics, English, history, political science, and sociology, and from the professions of journalism and public service, the perspectives on the past (and thus the future) that are shared in this volume naturally differ somewhat. Importantly though, common themes and points of understanding do emerge. This is partly because the contributors are all Canadianists, sharing not just a knowledge of Canada but also a sense that this country does have traditions, interests, and, above all perhaps, values that should be reflected in how Canada interacts with the international community.

With elegant realism Denis Stairs, in his introductory chapter on "Canada and the New World Order," provides context for the study as a whole. This derives not from any imagined new world order that might emerge with the year 2000 but, rather, from the passing of an old world order and its "ominous rattling of nuclear sabres"—the Cold War. The proposition that the antecedents of world order (or the lack thereof) in the new millennium are to be found in the post–Cold War era of the past decade is a theme that helps unite many of the essays in this volume. Another is that the post–Cold War era would witness the fostering of two powerful and contending forces that, following commentators on world politics, we might well dub ethnocentric nationalism and geocentric transnationalism.

Rooted in culture, ethnicity, and tribalism, ethnocentric nationalism helps to explain many of the bloody intrastate wars and their consequent atrocities that have marred the post–Cold War era. Nowhere perhaps has this phenomenon been more strikingly apparent than in Kosovo today. Geocentric transnationalism by contrast captures a rather diffuse mix of economic, environmental, social, and technological forces that, for good or ill, are pulling people away from the Westphalian nation-state that has served as their chief unit of security for the past four hundred years. That foreign policymakers in Canada (as elsewhere) have during the past decade shown themselves ill-prepared to cope with these contending forces is a third theme to be found in many of the volume's essays. A fourth is that Canadian foreign policymakers will have to begin to learn how to cope more effectively with these forces in the coming new millennium. If in markedly different ways, they may soon pose a formidable challenge to Canadian security.

Some, perhaps many, of the forces of transnationalism, as Denis Stairs points out, "lie far beyond the capacity of even the most powerful states to regulate." This may be especially true of the various forces of the global economy, nurtured, Stairs writes, "by electronic communications, modern modes of transport, and the development of the so-called information society.... This is the globalization of the market, of the right, of economic and professional establishments, of the epistemic communities of capitalism. But parallel to it, though trailing slightly behind," Stairs adds, "is the globalization of the culture of service—a globalization, that is, of the left, of what cognoscenti have come to call 'civil society." Transnational agendas have called forth transnational non-governmental organizations, or NGOs (non-governmental organizations)."

Scholars and practitioners on the military side to Canadian security policy have of late focused chiefly on the "new" threats posed by the sundry and brutish manifestations of ethnocentric nationalism. No consensus emerges from the contributions to this volume that touch on this theme, either as to the intensity of these threats or how they may impact upon Canada's security. Still, these essays address the problem of rampant internecine violence in rather poignant terms, and point to the reflexive commitment of Canadian security policymakers to try to help manage this violence simply in order to save lives.

This commitment, occasioned in particular by the suffering that post–Cold War intrastate conflicts have wrought upon civilian populations, has emerged as the policy of "human security." And as policy, the concept of human security has struck a responsive ethical chord amongst Canadians as a whole, especially at the level of non-governmental organizations. But nation-states, concerned chiefly and inevitably with their own national security, cannot adequately cope with many of the threats to human security. It is the transnational nature of these threats that, as Denis Stairs explains, has heightened the influence of transnational NGOs concerned with security issues.

While noble in intent, however, the policy of human security may also have spawned, in Stairs' words, a new "morality gap" in Canadian security calculations paralleling the "commitment-capability" gap that characterized Canada's over-extended alliance commitments of the Cold War era. The policy, as some of the contributors to Canada and the New World Order intimate, may have helped raise hopes and expectations in Canada and, more sadly, in war-torn societies themselves, that cannot be fulfilled.

Like its partner states in this effort, Canada has tried to help war-torn societies through military perhaps more than through diplomatic and other means, even where military means may well not have been the most effective. And Canada has chosen to focus on military solutions to pressing world problems at a time when, after the Cold War, it has exhibited profound uncertainty about the most appropriate role of the military in Canadian security policy. It may be ironic that no sooner had the problem of intrastate violence intensified with the end of the Cold War than Canadian policymakers, mandated to provide their public with peace dividends accrued partly from budgetary restrictions in Canada's security policy bureaucracies, set about paring the military resources by which Canada might have been able to help a troubled world more. Consequently, in its well-intentioned efforts to strengthen human security worldwide, Canada has at times failed to heed the realist maxim that foreign policy must be guided chiefly by calculations of national interest more than ethical prescriptions, and that the national interest must be defined in terms of the limits to national power.

Implicitly or explicitly these points emerge in this volume as a stern critique of current and probable future directions in Canadian security policy. While not the conscious design of the editors, this critique would focus almost inevitably on Canada as a peacekeeper. Peacekeeping and Canada's involvement therein thus emerge as central issues in many of the essays on military security. This reflects, of course, the very salience of peacekeeping in post-1945 Canadian security policy. But it also reflects a more troubling tendency on Canada's part to try to help achieve human security in a post–Cold War world perhaps largely through the mechanism of peacekeeping. As a leitmotif of Canada's policy of human security, peacekeeping has become a highly elastic concept. But it has also become rather mischievous.

In origin, peacekeeping was an instrument of Cold War diplomacy. Its chief object was to prevent local or "brush fire" wars from escalating and embroiling the Cold War nuclear adversaries—preventative diplomacy in essence. The means was the interposition of soldiers, usually under the banner of the United Nations, to keep the peace between the professional armies of interstate combatants. This role suited Canada, acting as part of an international "fire brigade" with other like-minded moderate middle powers. But, as Louis Delvoie and other contributors remind us, the Cold War policy rationale for peacekeeping has passed into history; so too, it seems, has the nature of the conflicts into which Cold War peacekeepers were sent.

Increasingly over the past decade peacekeepers have been asked to keep the peace not just Cold War–style between the professional armies of interstate combatants, but between guerrilla armies and their child-soldiers caught in the maelstrom of intractable civil wars. The dilemma, however, has not only been that professional soldiers in blue berets could not really "know" much less understand the combatants that they have faced. The dilemma, more fundamentally, has been the marked absence of any real peace to be kept.

In the absence of peace, however, or even the likelihood of civil war protagonists agreeing to peace terms, peacekeeping has not been jettisoned. Rather, the tasks confronting peacekeepers in the post–Cold War era have been broadened to encompass the ill-defined missions of "humanitarian intervention" and "peace enforcement." The former aspires to the reconstruction of war-torn societies, and the latter to finding peace by making war. Yet recent experience signifies that both middle-power and great-power peacekeepers are both ill-equipped and ill-trained for such missions, especially where they have no clear military rules of engagement. Still, where such missions have manifestly failed, as in Somalia, it has been the professionalism of the armed forces of peacekeeping countries that has been found wanting, not peacekeeping broadly conceived.

One of the contributors to this collection, Peter Desbarats, was clearly profoundly influenced by his role as commissioner on the inquiry into the role of the Canadian military in Somalia. In a thoughtful and deeply personal essay, Desbarats reflects on the lessons learned as a result of the aborted inquiry. Not only did he emerge from the months of testimony with a deep belief in the mismanagement of the Canadian military and a commitment to rethinking our international responsibilities on the eve of the millennium, but he also gained some insight into the domestic political situation. When the inquiry was unceremoniously ended before all the evidence had been heard, Desbarats clearly lost faith with Canada's politicians and identified problems that, upon reflection, have long existed. If Canada is to move with confidence into the millennium and onto the world stage, he argues, there has to be a renewed commitment to political accountability, and a real recognition that government is not only the servant of the public but also the reflection of our national experience and national values. That reflection, Desbarats argues, is a poor one in the wake of the Somalia affair, and immediate steps must be taken to clean it up.

Not surprisingly, the United Nations' recent forays into war-torn countries have provoked a heated debate over peacekeeping, especially in Canada where it has played such an important role in its foreign policy. J.L. Granatstein has written widely on Canada's role in peacekeeping and was among the first in this country to question our involvement in some of the UN's initiatives. In his contribution to this volume, he offers an analysis of what's wrong with it and suggests what he terms a "realistic agenda" for improving it. He suggests that in the past few years, there has emerged definitional confusion between peacekeeping, peace enforcement, and peacebuilding, which has put those soldiers involved at considerable risk. If casualties increase because the UN's role is not entirely clear, he wonders if countries such as Canada would be eager to participate in such missions? Because the task facing the UN is often peacemaking, the United States and other larger powers are increasingly expected to play a larger role and this sometimes means that these countries become involved only when it is in their interest to do so. He uses the Gulf War as an example. Moreover, Granatstein suggests that the UN has been ill-prepared for too many of its missions and that has been costly to several nations as well as to the reputation of the UN itself. And, of course, many of the soldiers sent to the war-torn areas are poorly equipped and poorly trained; some of them are simply racists, he suggests. As a result, he concludes that peacekeeping has not worked as effectively as it ought to.

However, he offers several practical suggestions to improve peacekeeping. First, peacekeepers need a clear mandate; they must know the rules of engagement before they are despatched to a war zone. Moreover, they must be impartial and uphold international law. Despite the growing influence of NGOs, Granatstein makes it quite clear that they should not be involved in peacekeeping efforts. However, regional organizations such as the Organization of African Unity must play an important role. They are usually more cost-effective and often less racist. Finally, he suggests that it is imperative that Canada and other nations work to develop rapid reaction forces to respond immediately to crises. That, he suggests, is what Canada's department of foreign affairs and international trade should be working toward.

It is in this vein that Louis Delvoie decries the absence of clear policy rationales in current Canadian approaches to peacekeeping. He provides a rather trenchant analysis of the Cold War rationales for peacekeeping, and for Canada's involvement therein. And he provides a useful typology of post–Cold War peacekeeping operations that includes traditional monitoring of ceasefires and troop redeployments, the reconstruction of states devastated by war, and humanitarian missions in aid of threatened civilian populations. Where Delvoie can see the rationales for Canadian involvement in Cambodia, Nicaragua, Namibia, Angola, and Afghanistan, he finds that the missions in the Former Yugoslavia and Haiti are more problematic from this standpoint. But it is the missions to Somalia, Rwanda, and Zaire that defy rationality, and thus impel in-depth critical analysis. These missions, Delvoie finds, raise more questions than can be satisfactorily answered. Were these, he asks, prime examples of "mission creep," or "selective interventionism"?

Michael Bonser and Marshall Conley also consider peacekeeping but they go much further than J.L. Granatstein and argue that traditional peacekeeping methods and military solutions alone are not enough to solve the conflicts in which the UN has recently become involved. Instead, they suggest that the UN must "embrace the concept of peacebuilding as a means of addressing the underlying economic, social, and political causes of conflict." They argue effectively that the UN efforts to avoid many of the conflicts produced in nationalistic, ethnic, and religious tensions must focus on such issues as human rights and freedoms, the rule of law, good governance, social equity, and sustainable development if it hopes to build lasting peace in countries ravaged by war. And, in their analysis, Canada can and must play a leadership role in the concept of peacebuilding.

Bonser and Conley argue that historically Canada has been innovative in developing the UN's peacekeeping role. It was a role that Canada played well and it's clearly served its own national interests. The UN remains the most important and effective avenue for Canada's continued participation in world affairs, they maintain, and, given the respect for Canada in the UN, its policymakers are among those best suited to promote the UN's acceptance of the concept of peacebuilding. However, given the current resource and financial restraints that face the UN, its members will have to become more generous in their political will and practical support if it is to carry out peacebuilding initiatives effectively.

Even so, a few nations, including Canada, are making that commitment to peacebuilding at the international level. Foreign Minister Lloyd Axworthy has embraced the concept of peacebuilding and established the Canadian Peacebuilding Initiative, which together with the Lester B. Pearson Peacekeeping Centre in Nova Scotia and Canada's promotion of anti-personnel landmines, indicate Canada's commitment to the process of moving away from simple peacekeeping. However, Bonser and Conley suggest Canada must do more. As just one example, they recommend that the UN follow through on Axworthy's call for significant structural reform to modernize its existing institutions. Canada's recent initiatives, they conclude, demonstrates its growing interest in and commitment to the concept of peacebuilding, and as a nation that benefits greater from its role in the UN, it can and must assume a leadership role.

In an examination of another international organization to which Canada has been a party since its inception, Dean F. Oliver offers a view that contrasts quite dramatically to that offered by Bonser and Conley. In assessing Canada's role in the North Atlantic Treaty Organization, Oliver finds Axworthy's insistence on significant structural reform of our international commitments a serious attack on the historic legitimacy of NATO as primarily a defence organization that demands military commitments from its member countries. While officials at the Department of Foreign Affairs and International Trade maintain that Canada is merely in the process of redefining our role in the post–Cold War international community, Oliver maintains that we are drifting away from commitments already made. Far from moving toward a new world order in which collective security becomes unnecessary and broader issues of economic and political associations are deemed more important, mounting evidence from eastern Europe and elsewhere suggests that the Cold War's end merely repositioned defence needs rather than eliminating them. Moreover, the current emphasis on Canada's role in international organizations as one of establishing "cooperative security" is little more than a camouflage, Oliver argues, for significant military retrenchment and a dramatic shift in security policy. If Canadian foreign policy strategists insist on pursuing the new objective of "cooperative security," Canada's already uncertain role in NATO will be even further undermined, as will Canada's presence within the global community more generally.

Similarly shrewd observations on the gaps in our security policy are provided by David B. Dewitt. Dewitt explores possible future directions in that policy, where Canada shifts "from a marginal actor at the centre to a central actor at the margins."Continued marginalization, he finds, may well ultimately derive from Canada's inability to frame "an overall strategic view" of its place in a post–Cold War world. But it has been fostered in a post–Cold War world by distant external conflicts that have impelled Canadian peacekeeping missions and by more direct threats to Canadian interests such as the fishery, for instance, but which have not engaged strictly military or "national defence" concerns. Thus it is, Dewitt writes, that the "idea of national defence seems to be of decreasing relevance to most Canadians".

Concepts of international security that embrace para and non-military threats will remain vital as we approach the millennium and, while these threats may remain marginal to Canadian national defence, they may well also continue to beg imaginative as well as constructive Canadian approaches to security dilemmas. But in addition, because military conflict will remain very much with us in a "world of war and peace," Canada will need to bring its commitments more in line with its military capabilities as the basis for a more effective security policy. Dewitt argues persuasively that what is needed is a strategic basis for Canada's security policy, that will provide a clearer sense of the missions, training, and equipment that will be appropriate and necessary for Canada's military in the turbulent years ahead.

As officials with the Department of Foreign Affairs and International Trade wrestle with the question of how much we should redefine our membership in traditional defence organizations, others grapple with establishing international alliances outside the parameters of security-based associations. Thus, the question of Canada's role in establishing global coherence in the new millennium extends far beyond the question of international security, as Ken Coates makes clear in his important article on "Indigenous Rights in Canada: An International Perspective." He shows that while there is a tendency to approach issues of natives rights from a domestic perspective, focusing on such things as treaties and land-claims and the right to self-government, from a different perspective "the indigenous rights movement is, ironically, less indigenous than Canadians typically assume." Although the Canadian experience followed a distinctive course, it did not do so entirely separate from the experiences of indigenous peoples elsewhere in the world. Patterns of protest and resistance to continued incursions into indigenous territory have been international phenomena but, Coates argues, normally viewed within the context of a particular national experience. In the years following World War II, however, as internationalist associations gained credibility and strategies for assimilating indigenous peoples fell into disfavour, indigenous cultures are gradually being "reconceptualized" in a global perspective. As Coates shows, the processes of globalization "have more recently provided both the technical capacity, organizational contexts, and the reassessment of Western/industrial values necessary for indigenous groups to reach beyond their hereditary boundaries in the defence of their life-ways." The global village of the new millennium has important implications for the course of indigenous rights, a topic to which Coates turns his scholarly attention in the essay included in this collection.

While most of the contributors to this volume have been concerned with the strategic, economic, and political interplay of Canada with the international community, Frances W. Kaye examines the interplay of international and global cultures. Using the arts of the Western Canada as a case study, she concludes that Canada—and much of the interior of North America, in fact—have been involved in a complex international arts dialogue that have had a profound impact upon indigenous culture and that of settler societies, which supplanted the earlier peoples. This study, like Ken Coates' on indigenous rights in Canada, provides a fine example of how cross-border or transnational contacts amongst people have deeply enriched both culture and human understanding. Disappearing national boundaries are a challenge to the sovereignty of Canada as it faces the new millennium. But, by enriching human contacts, disappearing boundaries may also help to strengthen

Canada's security. Kaye also suggests that Canada has a long tradition of internationalism within its own borders, and it is perhaps not surprisingly, that people such as Lester B. Pearson, one of Canada's best known and successful diplomats, assumed a leadership role in the creation of international bodies after the Second World War.

Canada's participation in a somewhat smaller continental village, on the other hand, has traditionally been exercised in the field of economic relations, and these North American agreements have often paved the way for broader international commitments in a variety of fields. One of the first steps that Canada took toward active participation in the global economy was to enter into freer trade arrangements with the United States, which has historically been Canada's most sought-after and most important trading partner. The decade-old trade alliance between the two countries is the Free Trade Agreement, a coup for the Mulroney government and a continuing source of angst for others dedicated to reducing rather than increasing the Canadian dependence on the United States. George J. De Benedetti directs his attention to an anniversary assessment of the effects of the FTA. He judges the agreement within the context of the problem it was designed to address, paying particular attention to its effects on the economies of various regions in Canada. Clearly, Canada's participation in the global economy cannot be achieved without a price, although De Benedetti refrains from assessing whether the price is too high.

The volume concludes with two articles on the impact of the changing world order on two of Canada's provinces: New Brunswick and Quebec. Louis Bélanger argues that the changes that are occurring in the international environment are having a profound impact on Quebec's desire for a distinct political identity abroad. After examining Quebec's recent involvement with La Francophonie and with Mexico and the United States, he concludes that Quebec is having considerable difficulty in getting the established nation-states to accept a larger international role for Quebec. He attributes this largely to the growing conservatism among the international community, particularly in North America, where there is little support for internal particularisms. Moreover, the established interstate order is fearful of the unknown and the potential problems created by the dismantling of multi-ethnic countries; rather, it would prefer to work toward solidifying the existing world order rather than trying to deal with the creation of new states. Even within La Francophonie there is a growing preference for state-to-state interaction rather than allowing French-speaking communities in countries like Canada greater participation in the organization. As for the impact of those changes in the new world order on the legitimization of Quebec's sovereign project, Bélanger offers a qualified response.

Chedly Belkhodja offers an intrastate comparative dimension when he examines the relations between the provinces of Quebec and New Brunswick regarding their involvement in La Francophonie. He suggests that historically there has been considerable tension between the two over their participation in the organization. Equally important, he argues, the behaviour of the two provinces has been influenced by the consideration of the dynamics of both globalization and fragmentation and, in his analysis, New Brunswick has been able to distance itself from the tensions within La Francophonie by emphasizing its economic interests rather than becoming embroiled in the enduring debate as Quebec has over its status on the international scene.

The essays in this volume not only provide an analysis of a wide range of subjects important to understanding Canada's role in the world but also offer much for Canadians and Canadian policymakers and political leaders to ponder. Collectively, the contributors examine and analyze various aspects of Canada's participation in the international community from peacekeeping to human security to indigenous people to international trade. That alone makes this volume an important one for those interested in the whole question of Canada's external relations. But the contributors go further here and offer practical suggestions on what Canada might do in a variety of policy areas.

The essays in this book came from a conference on Canada and World Order: Facing the Millennium organized by the Centre for Canadian Studies at Mount Allison University in Sackville, New Brunswick as part of its ongoing series of conferences on Contemporary Issues in Canada. The conference and this publication were made possible because of the continued support for Canadian Studies at Mount Allison from The Harold Crabtree Foundation. The editors would also like to acknowledge the support of the Social Sciences and Humanities Council of Canada for its grant in aid of scholarly conferences, the John Holmes Fund at the Canadian Centre for Foreign Policy Development, and the Academic Relations Office at the Department of Foreign Affairs and International Trade. At Mount Allison, Dr. Peter Ennals, Vice-president Academic, and President Dr. Ian Newbould provided valuable assistance as did Carolyn Smith, Joanne Goodrich, and the members of the Canadian Studies Students' Association.

Canada and the New World Order

DENIS STAIRS

Department of Political Science
Dalhousie University

The circumstances that we face as we approach the millennium are well known (or at least widely assumed) and the most commonly cited of them can be reduced to a series of recurrently trumpeted propositions. Some of these are blindingly obvious. Some of them are also, it must be said, a trifle vacuous. And a few of them are probably misleading, or even dead wrong. But to set a context for discussion, it may be worth our running quickly through them nonetheless.

The Context
Proposition 1: The Cold War, as we are usually (though not always) happy to observe, is dead, and its demise, for the time being at least, may have brought to an end (or so the optimists like to think) any serious prospect of our having to cope in the foreseeable future with big wars between big states—or certainly with big wars between *developed* states. The latter have discovered at last that, in the world they have engineered for themselves, big wars do not pay. Their domestic populations, moreover, show signs here and there—although not consistently and not everywhere—of having learned the same lesson, and of feeding it back as a reinforcing instruction to those by whom they are ruled.

Proposition 2: At the same time, however, the removal of the ordered discipline that came from the Cold War's bipolar structure, buttressed as it was by the ominous rattling of nuclear sabres, has made it possible for the lesser, and much older, demons of the human condition to renew their mischief. The conflicts of competing religions, cultures, and ethnicities have returned with a vengeance. Subordinated to forces larger than themselves, they had gone for a time unnoticed, while the practitioners of international politics focused on other things. But now their manifestations are as ugly and brutish as ever. They work their death and destruction not so much in wars *between* states as in wars *within* them (although they do a bit of the former, too). And the slaughters to which they lead are often lightly, if frenziedly, done—with machetes, and axes, and clubs, and handguns, and automatic rifles. The latter, it should be recalled, often originate as leftovers from the contracting armies of the greater powers. Surplus military debris, they have been recycled into black markets through the exotic, even the desperate, transactions of shadowy merchants of death.

But the slaughters, as we have all come to see, are no less deadly for being delivered by primitive instruments. Nor does it help the cause of proportionality—the cause that is, of bringing at least some measure of reason to the matching of practical means to political ends—that the killings themselves are so often executed by mindless adolescents, by role-playing youngsters whose childish motives would in Canada place them immediately under the protection of the *Young Offenders Act.*

Proposition 3: Notwithstanding these displays of darkness in the heart, or perhaps in part because of them, there is abroad the further observation that the threats to our welfare as a species have been greatly multiplied in our own time by modernity itself. The list is familiar enough. Among its more prominent and persistent components are "basket case" poverty in the non-developing world; famine, torture, and pandemically infectious disease; environmental decay; the depletion of resources; the diffusion of weapons, some of them conventional and some not, among the disorganized, the excited, and the aggrieved; the ruthless exploitation of women and children for purposes of work and pleasure alike; and the sundry predations of prejudice, superstition, and autocratic rule. In some parts of the world—certainly in our *own* parts of the world—we think we can see progress in the human condition. The Whigs are winning. But elsewhere the horsemen of the Apocalypse are multiplying, and some of them brandish their spears at our own gates.

In what measure, of course, these phenomena are really new, and to what extent they are *really* "products of modernity," are debatable questions. That so many of us seem to *think* of them as novel may be a reflection more of our own rising expectations than of real changes in the real world. We have come increasingly, after all, to the conviction that we need no longer automatically accept, as our ancestors routinely did, the catastrophes that the hand of Fate delivers. We think instead that we can fix them, or even prevent them.

Our new sense of new perils may reflect, as well, the McLuhanesque impact of electronic media, which have extended our awareness of the world around us to places that lie far beyond the communities we actually inhabit. Not all the threats we see are "new." They are simply "in our face." In any case, there are many threats—selected medical threats among them—that have actually *declined* in modern times, and they have done so not least of all because of modern technique.

But all such caveats aside, a few of the dangers that we now confront do seem to have become worse, or if not worse, then at least more urgent in our own time, and we have therefore advanced their placement on our priorities list.

Proposition 4: Superimposed on these sombre realities are the phenomena that we have come to describe in the vague vocabulary of "globalization." For some, this development has aggravated the challenges before us. This is partly because it has placed so many of the vehicles through which our wealth is produced and distributed into a realm of transnational forces that lie far beyond the capacity of even the most powerful states to regulate, and thereby to render reasonably benign. It is also because it has created a systemically interlocked world in which things that happen up close are caused by things that happen far away. Corner-cutters in the banks of Tokyo cause unemployment in British Columbia. Tree-cutters in Brazil cause skin cancer in Ontario.

But for others, the phenomenon of globalization is the harbinger of a *Nirvana* to come. It will generate more wealth. It will lead to a sharing of more values. It will create a commonality of more interests. Ultimately it will produce a world of liker minds. Those who think together work together, play together. They may even go to war together—but not against one another. Here is a bright future. The greater powers have seen the light. So have many of the smaller powers. It remains only to bring the other powers on side, and then to complete the task of making the vision real.[1]

Proposition 5: The term "globalization" is normally taken to refer to the workings of the global economy, as nurtured by electronic communications, modern modes of transport, and the development of the so-called information society, together with its profit-seeking offshoots, the knowledge-based industries. This is the globalization of the market, of the right, of economic and professional establishments, of the epistemic communities of capitalism. But parallel to it, though trailing slightly behind, is a globalization of the culture of service—a globalization, that is, of the left, of what *cognoscenti* have come to call "civil society." Transnational agendas have called forth transnational non-governmental organizations, or NGOs. For some, this is still a weak and dependent thing, a discordant assemblage of the conscientious and the willing, who must still rely on the beneficence of states and the state system for the successful pursuit not only of their objectives, but also of their overheads. For others, however, it heralds the beginning of a brave new world, a world in which the community to which we belong—and to which we acknowledge a moral obligation—is defined not by our citizenship, but by our species. The scope of our undifferentiated moral domain is thus a function of our membership in a humanity understood without reference to borders, or to the constitutional contrivances—the systems and mechanisms of state rule, together with the parochial frameworks for collective accountability that they represent—that are contained within them.

This is an eclectic array of phenomena—some good, some bad, but in any case all mixed up together. It should not be surprising, therefore, to discover that Ottawa's array of policies in response to them has been eclectic, too, and sometimes even contradictory. Of these, also, it may be said that some are good, and some are bad, but that in any case they are all mixed up together. The response to the demise of the Cold War has been to run down the defence establishment in order to help balance the budget and spend money on other things. The response to the resurgence of the "old demons" is to commit ourselves to modest military interventions in all sorts of places in which we have no direct national interest, and precisely *because* of the defence run-downs, to do so without the resources that are required to perform the task, with reasonable safety, reasonably well. The response to the arrival of the new perils, or at least of our new perceptions of them, is to include every one of them in our official conception of what our common security requires, and to promise accordingly to take a leadership role in dealing with them all.[2] The response to globalization is to celebrate and encourage it on the one hand, while fussing a little about the company it puts us in overseas on the other.[3] And the response to civil society is to keep it at a safe distance with the right hand (the hand that operates, for example, in the *economic* offices of the Department of Foreign Affairs and International Trade), while warmly embracing it with the left hand (the hand that operates most visibly in the office of Mr. Axworthy himself). My students are constantly disconcerted by displays of inconsistency in our foreign policy. I tell them that it is not an objective of foreign policy to be consistent; the real objective is to be effective. In the light of the evidence, after all, what *else* can I tell them?

Implications for Security Policy

These observations, it might be argued, are too short, too glib, and too flippant to be fair. That may well be true, although it would take relatively little effort to demonstrate the widespread prevalence of each of them in our public discourse were the space available to do so. In any event, the primary purpose of drawing attention to them here is to focus not so much on the merits of the argument in each case as on one or two of the implications that appear to flow from the way we are now interpreting and reacting to the external world around us. In so doing, I will say nothing more of departed Cold Wars, nor will I consider further the ambiguous consequences of globalizing economics. The latter is certainly where a lot of the action is, and some of the happy architects and engineers of our adjustment to it have enjoyed in the last decade or so a particular prominence and visibility in the federal public service (and often subsequently in the private sector, too). It may well be that their public philosophy is the emanation of a victorious capitalism at its zenith. But their tale is theirs to tell, not mine. I want therefore to concentrate instead on the *security* side of the world order agenda, and to raise some questions about our response to it.

It unveils no dark secret of state to observe that Ottawa has now come to view the problem of security as "security writ large"—as the problem, that is, of securing all of us at home, and as many as possible of our counterparts abroad, not against external military menace alone, but against the full array of perils defined above. It calls this cluster of threats, variously, the problem of *common* security, or *human* security, or *cooperative* security. In so doing, it has been responding in part to the representations that came from many of its attentive constituencies nearly four years ago during the conduct of its defence and foreign policy reviews.[4] Of the exhortations it received, the report of the Canada 21 Council was probably the most prominent.[5] It may also have been the most influential. But the change in both the conception of what "security" is and the vocabulary that we use to describe it took place against a backdrop of other inputs, the ruminations of Boutros Boutros-Ghali in his *Agenda for Peace*[6] and the communications of NGOs numbering now in the hundreds of thousands around the world not least among them.

The raw politics of vested interest aside, this amalgamating of the megathreats to human welfare under the single umbrella of "security" appears to have been driven by three factors.[7] Two of them are rooted in intellectual arguments. The third is concealed in political motivation. Of the two intellectual arguments, the first is founded in the observation that the new threats are every bit as dangerous as the old ones, the military ones. Wars can kill us in large numbers. But so, of course, can famine and disease. And a total depletion of the ozone layer could kill us all. It follows that perils of this kind warrant a priority in the attentions of government that is at least equivalent to the attention historically assigned to deterrence against military attack or to the defeat of military invasion. Security, in short, is multidimensional on its face.

The second of the intellectual arguments is rooted in the notion that the new threats are linked to the old threats by chains of cause and effect. Just as the alienations that come, for example, from poverty at home are often held to be responsible for the violence in our own cities, so the desperation and despair that come from hunger, or underdevelopment, or political oppression abroad are thought to be the progenitors of violence in the world at large. Radical politics feeds on misery, and war is radical politics. Dealing with it effectively thus requires (or so the argument goes) an attack, not on symptoms alone, but on the underlying causes as well. It also requires acting in support of the peace *before* it is broken, and *after* it is broken, and not merely *while* it is broken. Promoting economic development, therefore, is security policy. Encouraging democracy is security policy. So is nurturing the environment, or conserving resources. Whether these presumptions are "true"— whether, that is, there is *really* a cause-and-effect linkage between, say, a democratic politics and a pacific foreign policy—is a question that academic specialists still find reason in almost every case to debate. But that does not matter. What does matter is that the argument has a surface plausibility. It is this that gives it persuasive power.

The third factor underlying the campaign for a broader conception of "security" has been a trifle more self-serving. It has not, therefore, been much given to public advertisement. Specifically, it has been rooted in the desire of those who support the broader conception of what security requires to accomplish two interconnected objectives: first, to establish for the issues they hold dear an importance equivalent to the one traditionally associated with national defence, and second, to ensure, in consequence, that the financial resources that are freed up by the downgrading of traditional defence expenditures will accrue to their own policies of choice, rather than to some other public purpose. Spending money on development assistance is much easier to sell as a source of security—as "defence by other means"—than as a simple act of collective compassion.

The Intrusions of the NGOs

At first glance, it might be argued that none of these conceptual transformations really matters very much. We are dealing, after all, with little more than an artificial construct, a way of looking at things, a conceptual fabrication of the mind. As long as no one gets too caught up in the notion that controlling the atmospheric excretions of refrigerators and pressure cans is part and parcel of the problem of managing the army, we can probably live in reasonable comfort with our new analytical vocabulary for such time as it is firmly buttressed by political or academic fashion.

But there has been a political offshoot—a political handmaiden—of the new way of looking at things which is also worth noting. It is reflected in the massive intrusion of transnational NGOs into the politics of the foreign policy process. These, as indicated earlier, are the "civil society" embodiments of a globalized "culture of service." Their appearance is not a new development. There have been lots of antecedents, some of them going back to the interwar period and before. But the NGOs themselves are vastly more numerous than they ever were before. On Boutros Boutros-Ghali's own testimony, France alone registered 54,000 new associations between 1987 and 1996. In Italy, the number of such associations increased by 40 percent in the decade and a half between 1980 and 1995. Even Bangladesh has acquired 10,000 of them, the Philippines 21,000, and Chile 27,000.[8] A Canadian count would doubtless demonstrate a similar pattern. It would hardly be surprising if public servants in CIDA were beginning to argue in favour of some sort of organizational birth control!

However that may be, what is particularly interesting about the NGOs is that they are predominantly concerned with what might be described as "international public goods," as opposed to "interests" or "appetites" of the purely self-serving variety. These public goods are sometimes genuinely "transnational" in character (*everyone*, presumably, will benefit from the preservation of the ozone layer), but they are often aimed, too, at the relief of political, economic, social, medical, and other miseries that are located in sovereign jurisdictions far away, miseries that frequently have no discernible impact on Canada itself. The objectives of the NGOs, in short, seem to be guided by the desire to respond, not to the wants of the self, but to the needs of "the common," where "the common" is identified not with the citizenry of any given state, but with humanity at large. Since the needs are so dire, moreover, their urgency is impossible to deny.

But in responding to them, the nation-states and the state system often seem to get in the way—to be a part of the problem, but not of the solution. In the interest of humanity, therefore, those who are the custodians of the state, no matter how constitutionally defensible the process by which they have acquired their charge, must be evaded or brought to heel. Either way, their claim to primacy—their insistence on being "sovereign," on being the "last-say" decision-makers—must be attacked, and their supreme position in the hierarchy of legitimacy subjected to challenge.

So relentless and prevalent has this argument become—and I concede that I have expressed it here in its starkest form[9]—that at least some academic analysts are beginning to think that the NGO phenomenon (a kind of countervail from the left for multinational corporations on the right) may represent the beginning of the end of the Westphalian state system. Certainly some of the NGOs themselves appear to think so, and to hope so. The implication is that we are witnessing a transition to a new kind of international order in which the system of sovereign states will be succeeded by a considerably more diverse collection of international "regimes," presumably arranged in kaleidoscopic layers of authority, with each layer or segment differentiated from the others by the control it exercises over its particular functional domain.

But it may be premature to assume that the traditional nation-state is in such looming jeopardy. It has not yet given up, after all, its authority to "regulate" and to "enforce." More significantly, only the state has the power to tax, and with it the obligation to make the unavoidable trade-offs that the conduct of public policy requires, and hence to decide, in a world of unlimited demands and limited resources, who will get what, when, how. Since most of the problems on the contemporary security agenda will require a trifle more than a penny or two to resolve (if, in fact, they can be resolved at all), and since many of them will also involve the regulating of potential miscreants, these add up to pretty impressive assets.

But when all this is said and done, the voices of the NGO community are becoming increasingly difficult for governments to ignore. This is hardly because they have political clout. In practice, they do not control many votes, and their resources (which often come in any case from government itself) are piddling when compared with those at the disposal of captains of multinational industry and finance. Their influence results, rather, from their having become important sources of pertinent information and expertise, and from their practical capacity to deliver programming abroad on the government's behalf in a way that the government itself cannot hope to replicate. In addition, they can sometimes be mobilized as political ammunition by sympathetic ministers, who can make constructive use of them in out-flanking public servants or cabinet colleagues whose hearts are wedded to alternative agendas.[10] There should be no great surprise, therefore, in the discovery that they are now extensively courted through the increasingly elaborate outreach mechanisms of both CIDA and the Department of Foreign Affairs and International Trade.[11]

The long-term significance of this development is not yet clear. The so-called "Ottawa process" that led to the Landmines Treaty was a spectacular example of the process at work.[12] The trouble with spectacular examples, however, is that they are frequently atypical. Certainly it would be imprudent on the basis of an extrapolation from this case alone to argue that the influence over Canadian public policy of organizations like Oxfam equates to that of the Canadian Manufacturers Association or the BCNI.

Recalcitrant Dilemmas

Nonetheless, it does appear that the expansion of the security agenda, together with the monumental growth of the politics of transnational NGOs that surrounds it, are posing some profound dilemmas for us all—dilemmas that we will not be able to duck in the early years of the coming millennium. In one way or another they impinge on many, if not most, of the issues that are examined in this volume. I have answers to none of them. But I want to consider two or three of them all the same.

Of these, the first seems to me to be in many respects the most intractable. It has to do with the state system and with the concomitant principle of state sovereignty, which many rightly see as a fundamental impediment to constructive action in response to cataclysms abroad. We are increasingly haunted by the sense that we can no longer stand idly by when confronted by foreign horror. In the first place, we feel a moral obligation to act. In the second place, we have come to assume (as I have already pointed out) that the "human security" of others is essential to our own security, too.

And so now we are driven to intervene, whereas before we would have been driven (if driven at all) to mind our own business.

The dilemma this creates is the dilemma of humanitarian intervention.[13] When the horror we witness is confined within the boundaries of another sovereign jurisdiction, on the basis of what principle and by reference to what criteria can we defend a decision, uninvited, to intrude? This, at least, is how the dilemma is conventionally portrayed, and on these terms alone it is certainly difficult enough.

But this is not where the most serious difficulty really lies. Describing the problem in these terms is to describe it, after all, from the vantage point of the sovereign entitlements *of the target state*. And we can all think of mechanisms and principles by which the entitlements of sovereignty could be trumped. The politics may be daunting. Trusteeships, after all, might have to be resurrected. Great power imperialisms might have to be invoked. Concert systems might have to be legitimized. And no one really wants to give great powers *carte blanche*.

In the long haul, however, the sensitivities of the target states seem to me to be a far less onerous obstacle than are the sensitivities of those who are tempted to intervene. This is because of the limits that apply to the willingness, or the capacity, of the interventionist governments to transfer resources from the service of their own to the service of those who are *not* their own. It is worth reminding ourselves that the central purpose of representative and responsible systems of government is to ensure that those who govern do so in the interests of the citizens over whom they preside. In the real world, there are only two ways of squaring this core premise of the liberal democratic state with the voluntary acceptance of obligations abroad. The first is to demonstrate that serving the needs of "the other" works also, in the end, to the advantage of one's own. This is precisely what those who advocate the broader conception of human security are trying to do when they insist that relieving economic or political miseries overseas is conducive in itself to the prevention of war and hence to the preservation of international peace. They sense that the argument is politically effective because they know that Canadians perceive their own interests to be best served by the maintenance of a stable international order. The second way of squaring the circle is to arouse from the citizenry at home an altruistic instruction—an insistence that the government make generous and selfless use of the taxpayers' resources abroad because that is what a reasonable number of taxpayers want it to do.

These two mechanisms, however, suffer from obvious weaknesses. In the case of the first, the problem lies with the simple fact that the cause-and-effect linkage between the *foreign* "good" and the *Canadian* "good" often cannot be persuasively demonstrated. In the case of the second, it lies partly with the fact that, in politics, a little charity goes a long way and begins in any case at home, and partly with the fact that those who are the most eager to ensure that Canada is routinely generous in its support of good causes overseas may not be the ones who have to pay the price. Academics in Toronto, or even editorial writers at the *Globe and Mail*, can comfortably advocate the introduction of economic sanctions against China in defence of human rights in the happy conviction that their motives are pure, their purposes just; but it may be employees of Northern Telecom who end up carrying both the policy and such display of virtue as it may represent by losing their jobs.

It might be said of all this that it makes too much of too little, and that Canada has ambled along quite nicely in the postwar period with reasonably proportioned programs of development assistance, a series of constructive (or at least constructively intended) deployments of peacekeeping units abroad, a solid and consistent demonstration of support for the institutionalization of the international environment, and sundry other manifestations of responsible internationalism at work. And there is at least cosmetic truth in this. But the hard reality is that the price has been very small. By contrast, the agenda we are now contemplating, *if taken seriously*, would require expenditures well beyond anything Canada (or any other contributing state) has been prepared to contemplate thus far. It is a sobering thought, moreover, that the rhetoric of Ottawa's commitment to the amelioration of the manifold miseries of populations outside its own jurisdiction has intensified at a time when its actual expenditures on overseas programming of all sorts have been dramatically reduced.

I do not make this comment to be critical. I make it only to emphasize what I think is a rapidly accelerating "morality gap"—a gap between what we define as a responsible international security agenda for Canada on the one hand, and our real political and moral will to respond to it on the other. The gap is not peculiar to the Canadian case, although our growing disposition to Phariseean moralizing sometimes makes it appear a little worse in the Canadian context. But whether the gap is currently so widespread a phenomenon as I think or not, the task of closing it may well turn out to be one of the most complex of the political and institutional challenges that will confront us in the twenty-first century.

This problem, it seems to me, is complicated and compounded by another. For there is a sense in which the human security agenda, as we have now come to define it, is a latter-day product of the Enlightenment. It rests on a natural law premise—on the tacit premise, in fact, of all of the social sciences. Not to put too fine a point on it, it reflects our belief in social engineering. We think that dealing with most of the problems before us is a simple matter of combining resources with technique. Amazingly, we also seem to think that we can deal with them *quickly*. We assume, therefore, that we know how to make economies grow. The targets only have to follow the rules—*our* rules. We know how to make political communities democratic. The targets only have to set up the right institutions. We know how to establish the rule of law. The targets only have to let us train their police forces in Regina.

I exaggerate, of course, but not so grievously as to impoverish the point. For the fact of the matter is that we know surprisingly *little* of these things, and what we *do* know tells us that such notions are nonsense. Any second-year student in political science understands, for example, that if democratic institutions are established in a divided community without its inhabitants also being committed to a liberal political culture and to the principle of minority rights, there is a good chance that a ruthless tyranny of the majority will ensue. The logic is simple, and it has had a long and bloody history of practical expression. As manifested in the real world of politics, it goes like this:

"We're the majority.
"You're the minority.
"We've won.
"You've lost.
"Bang, bang.
"You're dead!"

Similarly, any first-year student in criminology can predict with confidence that if abusive policemen are given a knowledge of computers without the environment within which they operate having been appropriately transformed—transformed, that is, politically, economically, socially, and culturally—all that will ensue is a more efficient system for delivering police abuse. The problem, in short, with all such essays in "uneven development" is that they rearrange the internal distribution of power. The consequences are sometimes for the better, sometimes for the worse, but, in both cases, almost always unanticipated.

The two students, one in political science and one in criminology, would both quickly agree, moreover, that the adjustments that would have been missing in these not-so-hypothetical examples are by far the most difficult of adjustments to engineer. Indeed, it may not be possible to engineer them at all.

The point here, once again, is not to fire a cheap shot, or to make "the best the enemy of the good." The point is simply to emphasize that many of the items on our new "human security" agenda require, at the least, a commitment over the very long haul, and at most a capacity for social engineering that we may not in fact possess. This, too, is a reality with which we will have to cope in the twenty-first century.

Modest Suggestions

I said earlier on that I had no solutions to these dilemmas, or to others like them. I take this now to be obvious. In the grey light of such gloomy prognostications, can I say anything constructive at all? Probably not.

But I do have some modest suggestions. These may appear more Presbyterian in tone than Methodist, and this may be unkind to our current foreign policy, since it seems to be going through a distinctly Methodist phase. But there is probably little chance of their being taken seriously, and in any case they are too general to pose much threat to policymakers on the front line. I offer them, therefore, with little fear of significant retribution.

First: In none of these areas can it be said that there are either *simple* solutions, or *single* solutions. If progress is made, it will be made, as usual, by erratic combinations of careful foresight on the one hand, and reactive muddling through on the other. And the "feedback"—the lessons learned—will be gained most commonly through the expensive process of trial and error. It is the accumulation of small initiatives, many of them in response to accident, by a variety of actors working in a multiplicity of different areas over a very long period of time that will make the difference. Grand designs and visionary blueprints will not work, and in the end are likely to do far more harm than good. Progress in the human condition is like discovery in science: it is mostly serendipitous.

Second: In none of these areas, either, can Canada accomplish very much alone. It will have to work, as always, in coalition with others. With the Cold War gone, the coalitions within which it plays a part can now have a more varied composition, and where required they can, and almost certainly will, include non-state as well as nation-state actors. There are some in Canada, although happily not very many, who feel that we have recently become a "great" power, or a "principal" power, or some other kind of power capable of exercising a significant measure of unilateral will. But the reality is that the opportunities for our doing so are extremely limited, and we usually do things best when we do them in the company of others. Sometimes, moreover, a greater contribution can be made by pushing discreetly from behind than by leading ostentatiously from ahead. Modesty can be a source of power, too, and the influence it generates is often more durable than the influence that comes from claiming to have been there first.

Third: Our aspirations should not exceed our grasp. This relates, of course, to the limits of social engineering, to which I referred earlier. It also relates to the limits of our own political will. There is certainly a case for extending our reach—for pushing the frontiers just a little—since this is sometimes the only way of mobilizing the energy and other resources that are essential to change. But we need still to be realistic about what we can do. Otherwise, expectations, at home and abroad alike, get out of hand, fatalism and battle-fatigue set in, and cynicism—about our politics, our government, our political and bureaucratic leaderships, and our institutions—will further ensue, and further deepen.

Fourth: Our rhetoric should not exceed our aspirations. This fourth point, you may think, is no more than a variation on the third. And so in some degree it is. But an expansive rhetoric makes the problem worse. It gives encouragement to cynicism, and to the belief that everything, in the end, is a fake. Practised too long, it may even corrupt its own progenitors, either because they come to a fatal belief in their own myths, or worse, because they know their "spins" to be doctored, but still cannot help revelling in the manipulative nihilism of the game. In addition, a rhetoric of moralistic excess has the effect of depleting diplomatic credibility abroad. In the conduct of world affairs, high cant is counterproductive. When we see it in others, we think it facile. We should think the same when we see it in ourselves.

To the extent, moreover, that there are some in our own society who are magnetically drawn to the warm glow of what they hear, and who come in consequence to think that Canadians are not as others are, but are made instead of more holy and virtuous stuff, great damage is done to the very foundations of empathy and tolerance of which those who are attuned to Canada's politics so commonly boast. We need to be reminded over and over again that our capacity to make constructive, and seemingly selfless, contributions to the welfare of the international community is a product more of our good fortune—environmentally, geographically, and economically—than of our good character. If our behaviour in the turbot war did nothing else, it should at least have taught us this. When its implications are properly understood, moreover, a recognition of the true origins of the happy conditions in which we live can have a practical utility, if only because it can encourage us to tone down the sophomoric lectures that we seem increasingly to be giving to those whose circumstances are less convenient than our own. This, in the end, will increase, not diminish, our influence with others abroad.

Finally, and this point is directed more to the behaviour of NGOs than to the behaviour of government itself, the forces on the transnational "public service" left might wish to consider working more closely than they have done to date with the forces on the transnational right; and if components of the transnational left offer to do so, the transnational right might be well-advised to make the most of the opportunity. From the vantage point of the left, this is a hard injunction to follow. For many of them, after all, it means supping with the Devil, or at least with the Devil's demons. But we may have to get past this sort of polarization if, as a society, we are going to maximize our leverage—our real capacity to make a difference—in communities abroad. In any case, there may be far more complementarity of interest between NGOs and MNEs than we commonly assume. Certainly the question is worth putting to the test.

The promise of Presbyterian tone now having been fulfilled, the sermon is complete. Here, therefore, the lesson endeth.

NOTES

1. The most widely cited apostle of the optimistic view is, of course, Francis Fukuyama. See his "The End of History," *The National Interest* 16 (Summer 1989). The principal exponent of the view that the bottle is not half-full, but half-empty, and that the temper of world politics in the future will be governed more by civilizational differences than by civilizational commonalities is Samuel P. Huntington, whose pessimism finds expression in *The Clash of Civilizations and the Remaking of World Order* (New York: Simon & Schuster, 1996). A somewhat more dialectical assessment can be found in Benjamin R. Barber, *Jihad vs. McWorld* (New York: Times Books, 1995).

2. The most fully developed account of the official position can be found in *Canada in the World: Government Statement* (Ottawa: Canada Communications Group—Publishing, Public Works and Government Services Canada, 1995). Many of the speeches of Lloyd Axworthy, the minister of foreign affairs, pursue the pertinent themes. See, for example, "Notes for an Address by the Honourable Lloyd Axworthy, Minister of Foreign Affairs, to the 52nd Session of the United Nations General Assembly, New York, September 25, 1997," *Statement 97/36* (Ottawa: Department of Foreign Affairs and International Trade [hereafter DFAIT], September 25, 1997). In the current year, much of the emphasis has been on the development of human rights as an approach to peace. For the flavour of the *genre*, try "Notes for an Address by the Honourable Lloyd Axworthy, Minister of Foreign Affairs, to the Second Annual NGO Consultations on Peacebuilding, Ottawa, February 18, 1998," *Statement 98/10* (Ottawa: DFAIT, February 18, 1998).

3. The high-profile cases get the most attention. China is probably the most prominent example, the government's interest in trade-promotion leading to the cultivation of amicable relations with a regime whose internal political practices are not always in accord with Canadian preferences. The case of Indonesia follows closely along in second place. But there are many others.

4. The two reviews were conducted independently by two joint committees of the Senate and the House of Commons. The Report of the Defence Review Committee appeared first, under the title, *Security in a Changing World 1994: Report of the Special Joint Committee on Canada's Defence Policy*, and *Security in a Changing World 1994 (Appendices)* (Ottawa: Publications Service, Parliamentary Publications Directorate, 1994). The report on foreign policy arrived a little later. See *Canada's Foreign Policy: Principles and Priorities for the Future—Report of the Special Joint Committee of the Senate and the House of Commons Reviewing Foreign Policy*, together with two other volumes entitled, respectively, *Canada's Foreign Policy: Dissenting Opinions and Appendices* and *Canada's Foreign Policy: Position Papers* (Ottawa: Canada Communications Group—Publishing, Public Works and Government Services Canada for the Speaker of the House of Commons, 1994). On the defence side, the government's response came in the guise of the *1994 Defence White Paper* (Ottawa: Minister of Supply and Services Canada, 1994). The official reaction to the foreign policy review came in two separate documents: *Government Response to the Recommendations of the Special Joint Parliamentary Committee Reviewing Canadian Foreign Policy* (Ottawa: February, 1995), and *Canada in the World: Government Statement* (Ottawa: Canada Communications Group—Publishing Public Works and Government Services Canada, 1995).

5. The Council's offering can be found in Canada 21, *Canada and Common Security in the Twenty-First Century* (Toronto: Centre for International Studies, University of Toronto, 1994).

6. *An Agenda for Peace—Preventive Diplomacy, Peacemaking and Peace-keeping: Report of the Secretary-General Pursuant to the Statement Adopted by the Summit Meeting of the Security Council on 31 January 1992* (New York: United Nations, 1992).

7. The pros and cons of treating the various perils with which modern humanity is confronted as interlocking components of the same overarching problem of "security" are also discussed in Denis Stairs, "Contemporary Security Issues," *Canada's Foreign Policy: Principles and Priorities for the Future—The Position Papers*, especially pp. 1–6. The argument for distinguishing them, as opposed to lumping them together, appears not to have had much impact on members of the Joint Parliamentary Committee! Whether their judgment on the point was political or intellectual is not clear.

8. See his "Foreword" in *NGOs, the UN, and Global Governance,* ed. Thomas G. Weiss and Leon Gordenker (Boulder: Lynne Rienner, 1996), p. 7

9. The phenomenon is discussed in its current Canadian context at somewhat greater length in Denis Stairs, "The Policy Process and Dialogues with Demos: Liberal Pluralism with a Transnational Twist," in *Leadership and Dialogue: Canada Among Nations 1998,* eds. Fen Osler Hampson and Maureen Appel Molot (Toronto: Oxford University Press, 1998), especially pp. 34–48.

10. Such strategies have been deployed by Lloyd Axworthy on more than one occasion during his long and varied ministerial career. See *ibid.*, pp. 44–47, and in much greater detail, Herman Bakvis, *Regional Ministers: Power and Influence in the Canadian Cabinet* (Toronto: University of Toronto Press, 1991).

11. In the case of the latter, one of the principal instruments (although not the only instrument) is the Canadian Centre for Foreign Policy Development. For a recent account of its purposes and operations, see Steven Lee, "Beyond Consultations: Public Contributions to Making Foreign Policy," in *Leadership and Dialogue*, ed. Fen Osler Hampson and Maureen Appel Molot, pp. 55–67. Mr. Lee is the Centre's National Director.

12. The literature on this high-profile display of multilateral diplomacy, conducted, as it was, in close collaboration with interested participants from "civil society," is already burgeoning. A recent exposition by a Canadian foreign service officer who himself played a prominent role in the proceedings is Robert Lawson's "The Ottawa Process: Fast-Track Diplomacy and the International Movement to Ban Anti-Personnel Mines," in *Leadership and Dialogue,* eds. Fen Osler Hampson and Maureen Appel Molot, pp. 81–98.

13. A sensitive, but powerful, exploration of the ethical and other issues that are associated with this agonizing problem can be found in Michael Ignatieff, *The Warrior's Honour: Ethnic War and the Modern Conscience* (Toronto: Viking, 1998).

Canada and International Security Operations

The Search for Policy Rationales

LOUIS A. DELVOIE

Centre for International Relations
Queen's University

One of the boasts most frequently uttered by Canadian politicians of all persuasions is that Canada has participated in virtually every peacekeeping operation ever mounted by the United Nations. While the claim is essentially true, it begs an important question: why? Politicians rarely raise that question, and even more rarely provide any very satisfactory answers to it. That task is usually left to officials, academics, and journalists, and the responses provided, while often valid and interesting, rarely go to the heart of the matter. And yet for virtually all of the peacekeeping operations of the Cold War period (1948–88), it is perfectly possible to identify policy rationales firmly grounded in Canada's international security and political interests. What is far more problematic is to find equally substantive rationales for many of the international "peacekeeping" operations in which Canada has participated in the decade since the end of the Cold War (1988–98). In the midst of vast transformations to the international system and security environment, the Canadian government has failed to develop a new policy framework and criteria to determine why, when, and where Canada should engage its armed forces in what are now referred to as international security operations. There is in fact a policy vacuum that must be filled if the Canadian government is to avoid unproductive or unnecessarily dangerous undertakings that are of questionable value to the country, and may indeed be inconsistent with its interests. This is a serious challenge on the eve of a new millennium.

Rationales in the Literature

There is a large and impressive body of scholarly and semi-scholarly work on Canada's involvement in international peacekeeping. It includes numerous perceptive analyses of the reasons and the situations which prompted individual Canadian governments to respond in a particular way to individual international crises. Many of these analyses are solidly grounded in assessments of Canadian interests and of thrusts in Canadian foreign policy. When the time comes, however, to provide generic explanations of Canada's heavy engagement in peacekeeping over a period of decades, these writers adopt a different tack. They tend to fall back on essentially "soft" explanations related to domestic politics or to Canada's international image and reputation. Three examples will illustrate the point.

One of Canada's most prolific writers on peacekeeping is Alex Morrison, director of the Pearson Peacekeeping Centre in Cornwallis, Nova Scotia. Drawing on his experience as a military advisor to the Canadian mission to the UN in New York, Morrison explains in interesting detail the mechanics of Canadian decision making relating to individual UN operations. But in explaining why Canada has been so extensively involved in peacekeeping, he suggests that it is because peacekeeping has provided Canadian governments with an opportunity to put the functional principle into practice and to exercise leadership at the international level. He adds that peacekeeping has enjoyed the support of the Canadian public and allowed Canada to gain worldwide esteem.[1]

In an excellent new study of Canadian foreign policy, Professor Andrew Cooper of the University of Waterloo explains the phenomenon in similar terms, but somewhat more subtly. While occasionally making references to Canadian foreign and security policy interests, Cooper puts the emphasis on other factors. He suggests that "peacekeeping has been central to the definition of Canada's national identity, role and influence in the world," that it has become "a symbol of Canada's world view," "a staple tool for the application of constructive internationalism," and "an area of issue specific advantage." He adds that peacekeeping has provided Canada with international recognition, has been enormously popular domestically, and has provided Canada with repeated opportunities to exercise its talent for mediation.[2]

Finally, Professor Jack Granatstein, one of Canada's best-known historians, explains the phenomenon in terms that have more to do with Canada's collective psyche than its foreign policy. Contrasting it with Canada's participation in NATO and NORAD, he remarks that "peacekeeping at the same time somehow smacked of independence from the United States" and that peacekeeping became "the ideal role for Canada: responsible, useful, inexpensive and satisfying." He carries this latter theme further in suggesting that "peacekeeping was a satisfactory role for Pearson, one can surmise, because it was inherently useful, because it had good public relations value in Canada and abroad and because it struck a responsive chord in Pearson's and the national soul."[3]

While there are undoubtedly elements of truth in most, if not all, of the explanations offered by these three writers, do they represent the totality of the factors that motivated the Canadian government to become so heavily engaged in international peacekeeping throughout the period of the Cold War? If so, they would seem to constitute an insufficient basis for Canada's continuous engagement of its relatively small armed forces in human, political, and financial terms. If so, the country and its government would be deserving of Professor Granatstein's severe judgment:

> For too many Canadians peacekeeping has become a substitute for policy and thought. Some countries (but no longer our budget-strapped nation) try to deal with problems by throwing money at them; our people and, to some substantial extent, our governments try to deal with the world's problems by sending peacekeepers. This is not an ignoble impulse but it is one that has to be checked with realism. Governments, like individuals, are supposed to be capable of rational decision making. And automatic responses—whether "My country right or wrong" or "Send in the Canadian peacekeepers"—are no substitute for thought.[4]

The reality is, of course, that the Canadian government's policy on peacekeeping was not devoid of realism or thought. On the contrary, as one Canadian foreign minister put it, "we believe that our involvement in peacekeeping operations over four decades is a concrete reflection of our basic security and foreign policy interests."[5] What were those interests?

The Security Imperative

Throughout the years of the Cold War, the foremost security objective of the Canadian government was to preserve Canada from the effects of a global thermonuclear war involving the two world superpowers. This objective was at the heart of Canada's defence and security policies, of its membership in the NATO and NORAD alliances, and of much of its involvement in international peacekeeping. In the latter case, it involved a recognition that while a threat to the security of Canada might emanate from a direct threat to Western Europe or North America, it might equally arise from the escalation of regional conflicts in other parts of the world, especially ones where the two superpowers were either present or had important interests at stake. Thus in 1964, Canada's secretary of state for external affairs, Paul Martin, expressed the concern and the purpose in these terms:

In the thermonuclear world ... and in the world of newly-indepen-
dent states and under-developed countries in which conditions of
instability and disorder are apt to arise, an international force to keep
the peace or hold the ring while negotiations take place is vital if we
are to avoid the dangers of escalation to nuclear war. Whether we like
it or not, we live in a shrinking world. Local hostilities whether in
Southeast Asia, Africa or the Mediterranean, if not contained quickly,
can have as great an impact on our lives as an outbreak of hostilities
in the more familiar trouble spots of direct concern to NATO.[6]

The concern about the dangers of escalation was particularly evident in
relation to conflicts in the Middle East, where the Arab-Israeli dispute became
increasingly entwined in Cold War rivalries between the superpowers from
the mid-1950s onward. It certainly goes a long way towards explaining why
Canada participated in no less than eight separate peacekeeping operations
in the Middle East. As Canada's most eminent peacekeeper, General E.L.M.
Burns, was to write in 1985:

The parallel situations of 1956 and 1973 illustrate the special dangers
of hostilities in the Middle East developing into a confrontation
between the superpowers. ... It is fear of this world disaster which
basically moves Canada and other secondary powers to contribute to
the peacekeeping forces in the Middle East.[7]

The threat and fear of escalation was not only a powerful motivator of
Canadian action in the Middle East, but also in the case of peacekeeping missions in Asia and Africa. Thus in a statement to the UN General Assembly in
April 1961, the Canadian delegation addressed the question of the peacekeeping force in the Congo in these terms:

The involvement of the United Nations in the Congo was unques-
tionably right, and perhaps inevitable. The conflict which had
broken out in the Congo was internal, but outside intervention was
already a fact and the very real possibility of major international
conflict growing out of the Congo situation was evident to all.[8]

And later that year, the secretary of state for external affairs, Howard Green,
reiterated the concern in these words: "Were it not for the United Nations
presence, the Congo would probably sink into tribal strife and might even
become the scene of a great power conflict."[9]

Other Imperatives

But if the fear of escalation of regional conflicts was the central imperative in
determining Canada's participation in peacekeeping missions in the Cold
War period, it was by no means the only one firmly grounded in Canada's
security and foreign policy interests. Another closely associated factor was a
determination not to allow regional conflicts to have an adverse impact on

NATO, which successive Canadian governments regarded as the cornerstone of Canadian foreign and defence policy. This concern was uppermost in the minds of Louis St. Laurent and Lester Pearson during the Suez Crisis of 1956 and in the creation of the first UN Emergency Force in the Middle East. The cohesion of the Western Alliance was threatened by the divisions which the issue had precipitated in relations between the United States on the one hand and Britain and France on the other.[10] Similarly, in his efforts to establish a UN force in Cyprus in 1964, Paul Martin was chiefly concerned with the need "to contain an explosive situation which might have led to a major outbreak of hostilities involving two NATO allies."[11] It was, indeed, this determination to maintain the integrity of NATO and to safeguard its southern flank that led the Canadian government to contribute troops to the UN force in Cyprus for nearly thirty years.

Other more general Canadian foreign policy considerations were brought to bear in the case of several peacekeeping missions in the Middle East, South Asia, and Southeast Asia. One of these had to do with Canada's stance in the Cold War. Like other Western countries, Canada was interested in limiting the spread of Soviet influence in the Third World throughout the years of the Cold War. Thus, as early as 1948 Louis St. Laurent expressed the fear that the conflict between India and Pakistan might be exploited by the Soviet Union to its advantage and it was not coincidental that Canada's very first involvement in a UN peacekeeping mission was along the Indo-Pakistani ceasefire line in Kashmir.[12] And as Professor Granatstein has noted, "Our peacekeeping efforts almost always supported western interests. Certainly this was true in the Middle East, the Congo, Cyprus, Vietnam and Bosnia too."[13]

Finally, at least two of Canada's endeavours in the field of peacekeeping served to strengthen its bilateral relations with key partner countries. This was true of the first UN Emergency Force in the Middle East, whose deployment allowed Britain and France to save some face in the aftermath of the Suez Crisis of 1956. It was equally true of the International Commission for Control and Supervision established in 1973 under the terms of the peace agreement concluded between the United States and the government of North Vietnam. Although the Canadian government had serious reservations about the viability of this operation, it agreed to participate in order to help the United States extricate itself from Vietnam.[14]

The Sharp Principles

Virtually all of Canada's involvement in international peacekeeping operations during the Cold War can be explained in function of one or more of the security and foreign policy considerations outlined above.[15] These policy rationales came to be supplemented in the early 1970s with a series of political and technical criteria or guidelines to be used by the Canadian government in assessing the merits of Canadian participation in any particular operation. Deriving their name from the minister who first put them forward in the House of Commons, the so-called "Sharp principles" reflected the lessons learned from earlier bad experiences in the Congo, Egypt, and Indochina. The criteria stipulated that for Canada to participate:

- there should exist a threat to international peace and security;
- the peacekeeping endeavour should be associated with an agreement for a political settlement, or at least a reasonable expectation of a negotiated settlement;
- the peacekeeping organization should be responsible to a political authority, preferably the United Nations;
- the peacekeeping mission should have a clear mandate adequate to permit it to carry out its assigned function;
- the parties to the conflict accept the presence of the peacekeeping mission and agree to maintain a ceasefire;
- Canadian participation in the operation is acceptable to all concerned;
- there should be an agreed and equitable method of financing the operation.[16]

The Sharp principles were never intended to be hard and fast rules, and were not used as such by the Canadian government. They did, however, constitute a clear statement of Canadian government desiderata and were used to good effect in negotiating mandates and conditions of deployment with the UN Secretariat. They were also used to provide justification for Canadian withdrawal from operations that were inherently ineffective or had ceased to be effective.[17] In short, they added a further dimension of rationality to Canadian government decision making in relation to international peacekeeping in the Cold War era.

After the Cold War

The last major public iteration of traditional Canadian peacekeeping policy is to be found in the Defence White Paper of 1987, which put the emphasis on the avoidance of escalation of regional conflicts into superpower confrontations and on the prevention of rifts within the Atlantic alliance, and which repeated virtually all of the Sharp principles as conditions for Canadian participation in peacekeeping.[18] But like so much else in that white paper, this statement of peacekeeping policy was rapidly overtaken by events. The end of the Cold War and events surrounding it led to an explosion in the number of peacekeeping operations launched by the United Nations, and gave rise to the creation of types of missions that had never before been envisaged.[19]

The missions established by the United Nations during the decade 1988–98 fall broadly into three categories. The first are fairly traditional missions whose responsibilities involved the monitoring of ceasefires, and troop redeployments or withdrawals. The military observer groups deployed along the borders between Iran and Iraq and between Iraq and Kuwait, as well as those dispatched to Afghanistan and Angola fall into this category. A second group consists of missions charged with the political reconstruction of ruined or recently liberated states. Into this category fall the missions sent to Nicaragua, Cambodia, Namibia, Haiti, and the Western Sahara. Finally, there are what have come to be called "humanitarian missions" whose function is to aid and protect populations threatened by violence or starvation, usually in civil war situations. The operations in Bosnia, Somalia, and Rwanda, as well as the aborted operation in Eastern Zaire fall into this last category. In short, as Foreign Minister André Ouellet remarked in 1994, "the term 'peace-keeping' has taken on a rather elastic meaning."[20]

Most of the UN missions mounted between 1988 and 1992 can be seen as part of the process of winding down the Cold War. They came into being either as a result of the Soviet Union's new willingness to cooperate with the West in bringing longstanding regional conflicts to an end, or as a result of the Soviet Union's progressive withdrawal from regions of the Third World where it had been actively engaged in competitions for influence with the West.[21] This is true of the missions in Iran/Iraq, Afghanistan, Cambodia, Nicaragua, Namibia, and Angola. Thus Canadian participation in these missions, whether of the peacekeeping or reconstruction variety, fell well within the bounds of traditional Canadian peacekeeping policy. If the overarching national interest and policy rationale had until then been the containment of the Cold War through the limitation of regional conflicts which posed a threat of escalation, the actual termination of the Cold War in all of its manifestations served the same ends in terms of Canadian security interests.

The policy rationale for Canada's participation in the UN operations in the former Yugoslavia was somewhat different, but equally substantive. The Canadian government saw in the civil wars in Yugoslavia not only a series of humanitarian issues, but also a threat to the security and stability of Europe, which successive Canadian governments have identified as being in the Canadian national interest.[22] And in this broader security context, the Canadian government regarded its continued involvement in Yugoslavia as part of its commitment to NATO and its NATO allies.[23] The actual implementation of the mission, however, represented a singular departure from traditional Canadian policy and criteria, for as one recent study points out very accurately:

> The UN clearly made the choice to maintain the minimum involvement necessary to avert the worst effects of the war and to prevent a spillover of the conflict to surrounding countries. But once enacted, the Security Council incrementally increased the mandate over the next three and a half years, edging towards occupation and a forced solution. The problem is that it refused to support the increased mandates with a requisite military enlargement. Even worse, the UN sent forces to Bosnia under a Chapter VI mandate when it was clearly a Chapter VII engagement. This troublesome situation was acknowledged by the subsequent UN resolutions which left UNPROFOR to sort out the muddled mandates.[24]

It was, of course, precisely to avoid Canada becoming or staying involved in confused missions of the kind described here that the Sharp principles had originally been developed and subsequently elaborated. And yet despite the ineffectiveness of the operation and the dangers involved, to say nothing of the damage done to the reputation of the United Nations, the Canadian government maintained its commitment of troops to UNPROFOR in Bosnia until it was eventually replaced by a NATO force operating under very different conditions.

The experience UNPROFOR in Bosnia very graphically illustrated the point made in 1993 by one of the world's most respected experts on peacekeeping, Sir Brian Urquhart, when he said: "Peacekeeping is a very useful technique when the conditions are right. The trouble is that nowadays they mostly aren't right. ... The situations which characterize the post–Cold War world are really very different from the situations peacekeeping was set up to deal with, and they really mostly are quite unsuitable for the peacekeeping technique."[25] But rather than take this lesson on board and trim their sails accordingly, both the Mulroney and the Chrétien governments chose to dilute Canadian policy and to apply the peacekeeping technique ever more widely.

The Demise of Policy

Canadian government policy on peacekeeping changed incrementally, but not particularly coherently, between 1991 and 1995. In 1991 Prime Minister Mulroney virtually repudiated the traditional doctrine of non-intervention in the internal affairs of sovereign states, and made the case for Canadian and international interventionism in the interests of saving lives in domestic conflicts, advocating the need for a "rebalancing between international obligations and national sovereignty." While there were many factors that helped to explain this new activism, none of them had much to do with a re-thinking of Canada's foreign policy or national interests.[26]

But even when that re-thinking did occur with the Liberal government's foreign and defence policy reviews of 1994–95, the results were lacking in definition. The government's statement of foreign policy called for "a broadening of the focus of security policy from its narrow orientation of managing state to state relations" to one which would involve "working for the promotion of democracy and good governance, of human rights and the rule of law and of prosperity through sustainable development."[27] The government's defence white paper also made its contribution to further blurring the policy framework. Abandoning the use of the term *peacekeeping*, it spoke of *multilateral operations*, which encompassed the full range of military activity from preventive deployments to all-out war. And with few, if any, delineations along the way, it stated that the purpose of these operations should be to address not only "genuine threats to international peace and security" but also "emerging humanitarian tragedies." To this statement of objectives was appended what was inevitably a highly watered-down and conditioned iteration of the Sharp principles.[28]

This progressive broadening and dilution of the policy framework was accompanied by Canadian participation in three UN missions that underlined the questions and problems to which it could and would give rise. These were the missions to Haiti, Somalia, and Rwanda.

The overthrow of the democratically elected government of President Aristide by the leadership of the Haitian army was undoubtedly a regrettable event, but it certainly did not pose a threat to international peace and security, let alone to the security interests of Canada. Nor did it affect Canada's economic interests, since Canada's trade with and investments in Haiti were negligible, given that country's extreme poverty. What then explains the very high profile role adopted by the Canadian government in international diplomatic efforts and in the UN mission to restore President Aristide to power. The explanation might lie in the existence of a fairly large Haitian community in Montreal that supported Aristide, or in a wish to enhance Canadian diplomatic credit in Washington, where there was serious concern that further outflows of Haitian refugees would severely test the already tense race relations in parts of Florida. But both of these factors remained unavowed as the Canadian government gave the reasons for its initial and then its continued involvement in the UN mission to Haiti.

In fact, the reasons cited had everything to do with the inadmissibility of the overthrow of democratic governments by military force, with the need to restore democracy in Haiti and with the desirability of consolidating the democratic process and reinforcing national institutions in Haiti.[29] But by adopting a rationale divorced from Canadian foreign policy interests and based on a general principle, the Canadian government was either committing itself to a policy of global interventionism in support of that principle or leaving itself open to questions to which there was no logical answer. Why did the Canadian government consider that UN military intervention was warranted in the case of Haiti, but not in Algeria or Nigeria where the military had also intervened to thwart an ongoing democratic process? Why had the Canadian government in these cases contented itself with uttering cautious criticism, and no more?[30] In terms of the principle involved, there was and is no self-evident answer.

Different, but equally difficult, questions arise in relation to Canada's support for, and participation in, the so-called "humanitarian operations" in Somalia and Rwanda. For if it is difficult to discern any foreign policy foundations or logical consistency in the rationales advanced by the Canadian government for intervention in Haiti, it is virtually impossible to find any at all in the case of Somalia and Rwanda.

The civil war in Somalia began in 1989 and from the start gave rise to widespread violence, outbreaks of famine and the displacement of populations. The situation prevailing in 1992 was not qualitatively different from that which had prevailed in the previous three years.[31] Why was it that Canada and the UN only decided on military intervention in Somalia in 1992? Why did Canada remain committed to an intervention which represented a classical case of "mandate creep," evolving from a peacekeeping operation to protect humanitarian assistance deliveries into a peace enforcement operation whose goals were unachievable under the conditions prevailing in Somalia?[32]

Similar questions arise about Canada's involvement in the UN military missions in Rwanda. In explaining its decision to participate in these missions, the Canadian government offered no reason other than that "the world has been shocked by the human tragedy unfolding in Rwanda."[33] But this explanation begs the question as to why the Canadian government felt impelled to promote and participate in a UN military intervention in 1993–95 when it had never seen fit to do so during the numerous other outbreaks of ethnic conflict and massacres involving Hutus and Tutsis in Rwanda and Burundi during the period 1959 to 1991.[34] And why did Canada agree to the progressive expansion of the UN mandates in Rwanda, from a modest mission of monitoring the Uganda–Rwanda border to the formidable task of helping the Rwandan government "to re-establish a secure environment in the country," a task so obviously beyond the means of any short-term UN intervention given the history of relations between Hutus and Tutsis throughout the region?[35]

There is one much broader question which applies to both the Somalia and Rwanda missions. Why did the UN and Canada choose to intervene in the civil wars in these two countries but not in the bloody and destructive civil wars taking place at the same time in countries such as Sudan, Sierra Leone, Afghanistan, and Sri Lanka? In other words, why was the concept of "collective security" enshrined in the UN charter replaced by what might be termed a penchant for "selective interventionism"? The answer to these and most of the other questions raised above is to be found not in any coherent UN doctrine or in any analysis of Canadian foreign policy, but rather in what has come to be termed the "CNN factor." Events and developments in Somalia and Rwanda attracted the sustained attention of the Western mass media, especially television, which bombarded their audiences with heart-rending images of human suffering. This in turn provoked among Western governments and publics the sentiment that "something has to be done," and the result was a rush to often ill-thought-out action. The judgment of news organizations as to which civil wars and famines were newsworthy and which were not came to be substituted for rational policy making by governments.

The ultimate example of this phenomenon is to be found in the Canadian government's decision in late 1996 to play the lead role in mounting first a diplomatic initiative and then a multinational military intervention to assist several hundred thousand Rwandan refugees trapped in Eastern Zaire as a result of civil wars in both Rwanda and Zaire. On the basis of an extensive study of the decision-making process in Ottawa on this occasion, Professor John Kirton has concluded that the prime instigator of the Canadian government's action was Prime Minister Chrétien himself, and that "Chrétien was moved in the first instance by the television pictures of the plight of the refugees."[36] And it was Chrétien who carried the day in moving Canada forward from a diplomatic mission to a military intervention despite the obvious reluctance of the Departments of Foreign Affairs and National Defence in Ottawa, and despite the evident lack of enthusiasm of most of Canada's major allies.[37]

In trying to explain why Canada had taken the lead in addressing the refugee situation in Eastern Zaire, Foreign Minister Axworthy advanced no policy rationale, but seemed to suggest that Canada had to act simply because it was uniquely qualified to do so by virtue of "the credibility that Canada enjoys throughout Africa and in the Great Lakes region in particular, as a result of its bilingual capabilities and absence of colonial ties, as well as its longstanding and impartial involvement in programs of economic and educational cooperation."[38]

Even if taken at face value, this explanation hardly seemed adequate to justify Canada committing troops to, and taking command of, a military expedition into the heart of Africa, and especially one whose mandate was premised on the need for enforcement action rather than some form of peacekeeping.[39] In fact, the explanation was somewhat misleading. The reality was that the three African countries chiefly involved (Zaire, Rwanda, and Burundi) had never enjoyed a very high priority in Canada's foreign policy and international relations, and Canada did not have a particularly high profile in any of them. Canada had never seen fit to establish full-fledged embassies in either Rwanda or Burundi, and the Canadian embassy in Zaire had been closed since the spring of 1993.[40] Canada's diplomatic presence, as well as its consequent knowledge of local political realities, were well below the level of those of many other Western countries. As for Canadian aid programs in the three countries, they were in fact very modest. Thus in 1992–93 Canada's bilateral aid disbursements to Zaire, Rwanda, and Burundi combined amounted to only $20 million, slightly less than Canada contributed to Jamaica alone.[41] These aid programs were hardly of a magnitude likely to confer on Canada any particular status or influence in dealing with the governments concerned.

These realities became evident as planning and preparations for the mission to Zaire went forward. While the Canadian government might advocate the need to disregard the principle of national sovereignty in pursuit of humanitarian objectives, the African leaderships with which it was dealing clearly were not prepared to do so. Despite early indications that they might be willing to bend the principle, in the end the governments of Zaire and Rwanda, as well as the Zairian rebel leader Laurent Kabila, refused to cooperate in any external intervention in the regions they controlled.[42] And the

Canadian government had neither the influence nor the clout to make them change their mind, with the result that if the multinational military intervention had gone forward, it might have been militarily opposed by all three.

The actual preparations for the proposed Zaire mission also revealed two other fundamental flaws in the Canadian government's decision to put itself forward as the putative leader of this enterprise. The first was that Canada did not have the military capabilities, especially the logistical capabilities, to sustain that role in such a distant and unfamiliar theatre of operations. At every step of the way, it became more evident how totally dependent the success of the operation would be on the military and logistical capabilities of the United States (and consequently how the United States, not Canada, would have the final say on what was to be done).[43] Secondly, Canada was severely handicapped by a lack of detailed and reliable information about the situation on the ground in Eastern Zaire. Lacking the intelligence-gathering capabilities of the United States and Britain (satellite imagery and reconnaissance aircraft), the Canadian authorities often had to fall back on the fragmentary and sometimes contradictory information provided by the UNHCR and by NGOs working in the region,[44] or admit their total dependence on their allies. On both counts, the Canadian government's claim to be able to take the lead in mounting and commanding the Zaire operation proved to be unsustainable. It was lucky for both Canada and its soldiers that it was not put to the test in combat.

These and a host of other problematic issues are brought out very clearly in an unofficial document written by two Canadian government officials and entitled "Lessons Learned from the Zaire Mission."[45] The fact is, of course, that many of the problems discussed in this study were known and understood by government officials well *before* a decision was made at the political level to launch a military initiative for Zaire. What seems equally clear is that these issues were disregarded in an exercise that proved to be a triumph of good intentions and image building over coherent policy and rational decision making. (Although less relevant when written in 1991, Professor Granatstein's appeal for "realism" and "thought" had certainly become very pertinent by 1996).[46]

The Way Ahead

The main policy rationales and the criteria that underpinned Canada's participation in international peacekeeping during the Cold War period and its immediate aftermath have been largely overtaken by events. New realities require new approaches. In this regard, the Canadian government has been far from inactive. It has established the Pearson Peacekeeping Centre whose mandate is to explore and provide training in new forms of civil–military collaboration in the prevention and limitation of armed conflicts. It has sponsored and funded a major international study on ways to improve the United Nations' capabilities to intervene rapidly in nascent conflicts so as to limit their detrimental effects. Both of these initiatives are thoroughly worthwhile, but they deal with implementation techniques and mechanics. What is still lacking is an in-depth review of Canadian policy aimed at answering the questions why, where, when, and with whom should Canada envisage becoming involved in international security operations.

In its reviews and statements of foreign and defence policy in 1994–95, the Canadian government did not address these basic questions, but contented itself with diluting traditional policies and expanding the concept of security to include the promotion of democracy, human rights, social justice, etc. As Professor Joel Sokolsky has very aptly remarked: "What this approach often obscures is the reality that most cases of regional conflict will not even indirectly affect Canadian economic or security interests. Ottawa is often simply looking to participate actively in global affairs."[47] This approach also obscures two other important points. The first is that the capabilities of the Canadian Armed Forces have been dramatically reduced in recent years, as a result of a long succession of budgetary and personnel cuts; their ability to undertake new and more complex mandates is thus severely constrained.[48] The second point is that this approach ignores an even more fundamental question. The men and women of the Canadian armed forces are sworn to lay down their lives if necessary in defence of Canada, Canadians, and their interests. Is it legitimate to ask them to do the same in defence of others to whom they have no such obligations, in situations where there are no evident or important Canadian interests at stake?

All of this is not to suggest that Canadians or their government should remain indifferent to the suffering endured by populations confronted with civil wars, massacres, or famines. In these situations Canada can and should provide emergency relief assistance (food, medicines, and shelter), offer economic development assistance, participate with like minded countries in conflict resolution endeavours, support both politically and financially the efforts of international organizations and NGOs in relief operations and peacebuilding measures, and finally assist regional organizations in developing their peacekeeping capabilities. In short, there are many ways in which Canada can discharge its international humanitarian responsibilities without resorting to military intervention.

Decisions to deploy forces, to engage in military operations, and to put troops in harm's way are among the gravest which any government is required to make. They should never be taken casually, and should certainly not be based on the spontaneous reactions of politicians or publics to media images, no matter how dismal. They should instead be based on policies reflecting an accurate assessment of the country's interests and capabilities. On the eve of a new century which promises to be no less chaotic and conflict-ridden than the one drawing to a close, the time for the Canadian government to develop policies in tune with contemporary realities is now.

NOTES

1. Alex Morrison, "Canada and Peacekeeping: A time for reanalysis?" in *Canada's International Security Policy*, eds. D.B. Dewitt and D. Leyton-Brown (Scarborough, ON: Prentice-Hall, 1995), pp. 202–10.

2. Andrew Cooper, *Canadian Foreign Policy: Old Habits and New Directions* (Scarborough, ON: Prentice-Hall, 1997), pp. 173–77.

3. J.L. Granatstein, "Canada and Peacekeeping: Image and Reality" in *Canadian Foreign Policy: Historical Readings*, ed. J.L. Granatstein (Toronto: Copp Clark, 1986), pp. 232–37.

4. J.L. Granatstein, "Peacekeeping: Did Canada Make a Difference? And What Difference Did Peacekeeping Make to Canada?" In *Making a Difference? Canada's Foreign Policy in a Changing World Order*, eds. J. English and N. Hillmer (Toronto: Lester Publishing, 1992), p. 234.

5. Foreign Minister André Ouellet addressing a brainstorming session on peacekeeping in Ottawa on April 29, 1994, *Statements 94/18* (Ottawa: DFAIT 1994), p. 2.

6. *Statements and Speeches 64/20* (Ottawa: Department of External Affairs [hereafter DEA] 1964), pp. 6–7.

7. E.L.M. Burns, "Canada's Peacekeeping Role in the Middle East" in *Canada and the Arab World*, ed. Tareq Ismael (Edmonton: University of Alberta Press, 1985), p. 39.

8. *Statements and Speeches 61/4* (Ottawa: DEA, 1961), p. 2.

9. *Statements and Speeches 62/2* (Ottawa: DEA, 1962), p. 2.

10. *Statements and Speeches 56/26* (Ottawa: DEA, 1956), p. 4. See also Tom Keating, *Canada and World Order* (Toronto: McClelland & Stewart, 1993), p. 104.

11. *Statements and Speeches 64/20* (Ottawa: DEA, 1964), p. 7.

12. *Statements and Speeches 48/23* (Ottawa: DEA, 1948), p. 8. See also L.A. Delvoie, *Hesitant Engagement: Canada and South Asian Security* (Kingston: Queen's Centre for International Relations, 1995), pp. 17–20.

13. Quoted in Cooper, *Canadian Foreign Policy*, p. 181.

14. See Keating, *Canada and World Order*, p. 173.

15. The exceptions have to do with Canada's involvement in the missions in New Guinea (UNSF), the Dominican Republic (DOMREP), and Nigeria (OTN). These missions were, however, all of very short duration and involved no more than a dozen Canadians.

16. *Statements 73/23* (Ottawa: DEA, 1973), pp. 3–4.

17. For example, these included the Canadian withdrawals from the ICCS in Vietnam in 1973, from UNIFIL in the Middle East in 1978, and from UNMOGIP in Kashmir in 1979.

18. *Challenge and Commitment: A Defence Policy for Canada* (Ottawa: Department of National Defence [hereafter DND], 1987), p. 21.

19. See L.A. Delvoie, "Canada and Peacekeeping: A New Era?" *Canadian Defence Quarterly 20/2* (Autumn 1990), pp. 9–14.

20. *Statements 94/2* (Ottawa: DFAIT, 1994), p. 3.

21. See Delvoie, "Canada and Peacekeeping," pp. 9–10.

22. The most recent iteration of this policy interest is to be found in *Canada in the World* (Ottawa: DFAIT, 1995), pp. 29–30.

23. See *News Release 186/94* (Ottawa: DFAIT, 1994) and *News Release 62/95* (Ottawa: DFAIT, 1995). See also Cooper, *Canadian Foreign Policy*, p. 193.

24. Dawn Hewitt, *From Ottawa to Sarajevo: Canadian Peacekeepers in the Balkans* (Kingston: Queen's Centre for International Relations, 1998), p. 94.

25. Brian Urquhart, *The Role of United Nations Peacekeeping in the Post–Cold War World* (Kingston: Royal Military College, 1993), pp. 7–8.

26. See Cooper, *Canadian Foreign Policy*, pp. 183–86. See also Morrison, "Canada and Peacekeeping," pp. 212–13.

27. DFAIT, *Canada in the World*, p. 25.

28. *Defence White Paper* (Ottawa: DND, 1994), pp. 28–29.

29. See *News Release 192/93* and *193/93* (Ottawa: DFAIT, 1993), *News Release 189/95* (Ottawa: DFAIT, 1995), and *News Release 126/97* (Ottawa: DFAIT, 1997).

30. When the Nigerian military annulled the presidential elections in June 1993, the Canadian government simply expressed "deep concern" and an interest in promoting the democratic process in Nigeria. See *News Release 164/93* (Ottawa: DFAIT, 1993). It was not until two years later, when the Nigerian military regime had been found guilty of some gross and highly publicized human rights violations, that the Canadian government started to advocate a more robust reaction. But even then, this consisted of a call for Commonwealth sanctions, not UN military intervention.

31. See Charles Gurdon (ed.), *The Horn of Africa* (New York: St. Martin's Press, 1994), pp. 47–75.

32. See *Statements 93/11* (Ottawa: DFAIT, 1993), pp. 3 and 5. The phenomenon of "mandate creep" and some of the reasons for the ultimate failure of the Somalia mission are discussed in David Carment, "Rethinking Peacekeeping: The Bosnia and Somalia Experience" in *Canada Among Nations 1996: Big Enough to be Heard* eds. F.O. Hampson and M.A. Molot (Ottawa: Carleton University Press, 1996), pp. 224–36.

33. *News Release 127/94* (Ottawa: DFAIT, 1994), p. 1.

34. See Gerard Prunier, *The Rwanda Crisis 1959-1994: History of a Genocide* (London: Hurst and Co., 1995), pp. 50–114.

35. See *News Release 138/93* (Ottawa: DFAIT, 1993), p. 1 and *News Release 4/95* (Ottawa: DFAIT, 1995), p. 1.

36. John Kirton, "Foreign Policy under the Liberals" in *Canada Among Nations 1997: Asia-Pacific Face Off,* eds. F.O. Hampson et al. (Ottawa: Carleton University Press, 1997), p. 43.

37. *Ibid.,* pp. 42–44.

38. *News Release 200/96* (Ottawa: DFAIT, 1996), p. 1.

39. The UN Security Council resolution (1080) that authorized the creation of a multinational force under Canadian command was adopted under the provisions of Chapter VII, not Chapter VI, of the UN Charter. See *News Release 210/96* (Ottawa: DFAIT, 1996), p. 1.

40. The Canadian embassy in Kinshasa was not re-opened until January, 1998. See *News Release 17/98* (Ottawa: DFAIT, 1998), p. 1.

41. See *Annual Report 1992-1993* (Ottawa: CIDA, 1994), pp. 44–51.

42. Andrew Cooper, "Between Will and Capabilities: Canada and the Rwanda/Great Lakes Initiative" (Unpublished paper presented at a conference at the University of Waterloo, February 6–7, 1998), pp. 17–18.

43. *Ibid.,* pp. 25–26.

44. *Ibid.,* pp. 32–35.

45. James Appathurai and Ralph Lysyshyn, "Lessons learned from the Zaire mission" (Ottawa, 1997), 19 pp. The authors were members of the Interdepartmental Task Force created to coordinate Canada's response to the Zaire crisis, but the views expressed in this paper are those of the authors alone.

46. See note no. 4 above.

47. Joel Sokolsky, *The Americanization of Peacekeeping: Implications for Canada* (Kingston: Queen's Centre for International Relations, 1997), p. 39.

48. For a good analysis of this problem, see Joseph Jockel, *Canada and International Peacekeeping* (Toronto: Canadian Institute of Strategic Studies, 1994), pp. 27–46. The problem has, in fact, become far more serious since the publication of this study.

Somalia

The Long-Term Effects

PETER DESBARATS

Former Director
School of Journalism
University of Western Ontario

On March 16, 1998, two anniversaries occurred in North America. The date marked the thirtieth anniversary of the My Lai massacre in Vietnam when American soldiers gunned down some 500 Vietnamese civilians. March 16 also was, by a strange historical coincidence, the fifth anniversary of the cold-blooded murder of a teenager, Shidane Arone, by a Canadian soldier serving in Somalia, an act to which many other Canadian military personnel contributed.

It is instructive to compare how the two countries observed these anniversaries. In the United States, newspaper and television stories commemorated the event by belatedly making a hero of former Chief Warrant Officer Hugh Thompson. Thompson was a helicopter pilot in Vietnam on March 16, 1968, when he flew over the village of My Lai and noticed something unusual. He and his crew spotted a young Vietnamese girl lying wounded on the road. He dropped a smoke grenade to mark the spot and radioed for help. Then he watched in horror as an American officer on the ground walked over to the girl, flipped her over with his foot and shot her in the head.

Thompson then saw a group of wounded women, children, and older men huddled in an irrigation ditch. He landed his helicopter to request help for the wounded from nearby American troops. Instead, the American soldiers fired into the group of civilians. He then spotted some villagers crowded into a hut. An old woman was standing in the doorway, a baby in her arms, a child clutching her leg. Thompson asked the officer in charge to help him get the villagers out. The officer replied that the only thing the Vietnamese would get from his soldiers was a hand grenade.

After that, Thompson positioned his helicopter in front of advancing American soldiers and told his gunner to fire on them if they attempted to harm the civilians. He then called for assistance from two following helicopters and together they started to airlift the Vietnamese to safety. For this heroic act, Thompson was awarded the Soldier's Medal, given to those who risk their lives in a situation where an opposing enemy is not involved, although the award was given belatedly and grudgingly.

It was ten years ago that Thompson was interviewed for a BBC documentary on My Lai, and that interview was seen by a retired professor in the United States, David Egan, who started a letter-writing campaign on Thompson's behalf. It took eight years for the Pentagon to notify Thompson that he had been approved for the medal. He was faxed a copy of the citation. Even then, it took almost two more years for the American military to actually present the medal to Thompson at a ceremony last month at Washington's Vietnam memorial. The delay was blamed on bureaucratic procedure. On the anniversary itself, Thompson was in Vietnam with his former gunner, visiting the site of the massacre and receiving a hero's welcome.

Even after thirty years, Americans have difficulty confronting and accepting the truth about My Lai, but the important thing for Canadians to understand is that they do. The process started almost immediately after My Lai when an inquiry reviewed the original, inadequate military investigation of the massacre, and the whole story became known. Lt. William Calley, the officer in charge on that day, was found guilty by court martial and his name became synonymous with atrocity and disgrace. My Lai was acknowledged by the American people as one of the darkest moments in their military history.

By acknowledging it, and pledging at the time that it would never happen again, the American military reinforced a principle of accountability that has protected them ever since from a repetition of My Lai. There have been many individual examples of misconduct since then—and these have usually been dealt with swiftly and publicly—but nothing like My Lai.

Now contrast this with the observance of March 16 in Canada. Despite the fact that the atrocity in Somalia occurred only five years ago, and despite the fact that it has been in the news frequently ever since, particularly during the past three years, I'm not aware of any significant mention or observance of this anniversary in Canada. It passed unnoticed. And our equivalent of the American hero Hugh Thompson, former army Major Barry Armstrong, probably spent that day working as usual in his medical practice in the small Ontario town of Dryden, his name and story already slipping into obscurity.

Dr. Armstrong didn't have a helicopter gunship to place in front of Canadian soldiers who were running amok. His action was far less impulsive and dramatic but perhaps it took even more courage than Thompson's. It was Barry Armstrong who opposed single-handedly the combined forces of the senior military command in Somalia and the senior officers and bureaucrats at National Defence Headquarters in Ottawa who were in the process of covering up not only the murder of Shidane Arone but the killing of another Somali by Canadian soldiers earlier that month. And it was Barry Armstrong who faced abuse and ridicule from his military superiors as a result of his courageous action, and who continued to do so when he appeared before the Somalia inquiry in Ottawa last year. Instead of presenting him with the medal and the recognition that he deserves by the military high command and a grateful nation, he was slandered as being "almost certifiable," a term used by his former military commander in Somalia during our hearings.

The reason why Barry Armstrong is being ignored is that Canadians, unlike Americans in the case of My Lai, have not been allowed to come to terms with the murder of Shidane Arone, to acknowledge and accept their collective guilt, and to resolve that never again will Canadian soldiers commit similar atrocities. Instead, the Canadian government last year became the first in our history to interfere with and abort an independent public inquiry appointed by that government to investigate the murder of Shidane Arone and many less horrendous but significant problems associated with the deployment of Canadian soldiers to Somalia in 1992–93. And this blatant and unprecedented example of political arrogance was meekly accepted by a large majority of Canadians. That's the real reason why we don't want to be reminded of the March 16 anniversary.

I want to ensure that the issues raised by Canada's intervention in Somalia don't simply disappear and that the after-effects of our behaviour in Somalia and after Somalia don't contaminate our military establishment and our political life for decades to come. For the issue here is much larger than just the Canadian military. The many questions that remain unanswered in the wake of the Somalia experience relate to political accountability, the recognition by government that it is the servant of the public, and not the other way around, and the determination of Canadians as a people to insist on accountability from their governments. This is the larger theme of the Somalia experience.

Already we can see the government's blatant evasion of accountability in that case being repeated and replicated elsewhere in our public life. It isn't extreme to say that it is poisoning our domestic political life at all levels and weakening our ability to function independently and effectively on the international scene. It isn't too much to say that it is one of the most fundamental problems that our democracy faces at this stage in our development, rooted in our history and related to our various crises in national identity, Quebec, health care, and so forth, but much deeper and more difficult to resolve.

In this sense, what happened on March 16, 1993, in Somalia, and its consequences, was symptomatic of problems in Canada that extend far beyond the military.

Now some might say that I'm exaggerating this, that during the two years of the Somalia inquiry I became proprietorial about the process and a little obsessed by it. These people might say, as some said directly to us during the inquiry, with varying degrees of sophistication—What's all the excitement about? A couple of dead Somalis? How can you compare this with the 500 victims of the My Lai massacre?

Not only can I compare it with My Lai but I can say that, in every sense except the numerical, it was worse than My Lai. In Vietnam, the Americans were fighting a prolonged and bloody war against guerilla forces that seemed to materialize suddenly out of the civilian population and then, when confronted, to disappear into it just as quickly. It became almost impossible to distinguish between soldiers and civilians and, within the civilian population, between supporters and opponents of the Viet Cong and the many shades of neutrality in between. This certainly doesn't justify the My Lai massacre but it helps to explain it.

In Somalia our soldiers were not involved in a shooting war. They were part of an American-led intervention, authorized by the United Nations, designed to pacify the country in order to enable relief agencies to distribute aid and avert widespread famine.

The Belet Huen sector in central Somalia was one of the more peaceful before the arrival of the Canadians and throughout their stay. Food was being distributed in Belet Huen before our soldiers reached there in late December 1992. Not a single Canadian soldier was killed or wounded by hostile fire during the entire six-month occupation of Belet Huen. This isn't to say that the assignment wasn't physically uncomfortable or that an escalation of hostilities might not have occurred under certain conditions, but it wasn't Vietnam or even remotely close to it.

The only thing that the Canadian soldiers were required to do in Somalia was establish themselves on the ground, set up and maintain a base of operations, and patrol and monitor their sector. This should not have been a particularly difficult assignment, one would think, for a regiment reputed to be an elite formation.

Basic to this sort of mission is maintaining the security of your own camp. Particularly in a developing country such as Somalia, petty thievery is predictable. As soon as the Canadians arrived, in fact, it became evident that many Somalis regarded the presence of troops from one of the world's wealthiest countries as a heaven-sent opportunity to enrich themselves. They set about doing this in remarkably enterprising ways of varying degrees of legitimacy ranging from selling their services as labourers, guides, and interpreters to stealing everything that they could get their hands on.

There are also standard techniques for coping with this. You lay out a camp that can be guarded efficiently, you protect it with fences, barricades, lights, watchtowers, and so forth, and you patrol it regularly. With all these basic measures the Canadians seemed to have problems. Instead of creating one camp they created separate camps for each of their three commandoes, two English-speaking and one French-speaking. They had a fourth camp for the headquarters staff, a fifth for their engineers and a separate hospital area, all strung along a main highway and virtually indefensible in the case of serious attack. As I have noted on a number of previous occasions, it was a perfect illustration of Canada, divided into separate linguistic compounds with the bosses living in their own privileged enclosure. In the event of infiltration by thieves, the Canadians were in danger of shooting directly into one another's camps.

This was only one example of a serious breakdown and failure of leadership throughout the Somalia mission, starting with a hasty commitment to participate given to President Bush by Prime Minister Mulroney, and concluding with the ignominious fall-out from the mission that eventually included our aborted inquiry, the resignation under duress of a chief of the defence staff, and the reassignment of another to the federal Department of Fisheries.

Our soldiers were sent into Somalia with almost no knowledge of the situation they would encounter, without even the most elementary information about the country and its people, poorly equipped and badly disciplined. In Somalia they were inadequately maintained, the only element of the multinational force that existed on hard rations for its entire stay. And when thievery developed into a significant problem, the response of the most senior Canadian officers was not to improve camp security in a conventional fashion but to gradually relax the rules until Canadian junior officers and lower ranks understood that they were permitted to shoot thieves or even suspected thieves.

And when this resulted in the predictable unjustified killings, there was an immediate attempt in the field to cover this up, and to evade responsibility at the highest command levels, coinciding with an elaborate cover-up operation at National Defence Headquarters in Ottawa.

I haven't time here to go into all the questions that were left unanswered when the government ordered us to terminate our public hearings at the end of last March. I can hardly bother, at this stage, to repeat the inane explanations offered at the time by Prime Minister Chrétien and then Defence Minister Doug Young, ranging from the prime minister's "What cover up?" to Young's assertion that everything that anyone needs to know about events in Somalia was already known when he closed down the inquiry. Anyone who is interested in knowing what we would have investigated if we had been allowed to finish can find the list of unanswered questions in pages 1401 to

1440 of our report, in particular the questions related to the murder of Shidane Arone on March 16, 1993.

One of the unanswered questions is, "Why didn't anyone stop it?" Where was the Canadian counterpart of Hugh Thompson in Vietnam who broke ranks and said, in effect, "Enough is enough"? We do know, from testimony at court martials after the March 16 event, that the beating and torture of Shidane Arone went on for hours, that it was witnessed by a number of Canadian soldiers, that the screams of Arone were heard by perhaps hundreds of Canadian soldiers, including senior officers, and that no one lifted a finger to interfere with it or stop it.

Dr. Armstrong, incidentally, was not within earshot that night. He had already raised questions, verbally and in writing, about the earlier shooting of a Somali on March 4, a shooting that our inquiry clearly established to be unjustified. After the subsequent murder of Arone, it was his threat to go public with these questions, and the release of his suspicions to the media by his wife in Canada, that eventually blew the lid off a situation that was being suppressed up to that point. If Dr. Armstrong's concerns had been investigated immediately and thoroughly, it is likely that the murder of Arone would never have occurred.

One result of all this was the claim by the then minister of defence, Kim Campbell, that she did not learn of the murder of Arone until two weeks after the event. This was countered by the claim by former Deputy Defence Minister Robert Fowler, in an interview with me last summer in New York, where he is our ambassador to the United Nations, that he had told Ms. Campbell's chief of staff of the "foul play" involved in Arone's death within a few days of the event. This has been denied by Ms. Campbell's former chief of staff. Without going into all the complexities, it's clear that someone at National Defence Headquarters was covering up the truth about Shidane's murder and that the cover-up involved either the minister herself and/or senior members of her staff and/or senior bureaucrats and officers. In any case, the issue here is not a minor one. It involves the basic principle of political control of the military and accountability for the actions of the military.

Consequently, when the government aborted our inquiry, it rejected the principle of accountability, for its ministers, for the senior commanders of the armed forces, for the senior bureaucrats in the Department of National Defence, and for our senior officers in the field. The only people who were ever held accountable for the murder of Shidane Arone were the major who was in charge of that section of the camp that night, a small number of lower ranks and Cpl. Clayton Matchee who apparently killed Arone and then incapacitated himself permanently when he later tried to commit suicide. In this context of a massive failure of leadership in the Canadian mission to Somalia, from beginning to end, we can see Matchee and Arone, the Somali teenager and the young native Canadian soldier, as twin victims of a tragedy whose chief authors remain protected and unaccountable.

The results of this tragedy and the evasion of responsibility for it at the highest levels are very much with us today. They have certainly affected me, and I want to talk about this first on a personal level before I deal briefly with some of the political implications.

Little did I know, when the phone rang in my home in the spring of 1995, and I was asked to join the Somalia inquiry, that I was about to embark on a phase of my life that would have a profound effect on the way I think about this country. Today I look back on my "old self" of 1995 with amazement that I could have been as naive as I was after all those years in journalism. This new self that has emerged from the Somalia experience is not, on the surface, as attractive. I now belong to the group of people in Canada who have been betrayed and victimized by their own government. And in a sense, I also hold membership in the larger international group of people who have been the victims of unbridled political power.

I don't want to exaggerate this. I'm certainly not trying to compare myself to the hundreds of thousands who have suffered death, imprisonment, and exile because of arbitrary government action, or the failure of governments to give them the protection that was their right. But somewhere on the fringes of this large group there are people like myself, including many Canadians, whose rights have been violated or ignored by their governments and who have been permanently changed by that process.

For me, it was almost a physical sensation. When the government closed down our inquiry, I frequently said to myself—So this is what it feels like when raw political power is used against you. That was the word that kept recurring in my mind—*raw* political power. Political power not moderated and tempered by tradition, by basic civility and decency, by democratic or judicial processes.

This is not an abstract concept. When raw political power is used against you, believe me, you know it and you feel it. And when you become a victim of the misuse of political power, it separates you from everyone else. It marks you. You become a loser; and if you complain about this, you become a poor loser. Canadians in particular don't like poor losers, particularly those whose situation reflects badly on them as a nation.

A good example of poor losers, in the news again this past winter, were the patients at Montreal's Allan Memorial Institute in the 1950s who were victims of inhuman experimentation by a renowned psychiatrist funded in part by the Central Intelligence Agency in Washington. The CBC dramatized their story in an excellent mini-series on television entitled "The Sleep Room." Just as appalling as the professional misconduct of the psychiatrist in his treatment of those people was the failure of the Canadian government to help these victims for decades after they had been irreparably damaged. Only the persistence of an American lawyer eventually forced the CIA to offer compensation, followed belatedly by compensation from our own government. According to the CBC's version of events, Canadian diplomats in Washington were not only unhelpful but actively hindered the efforts of the American lawyer. For years, until the CIA was forced to pay compensation, Canadian politicians up to and including former Prime Minister Mulroney placed a higher value on maintaining good relations with the U.S. government, in particular with President Reagan, than on obtaining justice for these Canadian citizens.

Before 1995, I would have watched something like the CBC television program with a certain skepticism, and a degree of smugness. I would have thought, well, they're probably overdramatizing this. It probably wasn't that bad. Now I know that it was. When I watched Canadian politicians on the television screen ducking responsibility and evading accountability—they used real news clips in the drama—I recognized those people. They were exactly like some of the politicians and bureaucrats and senior military leaders whom we had encountered during our inquiry. I had a strong gut reaction to the CBC drama which I would not have had before 1995.

There was another moment of angry recognition when the lawyer for Alan Eagleson a few months ago presented a judge with about thirty letters of support testifying to the former hockey czar's good character and pleading for a light sentence. I could understand why some prominent and successful hockey players might have written letters, despite the obvious injustices suffered by some lesser known athletes. I could understand why some older sports columnists were still writing wistfully about good old Al. I could even understand why former prime minister John Turner wrote a letter, or at least why he tended to sympathize with Eagleson. I had a harder time understanding how the publisher of the Sun group of newspapers could personally support Eagleson. But to see a former justice of our Supreme Court, Willard Estey, making a formal plea of mitigating circumstances for a man who had admitted to lying, cheating, and stealing, to see a former judge dedicated to upholding the law pleading in public for a confessed thief, made me realize how far we have departed from fundamental values. It made me ask myself, "What's happening here?"

In the days following Eagleson's sentencing, I received calls from two journalists who were asking exactly this kind of question. What did Willard Estey's letter say about Canadian values? Was it significant that it was an American sports reporter and American investigators who finally exposed Eagleson and brought him to justice? Why were Canadian authorities so slow to act? Did the fact that Eagleson had many friends in high places protect him? Is that the way things work in Canada?

The reason why the reporters were calling me is that they were finding parallels between the Eagleson case and the Somalia inquiry. In both cases, it appeared that people with the right connections were able to evade responsibility. Eagleson ultimately was brought down to earth, but what about the senior people in the defence establishment who were responsible for the tragic events in Somalia and attempts to cover them up? These two reporters had noticed that the number two job at the United Nations, deputy to UN Secretary-General Kofi Annan, was about to be awarded to Louise Frechette who had been deputy minister of defence during the Somalia inquiry and who, in that role, had urged the government to take the unprecedented step of bringing the inquiry to an early and premature end. The reporters were also aware that the closure of the inquiry had meant that Ms. Frechette's predecessor as deputy minister of defence, Robert Fowler, was not required to testify about allegations of a cover-up of events in Somalia, particularly the murder of Shidane Arone. Mr. Fowler is now, as I noted earlier, Canadian ambassador to the United Nations where he undoubtedly lobbied for the appointment of Ms. Frechette to the deputy's job. The reporters wondered whether this was another illustration of the way things work in Canada.

I should mention that the reporters in this instance were Americans, one on the staff of the *Los Angeles Times* and the other with the *Washington Post*. Both of these American journalists had been intrigued by these apparent illustrations of Canadian elitism and cronyism at work. They seemed to regard it as characteristically Canadian. Why didn't the same facts provoke a similar reaction from Canadian journalists? Has this kind of thing become so conventional and accepted in Canada that it's invisible to us?

As the government prepared to close down our inquiry—the first time in history that this had been attempted—the prime minister became personally involved in an abortive effort to send an international force into Zaire. I must admit that I regarded this with a good deal of skepticism at the time. It seemed to me that our policy at that point was being shaped not so much by humanitarian concern about the plight of refugees in Africa but by a search for a mission that would overshadow the Somalia affair and rehabilitate the public image of the Canadian forces. When that failed, the Canadian government was left with an obligation to President Clinton who had supported the Zaire initiative although not with a great deal of enthusiasm.

That account came due when President Clinton undertook his latest showdown with Iraq and was searching for international support. This time, it was much more difficult for the United States to find justification for military intervention than it was in the case of Somalia, and Canadian participation for that reason was even more important to President Clinton.

The Iraq episode confirmed the impression that Canada will blindly follow the United States into almost any military adventure. All it requires is a phone call from the White House, regardless of the risks involved or our own capacity to respond, and this response seems to be growing more and more automatic.

As I said a moment ago, Canada was willing to make a commitment to action against Iraq with even less justification than in the case of Somalia. This time there were no starving faces on our television screens. On the contrary, the prospective bombing of Iraq threatened to put them there in large numbers. Canada had no direct interest in Iraq. All we had was the American insistence that military action was necessary to get rid of the dictator Hussein or at least bring him under control, and the Churchillian threat that appeasement would bring even greater perils in future.

Ever since the Second World War, the example of Munich and Churchill have been used to justify military action by the United States, from Vietnam to Grenada. Canadians seem to have forgotten that even in 1939, Canada deliberately delayed its declaration of war in order to underline our independence from Britain. By then, it had become important for us not to automatically say, "Ready, aye, ready," as soon as London called.

After the Second World War, this spirit of independence was expressed in our relations with China and Cuba in opposition to the wishes of the United States. In following this policy, we gained international respect, not to mention export customers, without seriously endangering our diplomatic or commercial relations with the United States. In both cases, our independent actions strengthened moderate forces in the United States and promoted a lessening of international tensions.

Now we seem to have slipped back into a diplomatic embrace that is more restrictive than anything we experienced under Britain in the nineteenth and early twentieth centuries. We have started to act as if alternative options are closed to us at the outset, as if the phone call from the White House is not an invitation to consider but an order to be obeyed. That kind of unthinking response doesn't serve us or the United States well. We saw that in Somalia and as a result of Somalia, we seem to have linked ourselves even more tightly to American foreign policy.

But there are many people at this conference who are far more knowledgeable than I about the history and intricacies of Canadian foreign policy. My purpose in this brief and very subjective paper has been to remind Canadians that foreign policy is a reflection of national experience and national values, and that the Somalia experience and its consequences have reflected a serious and growing problem of leadership and lack of accountability in this country.

All of us are aware of this and can think of many examples. At a time of continuing high unemployment and growing disparity between rich and poor in Canada, our political leaders at many levels have placed themselves at the head of the line seeking to skim off greater financial rewards for themselves from a growing economy. We have seen this in our national Parliament and we have seen it at the local level. In my own community of London, Ontario, there was something close to a taxpayer's revolt when members of city council recently proposed to increase their salaries within a few months of being elected. Doctors have complicated an already complex health care crisis by being unable to separate out concerns about their own incomes from concerns about the welfare of their patients, even to the point of striking against a system that already is in a precarious state in many areas. Teachers have had the same problem, appearing to be more interested in their welfare than in reforming an educational system that is simply not producing the results that we have a right to expect from it. In these and other examples of what we all used to consider the most honourable of professions, self-interest has taken precedence over the idea of service to the larger community.

We often heard during the Somalia inquiry that the classical ideal of a military officer was based on the principle of service. An officer places the interests of his soldiers ahead of his own. And we saw how this ideal was eroded and subverted and turned on its head, time and time again, in our armed forces. Since Somalia, we have continued to hear of salary increases for higher ranks, colonel and above, and simultaneously of the families of ordinary soldiers having to apply for welfare. And not content with generous salaries, pensions, and other perks, senior officers continue to make news when they are caught fiddling with their expense accounts and, just this past week, accepting benefits under the table from military contractors.

Many of these examples and incidents seem minor in isolation but their cumulative effect is to encourage skepticism among Canadians and a loss of confidence in our institutions. And this cripples our ability to function internationally with the kind of pride and self-confidence that others used to recognize as characteristically Canadian.

In this context, Dr. Barry Armstrong is the kind of military officer whom we should recognize and honour at this time and whose conduct has meaning far beyond the military sphere. When that recognition is given, perhaps we will then be able to face the March 16 anniversary of Shidane Arone's death with something more than embarrassed national silence.

What's Wrong with Peacekeeping?

J.L. GRANATSTEIN

Professor Emeritus of History, York University
Director and CEO, Canadian War Museum

Canadians know and understand better than any nation on earth how useful peacekeeping can be. We have done it for more than forty years in virtually every part of the world, thirty-six United Nations missions in all, I think, and Canada has also done non-UN missions in Indochina, the Sinai, Haiti, and Somalia. We do it as good international citizens and because we are good at it, and it overstates the case only a little to say that Canadians tend to believe that the Nobel Peace Prize for Peacekeepers in 1988 was really intended for them.

Lately, however, our numbers on peacekeeping operations and new UN missions in general have been declining, streamlined in size, or given shorter durations and conditional mandates by the Security Council. The reason is all too obvious: the UN's failures, as in Somalia and Rwanda, led to the hard tasks being taken over by more robustly armed coalitions, as in Former Yugoslavia, or transformed into peacebuilding exercises that are, if anything, even more difficult than traditional peacekeeping. In the circumstances, is it not time to ask what's wrong with peacekeeping?

I want to make nine points, not to knock UN peacekeeping off its pedestal, not to downgrade one of the central props in Canadian foreign policy, but to try to pose a more realistic agenda.

1. So what's wrong with peacekeeping? The definitional confusion in peace-keeping, peace enforcement, and peacebuilding

If peacekeeping is a child of the Cold War, peace enforcement is the product of the post–Cold War world that freed new nations and ethnic groups of superpower restraint. As a result, the line between peacekeeping and peace enforcement has blurred. This definitional problem is a major one, because without clarity we get a serious confusion of purpose. Today we also have peacebuilding—policies that are intended to help countries in conflict achieve stability by mobilizing civilian, military, governmental, and non-governmental expertise. There are preventive deployments such as in the Former Yugoslav province of Macedonia which imply a willingness to use greater force on the part of those nations contributing troops, even though that willingness may not be there, if and when the crunch comes. The UN also engages in human rights promotion, election monitoring, support for good governance, humanitarian assistance, refugee repatriation, disarmament and demobilization, and efforts at mediation to prevent conflicts.

Canada is a major booster of such efforts. For example, the Pearson Peacekeeping Centre in Nova Scotia now offers training for a "Neighbourhood Facilitators Project" in Bosnia. The Canadian government provides funding to the Guatemala Historical Clarification Committee (in effect, a truth commission), the preparatory commission for the establishment of the International Criminal Court, designed to try those accused of crimes against humanity, and for the work of the joint UN/Organization of African Unity Special Representative for the Great Lakes Region of Central Africa. The government has also put together CANADEM, a roster of Canadian experts on human rights and democracy, and it has expressed its willingness to give $500,000 to establish a non-governmental organization (NGO) foundation in Bosnia to develop civil society on the basis of multi-ethnic cooperation. I fear that more than $500,000, and more than neighbourhood facilitators, will be necessary for that.

We also have peacekeepers protecting NGOs—and increasingly NGOs seem to be setting the agenda of soft diplomacy—and not just in Canada: France is said to have 40,000 NGOs. The Department of Foreign Affairs and International Trade has had formal consultations with NGOs for several years now, and I think we can see the impact of these meetings on Canadian policies such as those mentioned. Denis Stairs has called the NGO network the "transnational public service left" and posited that the NGOs are trying to be a countervailing force to the corporations on the right. He is precisely correct.

All this definitional confusion and mission proliferation is occurring at a time when most conflicts seem to be within countries, not between nations, and civil wars, of course, are notoriously difficult to police. Does the UN need consent to intervene with peacekeepers or peacebuilders? Certainly the line between consent and no consent has blurred, and it should not. How does the UN make war and peace simultaneously on the same territory, as it tried to do in Bosnia? (The only answer, for those who have read the superb articles by Mark Danner in the *New York Review of Books* in late 1997 and early 1998, is badly.) How does it choose which side to support in Rwanda or Bosnia? Or does it decide to opt for strict neutrality and support for the status quo while the killing goes on? The world saw precisely this kind of shameful behaviour occur when the Dutch peacekeeping contingent in Srebrinica stood aside while ethnic cleansing was carried out under its nose. Similarly how does the North Atlantic Treaty Organization play the role of peacekeeper in Former Yugoslavia? Active or passive?

What this confusion too often produces is increasing risk to the peacekeepers. Canadian soldiers have suffered more than 100 killed on peacekeeping operations and more wounded. The rate of casualties seems to be increasing. Will the public here and in donor countries generally be willing to pay the price if the rules are fuzzy, if atrocities are not prevented, and if their soldiers are put at risk in a succession of political quagmires?

2. What's wrong with peacekeeping? The increasing American influence on and participation in UN and other operations

This is not an anti-American comment: Canadians know that the Americans are our best friends, as Social Credit leader Robert Thompson said thirty-five years ago in one of the great malapropisms of Canadian public life, whether we like it or not. It is simply a statement of reality.

The United States is increasingly world weary, fearful of casualties, and simultaneously playing a larger role, so much so that Joel Sokolsky has aptly called the whole process "The Americanization of peacekeeping." The recent peacekeeping operation in Haiti was understandable because of the immigration flow that would have flooded into the United States if the problems there were not resolved; but even there, once in, the United States wanted nothing but to get out (and leave the peacekeeping to Canada). The operation in Somalia was humanitarian in intent, but the American military insisted on running the show, an essential condition for all U.S. participation in order to appease Congress and satisfy the Pentagon. But the difficulty with U.S. participation is that the media is always on-site and in strength. This means that any petty warlord can get headlines and shape an issue by killing one —or more —U.S. soldiers, as so clearly happened in Somalia. The Americans then feel obliged to overreact or to withdraw; in either case, chaos can be the only result. Even so, for all its concerns about peacekeeping, the United States had 644 troops involved in UN operations at the end of December 1997, while Canada had only 254, the first time in at least forty years that there have been more Americans than Canadians involved in peacekeeping.

There is, nonetheless, a widespread sense that the United States only uses the UN when it suits its own purposes, as when it sought UN sanction for the war against Iraq in 1991–92. There is growing concern that Washington is willing to distort threats to regional peace (as defined in Article VII of the UN Charter) to include such crises as Haiti, which stretch the definition very far indeed. And all this goes on, moreover, at a time when the United States doesn't pay its bills to the UN for peacekeeping and, in the autumn of 1997, tried to "blackmail" the world organization into reducing the U.S. contribution to the UN from twenty-five to twenty percent (or so the Canadian ambassador to the UN characterized it in October 1997 with uncommon bluntness). The United States failed to reduce its assessment this time, and it has not yet anted up the billions it owes.

But if UN support can sometimes serve American interests, the feeling persists in the United States, as *Washington Post* columnist Charles Krauthammer wrote, that "peacekeeping is for chumps." In other words, the United States much prefers to be able to use force to "protect its own" and its own interests as defined by Congress and right-wing columnists like Krauthammer, not the UN. Why fool around with the polyglot processes of the United Nations when a simple surgical strike can fix a problem quickly?

Thus the sense has developed in many national capitals that the United States uses other nations when Congress blocks the Administration. For example, Prime Minister Jean Chrétien spoke only the truth when his table talk with the Belgian and Luxembourg leaders was picked up by a microphone at the Madrid NATO summit in 1997: "Clinton goes to Haiti with soldiers. The next year Congress doesn't allow him to go back. So he phones me. OK, I send my soldiers, and then afterward I ask for something in return." (What we might have received in return is hard to determine—certainly it was not a concession in the Pacific salmon negotiations!) Chrétien's partners clucked sympathetically, understanding exactly what he meant and how the game is played.

3. What's wrong with peacekeeping? The disorganization of the United Nations

The UN in 1994 ran eighteen peacekeeping operations with 80,000 soldiers from eighty-two countries on a budget of U.S. $3.3 billion. At the end of 1997, it was running seventeen operations with 23,000 soldiers on a U.S. $1.3 billion budget. The staff of the UN's Peacekeeping Operations Department in 1989 was six civilians and three military officers. Today, matters are somewhat better with 400 civilian and military personnel on staff and a UN undersecretary-general in charge of peacekeeping operations. There is, at last, a round-the-clock Situation Centre that should eliminate the answering machine that used to respond to commanders in the field calling New York for instruction after 5 p.m. EST.

There is also the generally sensible Canadian initiative to establish a UN Rapidly Deployable Mission Headquarters unit of sixty-one personnel for despatch on short notice to run a peacekeeping operation. But after two years of effort and diplomatic arm-twisting, only half the pittance of money needed to establish this unit has been pledged (perhaps because the countries providing officers pay their costs, not the UN). Moreover, with the plan calling for only eight officers to be recruited specially for this task, with twenty-nine to be provided by the UN's Department of Peacekeeping Operations and serving part-time, and with twenty-four to be designated but to remain in their home countries until needed for predeployment integration into the headquarters, one might well question if such a unit can work. How any headquarters can function effectively with officers from different nations and military traditions beginning from a standing start is unclear. There are also complaints from Less Developed Countries (LDCs), as the current euphemism for the Third World is styled, about this headquarters, even though Canada, Denmark, and the Netherlands have offered to finance LDC participation.

So there is some progress at the UN, but not enough. There still is difficulty getting orders at night; there still is insufficient planning and an alarming weakness in intelligence collection (as bedevilled UNPROFOR in Former Yugoslavia and the UN force in Rwanda), where the UN is literally dependent on U.S. sources that are sometimes withheld, contradictory, or unreliable. The UN's Standing Operation Procedures are still confused and confusing. And the UN Secretariat and its Department of Peacekeeping Operations still cannot be counted upon to back up its commanders or troops in the field.

Now that the UN frequently combines civilian and military personnel on operations and sometimes has to share responsibility in the field with other organizations—for example, in the Former Yugoslavia where UN and NATO both operate—the complexity of situations is multiplied dramatically. In such circumstances, what is clear is that the ad hoc, amateurish UN peacekeeping organization cannot any longer be tolerated. It is long past time for the UN to get its act together.

4. What's wrong with peacekeeping? The contracting out of logistical support for UN peacekeeping

One aspect of amateurish UN peacekeeping policy is that, incredibly, the UN continues to rely on civilian contractors to supply most peacekeeping operations. This is an inherently unreliable state of affairs, as with UNPROFOR in Yugoslavia in the first half of the 1990s where supplies could not reach deployed troops because civilian drivers and pilots refused to take the risk. This is one area where U.S. military assistance is likely more valuable than anything else the United States can provide—and, to be sure, the Americans have frequently provided such aid in a pinch. Indeed, it might well be that standby logistical units are more important than infantry for a country such as Canada to consider providing.

5. What's wrong with peacekeeping? The new phenomenon of countries selling troops for dollars

It should not be surprising that some nations have more soldiers than dollars. The Bangladeshis, for example, are frequent contributors to UN peacekeeping in substantial part because the U.S. $1000 a month paid by the UN for each peacekeeper is a very useful supplement to the country's holdings of scarce foreign exchange. But this can be true even for Canada. The Canadian Forces allow soldiers to keep the UN's monthly shilling, and because the military's pay is so low, many soldiers have eagerly sought UN service as a way of supplementing their income. In effect, Canadian soldiers were selling themselves for UN dollars. Poorly equipped armies can also get new equipment in the UN's service. Germany provided armoured personnel carriers to Pakistani troops in Bosnia, for example.

It is also true that the explosion of countries providing troops for peacekeeping has meant that many contingents are not well trained. As a result, some experienced nations have stepped in to assist. Sweden trained a Bulgarian unit prior to its despatch to Cambodia, and the Swedes incorporated Latvians into their IFOR unit in Bosnia, as did the Danes. Canada runs a peacekeeping centre to train officers and senior non-commissioned officers from many countries and is working directly with the combined Polish-Ukrainian peacekeeping battalion.

6. What's wrong with peacekeeping? The almost certain failure of efforts to improve the UN's rapid reaction capability

The UN has pledges of 80,000 troops on stand-by, but these are non-binding pledges that aren't worth the paper they're printed on. What is needed is a rapid reaction force that can be deployed quickly into a trouble spot. Such a force, for example, might have prevented the bloodbath in Rwanda.

The Canadian government has been pressing an initiative in New York for what it calls "Vanguard" forces, and Ottawa is calling for concrete changes at the UN to ensure speedy, efficient response to crises. There has been some progress, as noted above. The Canadian Vanguard proposal envisages up to 5,000 civilian and military personnel from member states ready for rapid deployment under control of the Rapidly Deployable Mission Headquarters, also suggested by Canada, which would be responsible for planning and advance preparations. The force would have no right to initiate the use of its weaponry but could defend itself vigorously.

Canada is not alone with such suggestions. Sweden's International Command is supposed to be able to deploy a rapid reaction force of 8,000-14,000 within a month, and there is also a joint Nordic rapid reaction battalion of 1,000. Unfortunately, no one in the Swedish military—or none whom I talked to in the autumn of 1997—seems to believe there is a realistic prospect of this being made operationally effective.

What do these plans matter when there is widespread resistance to the idea of UN rapid reaction force, and not least from the United States and China? Smaller countries are also suspicious that this proposal amounts to a supranational power grab by richer, bigger nations, and many others believe that such a rapid reaction force could entail a loss of national control over participation in UN operations. Others worry that the existence of such a force would encourage the Security Council to excessive interventionism or, just as bad, encourage the UN Secretariat to interventionist approaches. Then there are the costs—an estimated U.S. $300 million per year for 5,000-10,000 troops.

Nonetheless in December 1996, Canada and six other states led by Denmark signed a letter of intent to create a Multilateral UN Stand-By Forces High Readiness Brigade that would do Chapter VI peacekeeping (the least violent kind). SHIRBRIG, as it is called, has a cumbersome name and an even more unlikely future. Its initial operational and logistical capabilities were supposed to be up and running by January 1998, a deadline that was not met. Indeed, as of the end of November 1997, there had been seventeen drafts of a Memorandum of Understanding on the Operation, Funding and Status of SHIRBRIG—with no agreement in sight. SHIRBRIG is intended to be ready for instant deployment for a maximum six months period, *subject* to a *decision* on a *case-by-case basis* by *participating* countries. In effect, the rapid reaction force might see its contributors decide not to participate, something that effectively neuters the whole idea, even though the intent is for there to be sufficient forces on standby to replace a drop-out nation. Very simply, this will not work. As a result, the Canadian foreign minister, Lloyd Axworthy, sounded less than hopeful at the UN in September 1997: "These improvements ... are feasible, and they should be implemented without delay. Let us learn our lesson, not ignore it once again." But the lesson clearly hadn't been learned: the non-aligned member nations at the UN were quick off the mark with protests that SHIRBRIG is premised "on predetermined criteria [resulting] in pre-arranged exclusivistic linkages among a selected few." The non-aligned clearly see this initiative as contrary to the intent and spirit of the UN standby system because it has the potential to exclude a significant number of states from participation in UN peacekeeping. The message seems to be "better the shambles of peacekeeping in which all can join in than a more limited system that might actually work."

At the end of 1997, the Carnegie Commission on Preventing Deadly Conflict urged a different kind of rapid reaction force made up of Security Council members' troops, with it being a price of Security Council membership to contribute. The commission proposed that the United States have responsibility for logistics, communications, intelligence and air transport, and only sometimes for troops on the ground. While that recommendation is eminently sensible, the commission's proposal would be subject to veto by the permanent members of the security council. Moreover, such a proposal raises—and even more so—all the fears raised by SHIRBRIG and the Vanguard idea.

But what is abundantly clear is that continued "adhockery" in peace-keeping will not work. Something must be done, and the Vanguard/SHIRBRIG idea seems the best solution out there.

7. What's wrong with peacekeeping? Racism among troops doing peacekeeping

Canadian studies prepared for the Somalia commission of Inquiry found pervasive racism among Canadian, Belgian, Italian, French, and U.S. troops in Somalia. There seems no reason to doubt that this was so—or that black or Asian troops serving among white populations would be any different. With racism added to the usual effects of having young men and women serving away from home, namely drunkenness and prostitution, the result is that the local image of peacekeepers among citizens being "helped" is sometimes very bad indeed. This cannot be tolerated any longer, not least in the Canadian Forces, which have been hit with a succession of hammer blows involving racism, sexism, rape, and corruption. The question is how much longer donor countries will accept such behaviour and whether the nations being assisted by peacekeepers will agree to the stationing of UN troops on their territory. The answer is education, training, and discipline. What must be done to train/educate troops better?

8. What's wrong with peacekeeping? The cultivation of the "feel good" effect of peacekeeping

For fifty years, since 1948, the UN has had military observers in Kashmir in UNMOGIP, and India and Pakistan are as close to war today as they have been in the last two decades. For thirty years, Canadians served in Cyprus patrolling the Green Line separating Greek- and Turkish-Cypriots, and not until the Canadian government pulled its troops out of UNFICYP did the parties really begin to talk, though to no avail.

Simply put, endless missions that extend well beyond their original intended lifespan and in defiance of pledges by politicians are very damaging to the concept of peacekeeping. Everyone can "feel good" when the peacekeepers go in; no one feels good if they must stay in place for a generation with no prospect of a resolution of the crisis that brought them in in the first place. In other words, peacekeeping must not and cannot be an end in itself. Either it is accompanied by diplomatic efforts at a resolution or it should not be tried; and if diplomacy fails, then the peacekeepers should be withdrawn.

9. Finally, what's wrong with peacekeeping? The understandable donor fatigue that has gripped or begun to afflict those countries such as Canada that have provided troops to the UN for more than forty years

These points together add up to the sense that peacekeeping hasn't worked the way it ought to have and, moreover, that since the end of the Cold War, peacekeeping has become much more difficult, confusing, and stressful. Nations and their finance ministers want their peace dividends, a sentiment made all the more powerful as their publics feel the apathy born of bad results in UN service.

How can we fix these problems or at least ameliorate their worst effects?

First, is it not time to consider returning to the old conditions that used to govern UN peacekeeping? Consent by the parties involved was a requirement, as was the possibility of a resolution of the crisis. The peacekeeping force needed a clear mandate and a clear line of command and control; no superpowers could be involved on the ground; and the UN force had to be impartial and devoted to upholding international law. Those were sensible rules in the Cold War years, and I think we do need to retain some of them still, especially consent and impartiality. On the other hand, it makes sense in a post–Cold War world to involve Permanent Members of the Security Council in peacekeeping, primarily because they have the resources and reach to be of substantial use.

Second, the world has to begin to consider the appropriate role for NGOs. Should NGOs have a role in determining where and how peacekeepers will go and function, as some in Canada have suggested? I think not. The impartiality of NGOs is sometimes suspect, not least because some nations try to use them for intelligence-gathering or for other purposes. The risk of reprisals if NGO members speak out is sometimes great, and NGOs may require military protection. Moreover, and most important, who elected NGOs to make policy?

Third, it seems almost certain that peace enforcement—the toughest kind of peacekeeping permitted under Article VII of the UN Charter—works best outside the UN, most likely with a coalition of nations, operating under a Security Council green light. UN peacekeeping should be limited to the low end of the violence scale, to freeze a situation and give the parties a breathing space. In other words, it is time to define clearly what the UN will and will not do.

Fourth, it might also be time to consider subcontracting peacekeeping to regional organizations like the Organization for African Unity (OAU) and the Organization of American States, which might help make peacekeeping less racist, more sensitive, and even cheaper. The difficulties in using the OAU, for example, are obvious—weak militaries, tribal conflicts, and little money. The United States, to its credit, is trying to create an African Crisis Response Force of 10,000 troops with American and other funding, training, and logistics. But only a few countries have signed on, and there is massive criticism of the concept from, among others, President Mandela. The Africans and the UN desperately need such a force.

Fifth, countries must decide if they accept peacebuilding, not peacekeeping or peace enforcement, as the wave of the future. In Ottawa, officials are hard at work trying to uncouple peacekeeping from peacebuilding. Peacekeeping is a blunt instrument, they say, while peacebuilding is flexible and doesn't need peacekeeping first to succeed. Police officers, not soldiers; election monitors, not armies, in other words. Should we consider a UN standing police force of cops—an idea that is trendy at the moment? How can we mobilize civilian expertise for crises? How then do we protect civilian peacebuilders? Does this mean bringing NGOs directly into the peacebuilding policymaking process? Mr. Axworthy's department has said it will do so. Once again, it is time to ask who elected NGOs to make policy? And who anywhere believes that a Canadian Corps of Airborne Sociologists can resolve anyone's problems?

Sixth, the UN must realize that it cannot be too ambitious and cannot expect to resolve every problem. Hard choices about where to intervene and where not to will be necessary. There are signs that Secretary-General Kofi Annan realizes this. But with so many of the critical factors that affect the ability of peacekeepers to function effectively being within the UN administration or directly under UN control, the one task that cannot be shirked is bringing the UN Secretariat under control. Perhaps the appointment of a deputy secretary-general, the former Canadian deputy minister of national defence, will help this process. It must.

Seventh, however much better the UN administration becomes, the UN must recognize that there are serious perils in using force, especially in countries such as Somalia, where there was no larger political framework in place. The UN has to pick and choose its spots and determine which weapons in its arsenal to employ. Certainly, it is easier to minimize the use of force if the United States is not involved.

Finally, Canada and its friends must continue their efforts to develop rapid reaction forces. We must persuade the non-aligned and some great powers that this is essential, indeed much more important than banning landmines or trying to prohibit the sale of small arms. If Lloyd Axworthy can do this, he might prevent the next Rwanda or forestall the next Bosnia. If he can press the UN to do what it must, then he will deserve the Nobel Peace Prize that he failed to receive for his efforts to eliminate anti-personnel landmines. Nothing Canada can do at the United Nations is more important than to make rapid reaction forces a reality.

Canada, International Organization, and Human Rights

Elements of Peacebuilding

MICHAEL BONSER AND MARSHALL CONLEY

Department of Political Science
Acadia University

Since its inception, the United Nations and Canada have been inextricably linked. The UN has offered Canada a venue for active involvement in world affairs, and in return Canadian participation has arguably made the organization better than it otherwise would have been.[1] This is particularly true in the realm of international peace and security. Since Lester Pearson promoted the concept of peacekeeping in 1956, successive Canadian governments have participated in UN multilateral efforts to restore peace to troubled regions as a means of creating a more orderly international environment.[2]

In recent years, however, the changing complexion of international relations has led to questions regarding the UN's ability to manage potential threats to peace and security. The post–Cold War era has been characterized by a flourishing of new kinds of wars—conflicts that are fought within, rather than between, states. The root of these conflicts can often be found in long-standing nationalistic, ethnic, and religious tensions. They are notable for their violent nature and for the frequency in which civilians are targeted and forced to endure tremendous suffering.[3] In order to bring long-term resolutions to such conflicts, it is clear that military solutions alone are not enough. Instead the UN must embrace the concept of peacebuilding as a means of addressing the underlying economic, social, and political causes of conflict. It is only by broadening the definition of human security and focusing on issues such as human rights and freedoms, the rule of law, good governance, social equity, and sustainable development that the UN can successfully bring long-term peace to countries ravaged by war.[4] The success of future peace-building initiatives will ultimately depend on the UN's flexibility in respond-ing to new challenges and its credibility, in the eyes of member states, as an organization that can effectively address complex security issues. This analy-sis will argue that Canada must play a leadership role both in promoting the concept of peacebuilding among member states, and in championing the UN as an organization well suited to shape and coordinate international peace-building strategies.

In addressing the role that Canada should play in the promotion of peacebuilding, the goal of this analysis is threefold. First, this paper will pro-vide a historical overview of Canada's support for and involvement in the United Nations, particularly in the field of peacekeeping. This section will highlight the innovative role Canada has played in the past, and the value of the UN, from a Canadian perspective, as an important avenue for the con-ducting of foreign policy. Through this analysis it will be demonstrated that Canada has a vested interest in ensuring that the UN remains both flexible and innovative in its ability to deal with threats to international peace and security. Second, this paper will explore the concept of peacebuilding, both its potential, and factors that may hamper its success. Issues that will be addressed in this section include: the rapid increase in the number of con-flicts in which the UN is being asked to intervene, the legitimacy of UN action in largely internal state conflicts, and the ability of the UN to imple-ment peacebuilding initiatives consistently given its current resource and financial constraints. Finally, this analysis will examine recent efforts on the part of the Canadian government to advance the concept of peacebuilding as a necessary component of UN peace and security activities. A number of spe-cific examples will be highlighted, and certain recommendations for reform will be advanced. While it is beyond the scope of this paper to conduct a detailed analysis of UN reform, it is clear that the future of peacebuilding will depend on that organization's ability to improve and update both its struc-tures and institutions. In that regard, certain key issues will be discussed as they pertain to the legitimacy of the UN as a defender of international security.

Canada and the United Nations: A Strong Multilateralist Tradition

Canada emerged from World War II as a significant power in the world. Its economy had expanded substantially, it was strong politically, and Canadian policymakers employed a more activist strategy in world affairs.[5] It was also recognized, however, that Canada's foreign policy was shaped largely by the international system in which it operated. Its effectiveness, in other words, depended upon the willingness of other nations, principally the United States, to become involved in multilateral international regimes.[6] Policymakers understood, for example, that conflicts involving great powers would have direct repercussions for Canada, thereby underscoring the need to implement mechanisms to restrain these countries from acting unilaterally. As well, by the end of World War II, Canada relied heavily upon trade as a means of ensuring economic prosperity. However, because the government was incapable of imposing their vision of international order upon others either militarily or economically, it was clear that the only viable option was to establish credible institutions and procedures that would bring about an orderly interaction between states.[7]

For Canada, then, the primary objective in the post–World War II era was to secure the UN's legitimate place as a source of negotiation, compromise, and peace in the emerging world order. In that regard, Canadian efforts reflected a willingness to promote global objectives, rather than issues related to state sovereignty or a more narrow national perspective.[8] Through this approach, policymakers recognized that Canada's own national interests would be best protected and enhanced over the longer term. As Tom Keating points out in his book *Canada and World Order: The Multilateralist Tradition in Canadian Foreign Policy:*

> It was a ... strong concern with these national interests that tended to favour active support for an involvement in international organizations. Multilateral organizations would best protect Canada's interests in such matters as security, trade, and currency stablilization and would enhance political contacts.[9]

One of the most notable contributions that Canada has made as a member of the UN has been in the field of international peacekeeping. Canada was seen as generally acceptable on political grounds, and Canadians were recognized for their competence in the technical aspects of peacekeeping. For these reasons, Canada was able to step forward and play a leadership role in successive UN efforts to maintain international peace and security. From a Canadian foreign policy perspective, peacekeeping has also fulfilled an important political objective. This activity had about it an implicit sense that it served higher interests than simply those of the United States or the West. Despite the fact that Canada's efforts often coincided with U.S. interests, peacekeeping provided an opportunity for Canada to be seen, both at home and abroad, as pursuing an independent and globally responsible policy agenda.[10] In an era where superpower militaries called the shots, Canada had carved out a niche as a peacekeeper, an essentially "anti-military military role." [11]

Even during the late 1960s and 1970s when the Canadian government's commitment to multilateralism experienced a period of decline,[12] there is considerable evidence to suggest that Canada's support for peacekeeping remained strong. Within the United Nations itself, for example, the Canadian delegation continued to press to have peacekeeping operations placed on a more stable base of political and financial support.[13] Moreover, Canadian delegates stressed that:

> peacekeeping was an essential function of the United Nations, but was not in itself a substitute for the peaceful settlement of disputes; that peacekeeping costs should be borne by all United Nations members; and that practical measures as well as general guidelines were required to ensure the effectiveness of peacekeeping resolutions.[14]

In the present context, a strong and effective United Nations remains as a vital cornerstone of Canadian foreign policy. As a middle power, the Canadian government continues to have an interest in building a rules-based system of international relations.[15] The UN is the only organization capable of addressing threats to this system and continues to be the most important and effective avenue for Canadian participation in world affairs. Currently, however, the UN is at a crossroads. In order for the organization to continue to play a legitimate role in the maintenance of international stability, a fundamental rethinking of peace and security initiatives must be undertaken.[16] The legitimacy of the UN will rest, to a great extent, on its ability to demonstrate that it can be flexible and innovative in responding to the changing international environment. It is in Canada's best interest, therefore, to play a leadership role in this process. Just as Canada led the way in the development of peacekeeping, policymakers must now promote the concept of peacebuilding as a necessary component of future UN efforts to maintain and enhance peace and security.

From Peacekeeping to Peacebuilding: A Necessary Objective

The post–Cold War period represents a time of both great promise and growing uncertainty for the United Nations. As more and more issues find their way onto the global agenda, the definition of what constitutes a threat to international security has expanded greatly, and now includes issues such as: economic stagnation, poverty, overpopulation, human rights violations, and environmental degradation.[17] As well, the proliferation of new types of violent conflicts have reinforced the need for a rethinking of how to conduct peace and security initiatives. By the spring of 1997, for example, ten of the seventeen ongoing conflicts were taking place within rather than between states.[18] All too often, these conflicts have been characterized by long-term cycles of violence, with little or no capacity to sustain a peaceful society.[19] Fighting factions are often made up of undisciplined groups who, in order to achieve their aims, employ gross violations of human rights.[20] Civilians become primary targets in these conflicts, and approximately eighty percent of those killed in current wars are non-combatants, and even more disturbing, approximately half of these people are children.[21] For the UN this poses new risks and complex challenges that cannot be met by traditional peace-keeping methods alone. Clearly:

> political elites cannot cut workable deals on behalf of communities that do not trust each other, or that see each other as having fundamentally conflicting interests. What is required is extensive long-term, community level contact, consultation and confidence-building to generate a minimal trust between communities.[22]

In the face of these challenges, a number of positive trends have also emerged in recent years. Specifically the UN Security Council has shown itself to be willing to play a more activist and interventionist role in world affairs. With the coming to an end of the Cold War, the high degree of tension that once permeated Security Council discussions has been replaced by a growing sense of accommodation, and decision making by consensus.[23] For the first time since its inception, the Council has been able to operate more closely in a manner envisioned by those who originally drafted the Charter.[24] Not only is the Council addressing issues that would have been inconceivable during the Cold War, but it is turning with increasing regularity to Chapter VII enforcement actions—a measure once considered virtually unusable—in an effort to restore and maintain international stability.[25] While the Security Council must be careful to avoid becoming overly interventionist in its approach, its willingness to step in to protect and enhance human security is both necessary and desirable for the future of peacebuilding. As Canada campaigns for an elected seat on the Security Council this concept will become one of its main initiatives.[26]

Peacebuilding is a flexible concept, and efforts to build peace in regions marred by conflict can take many forms. These include: the disarming of warring parties, repatriation of refugees, advisory and training support for security and police forces, election monitoring, strengthening government institutions, advancing efforts to protect human rights, and promoting both formal and informal processes of political participation.[27] Furthermore, in the aftermath of a conflict between states, peacebuilding efforts may also focus on cooperative projects linking two or more countries together in mutually beneficial undertakings.[28] In recent years, the issue of peacebuilding has come to the forefront, and many would argue that all UN peace and security initiatives now require a substantial peacebuilding component. For example, the previous Secretary-General, Boutros Boutros-Ghali, in his 1992 report entitled *An Agenda for Peace*, stated:

> Peacemaking and peace-keeping operations, to be truly successful, must come to include comprehensive efforts to identify and support structures which will tend to consolidate peace and advance a sense of confidence and well-being among people.[29]

A number of key obstacles, however, continue to inhibit the UN in its efforts to build effective and lasting solutions. Specifically, these are inadequate financing, a lack of resources, and uncertainty over the degree to which member states possess the political will to involve themselves in longer-term missions; all serve to hinder the UN's ability to respond to new threats to international security. Clearly, if this organization is to contribute to long-term peace successfully, financial, organizational, and operational requirements will be needed in a much greater magnitude than what the UN currently has at its disposal.[30]

With respect to the issue of resources, many of the current difficulties facing the UN have resulted, quite simply, from the growing popularity of peacekeeping as the international community's tool of choice for conflict containment. For example, between 1947 and 1985, the UN undertook thirteen peacekeeping operations of varying scope and duration.[31] Conversely, between 1988 and 1996, twenty-nine new missions were undertaken.[32] Currently, there are sixteen missions operating.[33] This has stretched both the capability of the UN, and the ability for member states to contribute to these missions, to the limit. Compounding this problem is the degree to which the peacekeeping umbrella has expanded since the end of the Cold War. Missions now routinely include humanitarian aid agencies, professional police, human rights observers, and good government officials.[34] These multidimensional initiatives require a much higher degree of coordination and cooperation among UN personnel. This, in turn, has placed further strains on the organization's already limited resources.[35]

Closely linked to the lack of necessary resources, is the issue of inadequate financing. In recent years the cost of peacekeeping has risen at a rapid rate.[36] In 1990, for example, the annual UN peacekeeping budget stood at approximately $700 million. Yet, by 1995, this number had jumped fivefold to approximately U.S. $2.8 billion.[37] Since then, however, the peacekeeping budget has declined rapidly, and in 1997 it is expected to be less than the $1.3-billion regular budget. This decline has coincided with the development of a serious financial crisis for the UN, and has been further compounded by the fact that, as of April 30, 1997, unpaid peacekeeping dues to the organization stood at $1.65 billion.[38] While requests for UN intervention and assistance continue to rise:

> the organization can only be asked to do as much or as little as its members are willing to agree on and pay for. The difficulty of late is that they have been agreeing much more readily than they have been paying.[39]

This financial crisis will continue to determine the degree to which the UN can become involved in longer-term peacebuilding initiatives. Efforts, for example, to sustain postwar ceasefires and assist in the implementation and maintenance of peace agreements will require an increased financial commitment from the UN and its members. These costs, however, will undoubtedly dampen the enthusiasm of member states to participate in such initiatives. Unless the UN is able to draw further upon the resources of member states, or to find alternative sources of financing, the future of peace-keeping, let alone peacebuilding, will remain uncertain.

Finally, maintaining the political support of member states for wide-ranging peacebuilding initiatives will continue to be a difficult task. The question of political will has become even more critical as the UN encounters a growing number of intrastate conflicts where, not only has civil society broken down, but there is no clear sense of whether or not UN personnel are even welcome. Many developing nations, for example, continue to remain wary of UN efforts to intervene without the consent of a host country.[40] Fur-thermore, recent bitter experiences in the Former Yugoslavia and Somalia, may have served to underscore the difficulty facing the UN in generating the political will necessary to undertake a more activist peacebuilding role. In both of these instances, the Security Council undertook forceful humanitar-ian actions in order to save lives, but found itself entangled in no-win civil wars.[41] In the aftermath of these missions, "those who were vocal a few years ago in asserting that the Security Council has the right of humanitarian inter-vention seem to have fallen silent."[42]

Questions regarding the political will among member states have become further accentuated by a growing isolationist trend in the United States. The U.S. government's unwillingness to pay its $1.5 billion in arrears to the UN, its unilateral decision to cap contributions to peacekeeping budgets at twenty-five percent, and the recent decision by Congress to withdraw funding for U.S. forces in Bosnia, are all examples of a more inward looking perspective from the world's last remaining superpower.[43] If this trend continues, and the United States is perceived to be less supportive of UN activities, serious ques-tions will arise regarding the credibility and capability of this organization in the maintenance of international peace and security.

Clearly, the difficulties plaguing the UN have hindered its ability to play a more active peacebuilding role in world affairs. While member states regu-larly speak of the need for the UN to become more flexible and innovative in its actions, they often fail to provide the necessary resources, finances, and political backing to allow the organization to respond to the challenge. In order for the UN to retain its credibility on peace and security matters, member states will "have to demonstrate a good deal more political will and practical support than they have to date."[44]

An Innovative Role for Canada

In order to address the diverse challenges currently facing the UN, the Cana-dian government has joined like-minded nations such as Sweden, Norway, and the Netherlands at the forefront of efforts to promote the concept of peacebuilding at the international level.[45] Given Canada's strong background in peacekeeping and mediation, as well as the strong democratic traditions that typify Canadian society, this is a role that policymakers can and should pursue. In a 1996 speech to the UN General Assembly, Lloyd Axworthy, Canada's minister of foreign affairs, addressed the challenges currently before the UN. In his speech, the minister placed great emphasis on the concept of peacebuilding as a means of overcoming these obstacles. Citing the world's failure to prevent conflict in countries such as Rwanda, he stated:

> What is clear is the need for a new tool kit for the UN to respond. ....
> We have started to rework our own tool kit to improve our ability
> to initiate and support peacebuilding operations in areas such as
> preventive mediation and dialogue human rights monitoring
> and investigation, media and police training, judicial reform, and
> demobilization.[46]

In recent years, Canada has taken a number of measures in order to address those obstacles that have prevented the wider application of peacebuilding. In the area of financing, for example, the federal government in 1996 announced a $10-million Canadian Peacebuilding Initiative.[47] This program was designed in an effort to coordinate Canada's policies and programs in the areas of conflict prevention, peacebuilding, and postconflict reconstruction. Through this fund, Canada has supported a number of peacebuilding initiatives, including: assisting the Preparatory Commission for the Establishment of the International Criminal Court by underwriting the participation of delegates from developing countries, providing start-up funding for the Guatemala Historical Clarification Commission, contributing $500,000 to the new UN Trust Fund for Preventive Action, and announcing its intention to contribute an equal amount for the establishment of an NGO foundation in Bosnia to help develop a civil society on the basis of multiethnic cooperation.[48]

Certainly, the establishment of a peacebuilding fund is a worthwhile endeavour. Through such efforts, Canada has demonstrated its willingness to make tangible contributions to improve the potential for peacebuilding as a viable UN activity. There are, however, a number of factors which may serve to inhibit the overall effectiveness of this program. First, $10 million represents only a fraction of the actual financial resources needed to implement more comprehensive peacebuilding strategies. Furthermore, monies currently devoted to the peacebuilding fund are coming from Canada's larger Official Development Assistance budget.[49] Peacebuilding activities, in other words, may be conducted at the expense of, rather than in concert with, other important international assistance programs.

Second, while peacebuilding initiatives require both flexibility and long-term vision, the current government has adopted a shorter-term, project-oriented approach in determining the allocation of peacebuilding funds. Qualifying projects are short-term (maximum of eighteen months) in nature and are eligible to receive a one-time financial commitment of up to

$500,000.[50] Although such interventions are an important component in ensuring sustainable peace and allowing for longer-term development, there is a danger that the fund lacks the flexibility to be a truly effective peace-building tool. Peacebuilding, after all, is by its very nature rooted in the building of relationships and trust.[51] It is a process that requires both time and flexibility in approaches. In focusing on immediate objectives, which are often bound by parameters such as time and the completion of specific tasks, however, this initiative is in danger of falling short of its overall potential.

Aside from the peacebuilding fund, Canada has also taken a number of important steps to address the issue of inadequate resources, and particularly human resources, in order to further enhance the potential of peacebuilding. For example, as part of the Canada Peacebuilding Initiative, the government has created and submitted a roster of Canadian human rights experts available to the UN on short notice.[52] This initiative will assist the UN in its ability to provide a rapid and effective response when called upon. As well, in 1995, Canada tabled a report at the UN entitled *Toward a Rapid Reaction Capability for the United Nations*.[53] The report's main proposal calls upon the UN to assemble a multifunctional force of up to five thousand military and civilian peacekeepers in order to quickly deploy to preserve and restore peace and security.[54] Clearly, a key to the success of peacebuilding initiatives will rest on the ability of the UN to respond quickly and effectively in times of crisis. The sooner UN personnel become involved in conflict resolution, the better the organization's chances will be for securing long-term peace. If adopted, the recommendations put forward in this report will help achieve this goal.[55]

Furthermore, in recent years Canada has opened the Lester B. Pearson Peacekeeping Centre in Clementsport, Nova Scotia.[56] Canada's vast experience in the field of peacekeeping makes it well qualified to act as a centre for training UN military and civilian personnel earmarked for duty.[57] This type of training centre is critical as the UN assumes a larger peacebuilding role. Through enhanced training and education, military and civilian personnel can gain a better understanding of the need for a multifaceted and integrated approach to peacekeeping and peacebuilding. Participants can benefit, not only from an improved knowledge of the workings of the UN, but of other agencies involved in areas such as humanitarian relief and economic development, "activities which sometimes appear to be at cross-purposes with military action."[58]

Finally, Canada's efforts to promote human security through peacebuilding have led it to take a leadership role in the promotion of a global ban on anti-personnel landmines. Boutros Boutros-Ghali, in *Agenda for Peace*, called for a greater emphasis on de-mining as an important component of postconflict peacebuilding.[59] Canada has played an active de-mining role in countries such as Cambodia in recent years, and with this role has come a growing recognition of the danger these weapons pose to civilians worldwide. Not only do landmines represent an immediate danger to people, but "heavily mined areas cannot pursue economic development until they have been de-mined; and de-mining is a hopeless ... task if there is no treaty to prevent the laying of new mines."[60]

Canada's efforts, which culminated in an international signing ceremony in Ottawa on December 3, 1997, represent an important step forward in addressing the issue of human security.[61] Moreover, the government's pledge to contribute $100 million over the next five years to help make this treaty work is also commendable.[62] Canada must now continue to play a leadership role to ensure that the goals of the treaty are met. This includes providing assistance—both financial and technical—to those countries that lack the means to implement their commitments under the treaty, provide enhanced humanitarian assistance to victims of landmines, and work to achieve universal adherence to the treaty by lobbying those nations who continue to hold out. It is only by continuing to apply pressure on other member states can countries such as Canada ensure that this treaty represents a truly effective step in the process of peacebuilding.

Despite high-profile UN failings in countries such as Somalia, Rwanda, and the Great Lakes region of Africa in recent years, there is much evidence to suggest that peacebuilding has, in some instances, proven to be an effective tool in the maintenance of peace and security. For example, UN peacekeeping efforts in Haiti have entailed a substantial peacebuilding component: including the training of civilian police, coordination of institution building, and national conciliation and economic rehabilitation activities.[63] In addition, a number of other civilian peace missions that have been established in countries such as El Salvador and Guatemala are playing an important role in promoting stability, encouraging former belligerents to respect human rights, rebuilding state institutions, and bringing justice and lasting peace.[64] While these missions represent an important step in an effort to promote peacebuilding, clearly much more needs to be done. The UN continues to struggles to reconcile increasing requests for assistance with its often limited means to initiate long-term peace strategies. Peacebuilding efforts, therefore, tend to be ad hoc and reactive in nature. In order for the UN to retain its credibility as an organization well equipped to respond to new crises, a number of reforms must be initiated. These reforms should encompass both the practical workings of peacekeeping and peacebuilding initiatives, as well as address the more fundamental need to restructure the operations of the UN itself.

On the practical front, Canada should push for immediate action in two specific areas. First, Canadian officials must address the need for the development of a UN umbrella humanitarian agency. Major General Romeo Dallaire, in speaking of the UN shortcomings in Rwanda, and particularly the Goma refugee camps, argued that such an agency "could play a central role in planning, organizing, directing, coordinating and controlling the implementation of the humanitarian assistance plan."[65] This agency should fall under the mandate of the High Commissioner for Human Rights, and its focus must be on improving coordination between UN security and civilian personnel, and non-governmental agencies in order to provide humanitarian assistance more effectively both during and after periods of conflict and instability.

Second, as part of future peacebuilding initiatives, Canada should push for the development of an international media capability. Using television, radio, or newspapers, the UN must play a more active role in presenting the facts of a situation as a means of countering propaganda used to stir up both hysteria and hate among civilian populations.[66] However, given the current financial restraints hanging over the UN, there is little or no capability at the present time to create and fund a new branch of operations. In order to make this concept a reality, therefore, the UN must work with member states in order to develop a creative, low-cost alternative solution. For example, many nations, including Canada, the United Kingdom, and France already maintain international radio services. Perhaps, arrangements could be made with those member states that currently have the necessary communications infrastructure in place to allow UN access to these networks as a means of countering propaganda in regions marred by conflict or instability.

In order to ensure the UN is able to promote comprehensive peacebuilding initiatives over the long term, however, Canada must also push for a more fundamental rethinking of how the UN currently operates. For example, in examining the role of the United Nations on matters of international peace and security, policymakers must stress the need for the UN to work more closely with like-minded regional organizations. Given the current resource and financial constraints facing the UN, the use of regional bodies may prove to be a practical and attractive alternative. Critics of this approach will undoubtedly point to the fact that these organizations are far less capable than the United Nations in the maintenance of international peace and security.[67] This should not, however, deter the UN from improving its working relationship with regional multilateral organizations. An improved regional presence during periods of instability may serve to accomplish two important goals. First, it would clearly strengthen the UN's early warning capability by allowing for more timely updates and reports from regional agencies which may already have representatives on the ground. Second, the assistance of regional agencies may encourage greater transparency in efforts to restore peace within the region, and instill greater confidence among conflicting parties.[68] The UN must strive to share its experience in peacekeeping and peacebuilding in order to allow regional organizations to play a more effective role in resolving conflicts. In doing so:

> The UN will become a stronger force for peace if it persists in efforts for a more productive relationship with the regional groupings and for improved effectiveness on their parts even if the results are some time in coming.[69]

At the same time, however, more attention must be given to early warning. A number of secretaries-general have dealt with this particular issue.[70]

Finally, in order for the UN to continue to play an effective peacekeeping and peacebuilding role, certain fundamental issues of reform must be addressed. Member states have long recognized, for example, the need for improved efficiency within UN operations. In recent months, Secretary-General Kofi Annan has announced a series of wide-ranging reform measures aimed at addressing these concerns.[71] This is a process that Canada must wholeheartedly support. Without significant institutional reform and cost-saving measures, the future viability of the UN, let alone its peacebuilding capabilities, is very much in doubt. Moreover, given Canada's own efforts to streamline government and make programs more efficient in recent years, Canadian officials are in an ideal position to offer technical assistance during this reform process.

Budget cutting alone, however, is not the answer. Minister Axworthy, in his 1997 speech to the UN called for significant structural reform in order to modernize existing institutions.[72] One institution of particular relevance to the future of peacekeeping, and ultimately peacebuilding, is the Security Council. In recent years, many member states have expressed concern that, despite the rapidly changing international environment, the Security Council remains dominated by members largely sympathetic to Western interests. Without genuine structural reform of the Security Council—and specifically the makeup of the Council's permanent membership—the UN will ultimately lose credibility in the eyes of member states.[73] This issue has gained particular urgency in light of more recent UN peacebuilding efforts. For this organization to truly embrace the concept of peacebuilding, its presence will be required in unstable regions for longer periods of time. If member states are to approve of a more proactive UN, then, in return, its main peace and security organ must become more representative of the international environment in which it operates. Canada's desire to be elected to the Security Council in 1999 is indicative of the role this country desires to play in reform of the Security Council.[74]

Conclusion

The nature of international relations has changed profoundly in recent years. New types of wars have brought complex challenges as well as new types of threats to regional stability and international security. Traditional peacekeeping methods alone may no longer prove to be effective in bringing an end to such conflicts. However, while there is a greater need to focus on the economic, social, and political causes of conflict and the subsequent abuse of human rights, many obstacles continue to impede the UN from addressing these issues on a consistent and effective manner. Namely, these are the high financial costs involved in investing in long-term peace initiatives, a lack of adequate resources, and the often low levels of political will among UN member states to play a more active role in intrastate conflicts, will continue to hinder efforts to restore and sustain long-term peace. In order to secure peace in regions marred by conflict, however, UN member states must embrace the concept of peacebuilding. Although the costs involved with increased UN action are certainly prohibitive, there is a greater price to be paid if the UN does not play a more activist peacebuilding role. After all, "we are not impaired by a lack of resources, if we choose to invest wisely and practically in peace. We are limited only by how far we are willing to cast our vision."[75]

For Canada, the question becomes how to address these current challenges in such a way that will ensure the UN retains both its credibility and capability on peace and security matters? The UN continues to be an important avenue for the pursuit of Canadian foreign policy objectives, and is a critical venue for the achievement of multilateral cooperation on a wide range of international issues. However, unless the UN can demonstrate its ability to address new types of threats to peace and security, its legitimacy, in the eyes of member states, will be diminished. Recent experience has shown that Canada has the capacity to play a critical role in the evolution of international peacebuilding within the UN system. It is a country with a strong history of contributing to UN peace and security efforts and is recognized internationally for its expertise in this field. Moreover, the current government has demonstrated a growing interest in, and commitment to, the concept of peacebuilding in recent years. As a nation that continues to benefit greatly from its involvement in the UN, this is a role that Canada can and should play.

NOTES

1. James Patrick Sewell, "A World Without Canada: Would Today's United Nations Be the Same?" in *Making a Difference? Canada's Foreign Policy in a Changing World Order*, eds. John English and Norman Hillmer (Canada: Lester Publishing, 1992), p. 188.

2. See << http://www.dfait-maeci.gc.ca/virtual/foreignpolicy/english/main.htm>>

3. David B. Dewitt and David Leyton-Brown, *Canada's International Security Policy* (Scarborough, ON: Prentice-Hall, 1995), p. 199.

4. DFAIT, "Notes for an Address by the Hon. Lloyd Axworthy, Minister of Foreign Affairs, to the 51st General Assembly of the United Nations, September 24, 1996," <<http://www.dfait-maeci.gc.ca>>, accessed on 17/11/97.

5. Tom Keating, *Canada and World Order: The Multilateralist Tradition in Canadian Foreign Policy* (Toronto: McClelland & Stewart, 1993), p. 16.

6. *Ibid.*, p. 176.

7. *Ibid.*, p. 16.

8. *Ibid.*, p. 36.

9. *Ibid.*, p. 18.

10. J.L. Granatstein, "Peacekeeping: Did Canada Make a Difference? And What Difference Did Peacekeeping Make to Canada?" in *Making a Difference?*, eds. English and Hillmer, p. 235.

11. *Ibid.*, p. 231.

12. See Michael Tucker, *Canadian Foreign Policy* (Toronto: McGraw-Hill Ryerson, 1980), pp. 9–22.

13. Keating, *Canada and World Order*, p. 166.

14. *Ibid.*

15. Liberal Party of Canada, *Securing Our Future Together: Preparing Canada for the 21st Century* (Ottawa: Liberal Party of Canada, 1997), p. 97.

16. Joseph Jockel, "Canada and International Peacekeeping: An American View" in *The New Peacekeeping Partnership*, ed. Alex Morrison (Canada: Government of Canada, 1995), p. 153; see also <<http://www.un.org/reform/>>

17. Government of Canada, *Towards A Rapid Reaction Capability for the United Nations* (Canada: Government of Canada, 1995), p. 4; see also <<http://www.dfait-maeci. gc.ca/english/news/newsletr/un/rap1.htm>>

18. Bhaskar Menon, "Making and Keeping the Peace" in *A Global Agenda: Issues Before the 52nd General Assembly of the United Nations,* eds. John Tessitoire and Susan Woolfson (Totowa, NJ: Rowman & Littlefield, 1997), p. 5.

19. DFAIT, "Notes for an Address by the Hon. Lloyd Axworthy, Minister of Foreign Affairs, to the 52nd Session of the United Nations General Assembly, September 25, 1997," <<http://www.dfait-maeci.gc.ca>>, accessed on 17/11/97.

20. See <<http://www.igc.org/igc/conflictnet/index.html>>

21. Menon, "Making and Keeping the Peace," p. 7.

22. Ernie Regehr, "The Future of Peacekeeping" in *The Changing Face of Peacekeeping*, ed. Alex Morrison (Canada: Government of Canada, 1993), p. 29.

23. James O.C. Jonah, "Differing State Perspectives on the United Nations in the Post–Cold War World," <<http://www.brown.edu/Departments/ACUNS/New_publications/ 2.7/2.7.Chap.2shtml>>, accessed on 02/11/97.

24. Dewitt and Leyton-Brown, *Canada's International Security Policy*, p. 216.

25. Jonah, "Differing State Perspectives"

26. <<http://www.dfait-maeci.gc.ca/onu2000un/fa-01txt-g.htm>>, accessed on 15/03/98.

27. <<http://www.unicc.org/unrisd/wsp/index.htm>>

28. Boutros Boutros-Ghali, *An Agenda for Peace* (New York: United Nations, 1992), p. 32. Also available at: <<http://www.un.org/Docs/SG/agpeace.html>>; supplement available at: << http://www.un.org/Docs/SG/agsupp.html>>

29. *Ibid.*

30. William J. Durch, *The Evolution of UN Peacekeeping: Case Studies and Comparative Analysis* (New York: St. Martin's Press, 1993), p. 2.

31. *Ibid.*, p. 7.

32. Menon, "Making and Keeping the Peace," p. 3.

33. <<http://www.un.org/Depts/dpko/faq.htm>>

34. Dewitt and Leyton-Brown, *Canada's International Security Policy*, p. 217.

35. Tom Keating, "The Future of Canadian Multilateralism" in *Canada Among Nations 1994: A Part of the Peace,* eds. Maureen Appel Molot and Harold von Riekhoff (Canada: Carleton University Press, 1994), p. 61.

36. See N.D. White, *Keeping the Peace* (Manchester: Manchester University Press, 1997, especially chapter nine).

37. Menon, "Making and Keeping the Peace," p. 9. As well, updated figures can be obtained at: <<http://www.un.org/Depts/dpko/faq.htm>>

38. Durch, *The Evolution of UN Peacekeeping*, p. 2.

39. Regehr, "The Future of Peacekeeping," p. 30.

40. Menon, "Making and Keeping the Peace," p. 1.

41. *Ibid.*

42. Andrew Cohen, "World-Weary U.S. Looking Inward," *Globe and Mail*, 22 September 1997, p. A1.

43. Keating, "The Future of Canadian Multilateralism," p. 65.

44. DFAIT, <<http://www.dfait-maeci.gc.ca/ONU2000UN>>, accessed on 04/12/97.

45. DFAIT, "Notes for an Address by the Hon. Lloyd Axworthy, Minister of Foreign Affairs, to the 51st General Assembly of the United Nations, September 24, 1996."

46. DFAIT, "Notes for an Address by the Hon. Lloyd Axworthy, Minister of Foreign Affairs, to the 52nd Session of the United Nations General Assembly, September 25, 1997."

47. DFAIT, "Notes for an Address by the Hon. Lloyd Axworthy, Minister of Foreign Affairs, At York University 'Building Peace to Last: Establishing a Canadian Peace-building Initiative,' October 30, 1996," <<http://www.dfait-maeci.gc.ca>>, accessed on 17/11/97.

48. DFAIT, "Notes for an Address by the Hon. André Ouellet, Minister of Foreign Affairs, to the 50th General Assembly of the United Nations," <<http://www.dfait-maeci.gc.ca>>, accessed on 17/11/97.

49. DFAIT, "Canada and Peacebuilding," <<http://www.dfaitmaeci.gc.ca/peacebuilding/index-e.asp>>, accessed on 20/06/98.

50. *Ibid.*

51. John Paul Lederach, *Building Peace: Sustainable Reconciliation in Divided Societies* (Washington, DC: United States Institute of Peace, 1997), pp. 130–35.

52. Geoffrey Pearson, "Peacekeeping and Canadian Policy" in *United Nations Reform: Looking Ahead After Fifty Years*, eds. Eric Fawcett and Hanna Newcombe (Toronto: Dundurn Press, 1995), p. 120. See also <<http://front.web.net/canadem>>, accessed on 30/03/98.

53. David Cox and Albert Legault, eds. *UN Rapid Reaction Capabilities: Requirements and Prospects* (Clementsport, NS: The Peacekeeping Press, 1995).

54. *Ibid.*, p. 120.

55. <<http://www.un.org/plwebcgi/idoc.pl?6+unix+_free_user_+www.un.org.. 80+un+un+webdocs+webdocs++early%26adj%26warning>>

56. <<http://www.cdnpeacekeeping.ns.ca/>>

57. Geoffrey Pearson, "Peacekeeping and Canadian Policy" in *United Nations Reform: Looking Ahead After Fifty Years*, eds. Eric Fawcett and Hanna Newcombe (Toronto: Dundurn Press, 1995), p. 120.

58. *Ibid.*

59. Boutros-Ghali, *An Agenda for Peace*, p. 33.

60. DFAIT, "Notes for an Address by the Hon. Lloyd Axworthy, Minister of Foreign Affairs, to the 52nd Session of the United Nations General Assembly, September 25, 1997."

61. See << http://www.dfait-maeci.gc.ca/peacebuilding/index-e.asp>>, accessed on 29/03/98.

62. Canada Office of the Prime Minister, "Canada Pledges $100 Million to Implement Global Ban on Anti-personnel Landmines," <<http://pm.gc.ca/cgi-win/ pmo_view.exe/ENGLISH?693+0+normal>>, accessed on 15/03/98.

63. DFAIT, "Notes for an Address by the Hon. Lloyd Axworthy, Minister of Foreign Affairs, At York University 'Building Peace to Last: Establishing a Canadian Peace-building Initiative,' October 30, 1996"; also see United Nations Department of Peacekeeping Operations at << http://www.un.org/Depts/dpko/>>, accessed on 18/06/98.

64. United Nations Peacekeeping Operations, "Studying the Past While Planning for the Future," <<http://www.un.org/Depts/dpko/yir96/study.htm>>, accessed on 17/11/97; also see MINUGUA United Nations Mission for the Verification of Human Rights in Guatemala, <<http://www.un.org/Depts/minugua/>>, accessed on 20/06/98.

65. Maj. Gen. Romeo Dallaire, "The Rwandan Experience" in *The New Peacekeeping Partnership*, ed. Alex Morrison (Canada: Government of Canada, 1995), p. 24.

66. *Ibid.*

67. Roger A. Coate et al., *The United Nations and Changing World Politics* (Boulder, CO: Westview Press, 1994), p. 35.

68. James B. Sutterlin, *The United Nations and the Maintenance of International Security: A Challenge to be Met* (New York: Praeger Publishers, 1995), pp. 109–10.

69. *Ibid.*, p. 111.

70. As an example see <<http://www.un.org/Docs/SG/ag_index.htm>>, especially paras. 155–74.

71. United Nations Reform, "Renewing the United Nations: A Programme for Reform," <<"http://www.un.org/reform/>>, accessed on 03/11/97.

72. DFAIT, "Notes for an Address by the Hon. Lloyd Axworthy, Minister of Foreign Affairs, to the 52nd Session of the United Nations General Assembly, September 25, 1997."

73. Coate et al., *The United Nations*, p. 93.

74. See <<http://www.dfait-maeci.gc.ca/onu2000un/>>, accessed 30/03/98.

75. Lederach, *Building Peace*, p. 152.

Canadian International Security Policy and the North Atlantic Treaty Organization

A Contradiction in Terms?

DEAN F. OLIVER

Canadian War Museum

Ⅰn the aftermath of the Cold War, Canada retreated from many of its formal obligations to the North Atlantic Treaty Organization (NATO).[1] The critical turning point was the February 1992 decision of Prime Minister Brian Mulroney's Progressive Conservative government to withdraw the last of Canada's overseas forces from NATO Europe. Events after 1992 witnessed the further gradual erosion of Ottawa's rhetorical commitment to the alliance, as well as a precipitous decline in Canada's military capabilities. It remains the case, as David Haglund and others have noted,[2] that more dramatic alternatives, like withdrawing from the alliance altogether, were never in the cards, but Canada's actions on several fronts left considerable doubt, at home and overseas, as to the nature of its residual commitment. When a senior academic stated at the Atlantic Council of Canada's annual meeting in 1996 that Europe was being "drastically undersold" by Canadian foreign policy practitioners in favour of Asia-Pacific, Africa, and Latin America, most listeners understood implicitly that growing disinterest in NATO was a critical component of his verdict. Indeed, at the same meeting a senior official of the Department of Foreign Affairs and International Trade (DFAIT) berated the alliance for its failure to adjust more quickly to the post–Cold War period, all but ignoring the changes in organization, doctrine, and mission that had occurred since 1991.[3] Formal defence and foreign policy reviews by the governing Liberal Party in 1994 and 1995 downplayed the salience of NATO to Canada's international security, just as the previous Tory government had emphasized the United Nations as the more appropriate vehicle for Canada's pursuit of its international interests. Canada retained its activist international agenda in the later 1990s, but it was no longer complemented necessarily by its membership in NATO.

More recent actions give added reason to question Canadian commitment. Ottawa's unilateral attempt in the fall of 1997 to cut funding for NATO's admittedly troubled science program, a decision later rescinded after vigorous protests from alliance members and by the Canadian scientific community, epitomized the seemingly ambiguous attitude of successive Canadian governments towards NATO.[4] As the Canadian Mathematical Society (CMS) asked caustically of the science program decision,[5] "how does this fit with Canada chiding the United States about its UN dues?" NATO, the CMS reminded its members, "offers Canada a unique window to Europe scientifically." Moreover, the lack of consultation with allies preceding the decision called into question Ottawa's commitment to the alliance's consultative mechanisms. If even relatively minor fiscal decisions did not warrant a cursory nod to multilateral due process, worried some of Canada's allies, what might this portend for Canada's continued membership? As one diplomat noted, even in the absence of dramatic pronouncements, Ottawa's poor handling of the science programme seemed further proof that Canada was gradually "drifting away" from its alliance obligations.[6]

Cutting back on cooperative algebra might not adversely affect national security, but the longer-term impact of other decisions, including the pullout, a declining defence budget, troop reductions, and the infrequency of major training exercises with alliance partners, is nevertheless potentially severe. To the extent that such actions harm Canadian interests, blame is widely distributed. Many Canadian Forces' (CF) senior officers argued in the early 1990s that returning forces from Europe would save money and allow greater resources to be devoted to equipment replacement and other needs. Instead, budgets withered, kit replacements were slow in coming, and overall numbers declined by more than one-third. Privately, senior officers now insist that readiness, training, and interoperability have declined, in some cases severely, due to the infrequency of training exercises with allies. More importantly, some argue, the curtailment of ongoing personal and professional contact occasioned by the withdrawal from Europe has had a long-term and deleterious impact on Canada's ability to operate on future battlefields with alliance partners, a weakness aggravated significantly by continuing reductions in the overall size of Canadian forces. Canada's long deployment to Europe permitted the CF a degree of familiarity and integration with allies that prolonged absence from Europe will quickly erode.[7] As French formations discovered during the 1990–91 conflict in the Persian Gulf, there is no doctrinal or motivational substitute for constant practice with likely allies. Canadian formations can still operate in alliance missions, as the air campaign over Serbia demonstrates, but in the absence of frequent interaction it is an increasingly difficult exercise, especially for ground forces.

Highlighting these examples, the science program and military training, from among the broad range of interactions that occur within NATO admittedly implies a narrow (and perhaps even simplistic) view of the changing nature of Canada's alliance membership. The impassioned pronouncements of Canadian diplomats and politicians from the alliance's formative period stand against such a utilitarian interpretation of membership, as does the position of the current government on NATO's conflict in Kosovo.[8] Moreover, it is by no means obvious that cuts to Canada's defence budget or to its NATO commitments necessarily reduce access to the less tangible benefits deriving from having a "seat at the table". The whole, in other words, might yet be more impressive than the sum of its parts.

The ability to secure through the alliance broader strategic, political, or economic objectives has nevertheless always been predicated upon the perception that alliance members were "pulling their weight," either across the spectrum of alliance activities or in areas of special expertise, resources, or commitment. As an American official noted recently at a conference in Montreal on alliance enlargement, "NATO is not a recipe for automatic consultation. You only get out [of it] what you put in. Don't forget that."[9] Or, as Harlan Cleveland noted three decades earlier, "in international as in domestic politics, there is a tendency over time for taxation and representation to come into balance. Those who are reluctant to take responsibility tend to be left out of the meetings where decisions are made."[10]

Whether or not Canadian officials are now left out of the meetings where decisions are made, and whether, if true, such exclusion results from the perception that Canada no longer pulls its weight, is debatable, but the recent record fails to show many successes for Canadian initiatives. Canada was criticized by all allies for its NATO pullout, for example, Canada was left off the Contact Group for former Yugoslavia, and was at times left alone in opposing air strikes in support of United Nations efforts in Bosnia. More recently, the report of a parliamentary committee on nuclear weapons issues, initiated at the request of the foreign minister, received a cool reception from most allies, but especially the nuclear weapons states, for courting NATO's possible adoption of No First Use of nuclear weapons after a full alliance debate. As one official remarked privately, "you were outvoted eighteen to one."[11] Canada did succeed in winning support from all NATO allies except the United States and Turkey for enacting a global ban on antipersonnel landmines, but even here many allies complained privately that Canadian tactics were considerably more disruptive of alliance relations than need otherwise have been the case.

It would be grossly inaccurate to ascribe this state of affairs solely (or even primarily) to the current federal government. Since the late 1960s, Canada's military contribution to NATO has eroded almost steadily. Exceptions to the trend, like the 1987 White Paper on Defence, died with such indecent haste as to confirm the general rule. Even before Pierre Trudeau's review of foreign and defence policy dramatized the fact, Canada's political and military commitment to the Old World had been questioned and, occasionally, found wanting by its allies. Paul-Henri Spaak remarked in 1958 that "Canadians are the Yugoslavs of NATO," non-aligned and uncommitted. Although Canada has frequently been NATO's "odd man out," more recently, as one scholar has noted, its Atlantic "vision" has been replaced by an "Atlantic astigmatism" and its current distance from the alliance, Kosovo notwithstanding, has perhaps never been greater.[12] Even as Canadian warplanes flew strike missions against Serbian targets in April 1999, Canadian pressure for the alliance to revisit the issue of nuclear weapons in its Strategic Concept continued to evoke the displeasure of key allies. Its apparent inability to contribute more than 800 ground troops to a possible invasion force in Kosovo likewise demonstrated the weaknesses in Canada's force posture.

Must NATO obligations dictate a military return to Europe, or some similarly dramatic gesture of renewed Canadian faith? Clearly it is militarily unnecessary, politically unlikely, and economically unwise. Indeed, Kosovo at least demonstrates that given time and alliance consensus Canadian forces will, in all likelihood, again enter the lists in aid of European security. The presence of eighteen CF-18s at Aviano, Italy is the best indication in years of Canada's continued interest in European affairs. It is to point out, however, that the relationship between the costs and the benefits of alliance membership has not substantively changed since 1949. If one can safely countenance the likely risks of reduced engagement in peacetime, the calculus must surely be grounded in the knowledge that in the post–Cold War period the advantages of commitment no longer outweigh to any significant extent the effort. In other words, the seat at the table must now be deemed less valuable than the cost of admission. To the view of some that NATO was once a provocative and militaristic expense—an institutional tail vigorously wagging the foreign policy dog[13] is now added the charge that it is an asset of steadily diminishing value. One cannot (yet) afford to ignore the forum entirely, if only because of its importance as a way-station in the post–Cold War evolution of transatlantic and European relations, but one can feel relatively comfortable in presiding over its slow demise, or at least its radical transformation. If NATO fails in Kosovo, this process might well be accelerated.

As long as NATO remains, a Canadian contribution, however paltry or symbolic, will be necessary, if only to avoid charges of hypocrisy from impatient allies. National commitment will gradually erode, however, and participation will act as a springboard or pulpit for the promulgation of Canada's new international security mantra: human security and the "new" diplomacy. NATO membership, by this reckoning, is simply a convenient platform for the promulgation of an "alternative lifestyles" approach to security, a legitimizing structure that ensures a hearing even if the message conveyed is inimical to the organization itself.

To a large extent, this transformation in the rationale for Canada's continued NATO membership has already occurred, as official explanations for Canada's Kosovo policy repeatedly maintain. In developing new touchstones for Canadian international security policy like public diplomacy, cooperative security, and human rights, the Liberal government of Jean Chrétien has presided over a thoroughgoing revision of the declaratory basis of Canada's NATO membership. DFAIT representatives, including the current minister, Lloyd Axworthy, and successive deputy ministers, regularly tout the end of the Cold War as the occasion for a signal redefinition of the alliance's organization, rationale, and operations. The recent evolution of Canadian international security policy echoes the evolution of NATO itself in the 1990s,[14] but Canadian enthusiasm for the 'new' agenda outstrips that of either the alliance or most of its key members. Ottawa's military commitment in Former Yugoslavia, long explained to skeptical Europeans as evidence of Canada's long-term reliability as a partner in continental security, is in truth nothing of the kind.[15] It is, instead, a temporary concession, subject to regular renewal and revision, and one whose origin and continuation lie more in the realm of temporary necessity than substantive consensus or formal obligation. As *Globe and Mail* columnist Jeffrey Simpson once noted, this attempt to equate Canada's NATO contributions with verbal commitments and United Nations peacekeeping represented "political flap-doodle designed for domestic consumption."[16] Canada committed itself to the Balkans to rejuvenate its image with NATO allies after its departure from Europe, but the attempt proved unsuccessful. As the United Nations mission in Former Yugoslavia gave way to a NATO-led intervention force, Canada's military sleight-of-hand gained added credence (now, after all, it *was* a NATO mission), but other alliance members never accepted the view that the two missions were one and the same.

As NATO further defines its international peacekeeping obligations, this relationship will surely change, perhaps in Canada's favour. For the present, Canada's Balkan commitment remains, in the eyes of many allied observers, welcome but insufficient, a distressing indication not of what is and will likely be, but of what was and will be no more. Ottawa's willingness to extend the Balkan deployment is an encouraging development, but its predictable failure to convince allies that ground troops essentially held over from a former United Nations commitment compensate for real NATO participation continues to erode the diplomatic credit that might otherwise flow from the mission. When the current Canadian battle group eventually redeploys, it will be to Canada and not to its former bases in Germany, so close to likely trouble spots in Europe, Africa, and the Middle East. At that point, Canada's in-theatre commitment to the alliance, will revert to what it has been since the Mulroney government's reductions six years ago: a handful of staff officers in Brussels and one hundred or so air force personnel with the AWACs component at Geilenkerchen. Kosovo has added 18 CF-18s with ground crew plus up to 800 troops to this total, and Canada is likely to contribute to any follow-on peace implementation force, but the numbers will likely be small and the commitment conditional.

The cost of reduced participation in the alliance is reduced influence. The addition of Poles, Czechs, and Hungarians to the organization's permanent staff will leave far fewer positions for Canadians. Poland alone enters the alliance with 250,000 troops, all of them in NATO Europe. Although this number will soon fall to 180,000, even Poland's postaccession military will remain three times the size of Canada's regular armed forces, and twice that of Canada's regular and reserve forces combined. Barring large-scale participation in new peacekeeping missions, Canada's future commitment to European security will thus hang on a thin military thread even as its share of the alliance's valuable (and well-paid) staff appointments diminishes.[17] Without dedicated military capacity or significant senior positions on NATO staffs, Ottawa's capacity to affect the alliance's security discourse and, by obvious association, the broader Euro-Atlantic security discourse will remain marginal. For a trading nation whose longstanding obligations and interests are so directly affected by events in that theatre, it is an astonishingly weak position.

This weak position might matter less if Canada's rhetorical position on the alliance were in harmony with its commitments, perhaps through a less strident, more coherent sophisticated iteration of the country's security needs. It might also be mitigated by a more modest, more subtle appreciation of the growing dissonance between Ottawa's words and deeds as perceived by allies whose core security interests remain unaffected, and largely unimpressed, by either megaphone diplomacy or passionate invocations that a new security age has dawned. In deciphering current Canadian policy towards NATO, however, one finds neither clarity of commitment nor modesty of tone; instead, one finds an erstwhile free rider whose qualified disinterest juxtaposes ardent reformism, strong support for enlargement, and fearless advocacy of new commitments, new agendas, and new stratagems. Reform and innovation are commendable assets in one's security arsenal but, in the absence of clarity, commitment, and capacity they risk attracting the condescension of allies even as they generate confusion as to our policy's main purpose and incredulity at our willingness to stay the course.

Ottawa's support for an "open door" policy on enlargement, irrespective of the likely security challenges enlargement might entail, is an example of the extent to which reformist zeal now precedes practical responsibility.[18] Indeed, Ottawa fast-tracked ratification of NATO's accession protocols for the three states in enlargement's first *tranche* to ensure Canada pride of place as the first member government to approve the project, an artifice repeated in ratifying the December 1997 agreement to ban anti-personnel landmines.[19] The necessity of garnering pride of place in each case is hardly self-evident. Enlargement's ratification even proceeded without the formal parliamentary debate promised by Minister of Foreign Affairs Lloyd Axworthy during a March 1997 session of the House of Commons Standing Committee on Foreign Affairs and International Trade (SCOFAIT). "Of course I want to underline that once decisions are made by the leaders as to the direction that will be taken," Axworthy said of the impending Madrid summit, "we will then engage in a thoroughgoing consultation with Parliament again to ratify any decisions that are taking place at that time."[20] Without the debate promised by the minister, Canada rushed to judgment.

Likewise, despite repeated assurances of Canada's commitment to the alliance, Axworthy urged SCOFAIT to study and report on the implications for Canada under international humanitarian law of an advisory decision by the International Court of Justice on the possession and threatened use of nuclear weapons by the alliance. To be sure, there was no legislative or treaty impediment to Axworthy's referral, but the likely practical, political, and military ramifications of the committee's deliberations ought probably to have cautioned the minister against the move.[21] The diplomatic and military interest shown in the committee's hearings by the United States and other allies soon testified to their potential to wreak havoc on an organization that still reserves the right to a nuclear response in certain exceptional circumstances. The committee report, released in December 1998, failed to recommend No First Use (NFU) of nuclear weapons, but it did advocate its study and elaborated a sophisticated critique of the West's current nuclear policies. NFU did enjoy support from several committee members, despite the discomfiture it would undoubtedly have caused in Brussels, London, and Washington.[22] The fact that the alliance's nuclear strategy is clearly in need of revision and that several influential Canadians have already proposed such a policy would hardly alleviate the hostility likely to be engendered by Canada's possible championing of the NFU cause.[23] Coming hard on the heels of Ottawa's leading role in the campaign to ban anti-personnel landmines (a movement whose tactics riled alliance members even as they signed the accord), simply suggesting No First Use could have been a costly, disruptive exercise. To the extent it might have soured relations between Canada and key European allies, it would also spell trouble for Ottawa on other fronts, including its efforts to promote alliance flight training in western Canada.

Speculations of this type are perhaps more entertaining than edifying, but they derive from a genuine confusion in Canada's current NATO policy, a strain of contradictory impulses that cuts a broad swath through both official statements and policy initiatives: on the one hand, continued engagement in and enlargement of the organization, but on the other, disinterest bordering on virtual sabotage. It bears repeating that crises, real or perceived, in the Canada-NATO relationship are nothing new. Yet when the overwhelming impression carried away by senior NATO officials after a recent visit to the capitol is that Canada is drifting inexorably away from the alliance fold, it would appear that Ottawa's repeated entreaties of good faith are, of late, falling on deaf ears.[24] If Canada is indeed perceived by some of our allies as drifting away from the alliance, however, from what exactly are we drifting? Moreover, and perhaps more importantly, from what exactly might Canadian decision-makers *think* they are drifting? Surely it cannot be an organization that, in the aftermath of the Cold War, is in tune with the tenor of Canada's evolving security objectives.

This assumption, of course, is not shared by all observers of Canada's NATO policy. As DFAIT officials pointed out in response to a recent presentation criticizing the department's alleged neglect of NATO, Ottawa remains steadfastly committed to European security in general, and to the alliance in particular, even as it moves ahead with a more confident, more activist agenda on other fronts.[25] Moreover, far from being contradictory, the two projects—NATO reform and the renaissance in Canadian international security policy—are closely related and mutually supportive.

The future, by this interpretation, yields an alliance in which Article II of the treaty is not just more carefully articulated than during the Cold War, but one in which NATO has evolved inexorably away from collective defence and Article V security guarantees towards cooperative security and Article II. In this construction of Canada's role in NATO's postenlargement, postreform future, Ottawa is successful in transferring its newfound security priorities to the alliance. It assumes a role of intellectual and political leadership just as the organization revisits its Strategic Concept, welcomes new members, and reformulates its role in response to both traditional and non-traditional security threats. Rather than leading by example or force, it is leading by rhetorical brilliance and "soft power" manipulation. This is a NATO, in other words, whose security challenges are those most likely amenable to the military and political wherewithal left to a cooperative security alliance, and a NATO whose primary security risks arise from non-traditional areas of the sort now described so frequently by Mr. Axworthy. Significantly, it is also a NATO wherein Canada's current "enlightened" security vision is shared without rancour or regret by the other allies, a world, in short, where the persuasive logic of cooperative security holds sway, unblemished by countervailing evidence from crises, wars, or expediency.

Is this an accurate reading of the alliance's evolution to date? Will it come to pass in the near future? The view that Canadian international security policy will be vindicated (and complemented) by the alliance's own reformation has been developed brilliantly by political scientist David Haglund.[26] Arguing that the "new" NATO is, in fact, the NATO "of Canada's dreams" because of its fortuitous correspondence with Ottawa's cooperative security outlook, Haglund further suggests that, far from a revolutionary new departure, cooperative security is fully consistent with the traditions of "Pearsonian internationalism." It constitutes, in effect, a Canadian "grand strategy." "[W]ith its emphasis on inclusiveness (and its assumption that this must mean negotiation and the search for compromise) and the stress it places on conflict management, co-operative security can be linked to a Canadian foreign policy that is synonymous with a 'Pearsonian tradition' itself characterized by a distrust of dogma, an abhorrence of grand designs, a belief in compromise, and a disposition toward pragmatism ... in other words, co-operative security, construed as a "realistic" alternative to collective security, *is* Pearsonian internationalism [emphasis added]."[27] Haglund admits that there are caveats to this depiction. Does the attractiveness of the new NATO to Canadian foreign policy mandarins reside in its relatively low cost? How much depends on the specific definition of cooperative security? What is the potential for postenlargement security problems, perhaps arising in response to renewed American demands for expanding NATO's arc of geographic responsibility? But his broadly integrative analysis of current trends in Canadian and NATO "doctrine" contradicts, with considerable aplomb, most interpretations of Canada's drift away from the NATO orbit in recent decades.

Haglund provides a useful corrective to the "sky is falling" school of analysis first generated by Trudeau's anti-NATO foreign and defence policy reviews thirty years ago.[28] It is not clear, however, that his explanation depicts accurately the relationship between current Canadian policy and NATO's evolving mission. The problems lie not with the various elements of Haglund's proposal, but rather with the interrelationships posited among them and with the allocation of resources and commitments that this interchange would entail. Canada's experience to date in operationalizing cooperative security instills little confidence that the concept, as understood and practiced by the Department of Foreign Affairs and International Trade, is either internally coherent or universally applicable. Instead, it appears in all too many instances as a protective sheen for military retrenchment, a trade-driven policy agenda, and the selective championing of international causes by senior government officials.[29] Haglund, unlike DFAIT, acknowledges as much in his careful discussion of the concept itself and in his timely admonishment that new signposts for Canada's security order "have yet to be erected." But ascribing even tentatively to this melange of artifice and adhockery a strategic appellation seems slightly generous: it may well be grand, but is it really strategy?[30] Fashioning from current Canadian policy threads of consistency and direction is a daunting challenge, despite the integrative effect of broad principles like human security brought to the subject by Mr. Axworthy. Equating the practical realism and consummate professionalism of Lester Pearson's generation of hard-nosed but discerning diplomats with the uncompromising idealism of Mr. Axworthy and his coterie of young advisers, especially ministerial staff and appointees, is seriously misleading.

Addressing the alliance's public pronouncements on new missions and security challenges, Haglund's argument assumes an equality among the broad range of security risks currently envisaged by NATO planners and, more importantly, a basic symmetry between this shopping list of challenges and the agenda now advanced by Canada. The former acknowledges but downplays the protracted skirmishing over alliance roles and missions currently bedevilling the alliance, particularly as it derives from America's continued insistence on NATO's core defence function, even as it prejudges the outcome of that debate by proclaiming (guardedly, to be sure) impending victory for its Canadian and Canadian-like practitioners. The latter assumes, this time in an international context, both the intellectual cohesion and the political wisdom of the cooperative security project. Both assumptions are intriguing but debatable, as Canadian policy on and NATO's response to events in Kosovo attest. Thus, while the articulation of Canadian interests in relation to NATO's evolution is superb, it also presumes a congruity or constancy between word and deed that is extraordinarily flattering to the Canadian side; moreover, the linkages between Canadian and NATO security perhaps remain slightly more opaque than the analysis implies.

A recent speech by General Klaus Naumann, NATO chairman, provides a markedly different take on NATO priorities and differs radically from the security agenda routinely advanced by Canadian officials.[31] General Naumann prioritized four uncertainties and risks clouding NATO's horizon: Russian instability; unresolved disputes along Europe's frontier "from Morocco to India"; proliferation of weapons of mass destruction; and, finally, "the new risks" to security, including mass migration, competition for strategic resources, transnational crime, terrorism, and the use of high technology by non-state actors. Far from trumpeting the way in which diverse risks herald revolutionary change, Naumann was at pains to suggest that the responses and capabilities required of the alliance would, in effect be of the more traditional variety, including rapid reaction military forces, passive and active counterproliferation, arms control, information sharing, and "the means [for NATO] to defend itself including the irreplaceable transatlantic link." He even enlisted former Canadian diplomat and prime minister Lester B. Pearson in his aid, citing Pearson's sophisticated understanding of security to make the case that NATO's purview must extend beyond the mere defence of members' territory "to project stability and enhance security." Moreover, Naumann's priority list turned on its head the list of priorities usually advanced by Canadian officials. "New security risks" was relegated to fourth place and Naumann highlighted capabilities and techniques usually downplayed, if not dismissed outright, by Mr. Axworthy, most notably the continued possession of robust, mobile, and credible military assets. Given the stark difference between Naumann's portrayal of NATO priorities and those of the current Canadian government, in fact, it would not be far wide of the mark to fashion Naumann's address as a subtle critique of the Canadian position, especially given that the talk was delivered in the Lester B. Pearson Building, headquarters for Canada's Department of Foreign Affairs and International Trade.[32]

As numerous commentators, most of them American and European, have already pointed out, NATO can only evolve so much in the direction of cooperative security and organizational reform without losing meaning and effectiveness as a collective defence organization.[33] It is precisely the alliance's continued military capacity that makes it the essential instrument in ensuring European security for the foreseeable future. As Carl Hodge noted recently:

> the Atlantic Alliance remains the brain, sword, and shield of the Old Continent's Defence. It is and has always been simplistic to regard military power as the prime factor in all international relations, but to shunt it from its central position in understanding security and the credibility of any foreign policy is determinedly romantic.[34]

It is also precisely this aspect of NATO's mission—its core function—that fits with Canada's evolving international policy most poorly and, in particular, with the well developed and carefully articulated views of the current foreign minister. As Haglund suggests, most Canadian policy-makers are comfortable with reforming NATO, even as—through enlargement—they add to its security responsibilities, both current and as yet unforseen. It is equally the case, however, that their comfort level appears to be defined with extraordinary narrowness and tautological precision. NATO works, in other words, to the extent it coincides with a new security agenda and reduced hard-security commitments; to the extent it does not, NATO is a relic of the Cold War and an obstacle to progress. Kosovo has perhaps forced uncomfortable truths upon some Canadian decision makers, especially with regard to the application of force, but it is unlikely that renewed confidence in NATO's military vocation will emerge from the present crisis. Skepticism will perhaps be richly deserved, but surely the lessons from the Kosovo operation include the need for rapid reaction military assets and the extent to which military capability enhances one's position in inter-allied counsels.

These contradictions, aggravated by Canada's current activism and almost embarrassing international self-confidence, weaken any assumption of inherent symmetry between Canadian and NATO security policy, at least in the short term. In this environment—Canada's disdain for traditional security, its rejection of the old diplomacy, and its uncritical espousal of soft power methods—it is possible to style Canada's current position on NATO not as a fortuitous meeting of minds, but as a subtle usurpation of the alliance in favour of the more benign, more circumscribed organization envisaged by cooperative security's proponents. This can hardly be counted as continued support for NATO, especially in view of events like the attempted unilateral abandonment of the science program. If multilateral science projects fail to qualify as cooperative endeavours, after all, then what does? Participation in the Kosovo mission offers considerable hope that, as Haglund has argued, Europe's stock is again rising in Ottawa, but Canadian policy has too frequently been at odds with the NATO consensus in recent years to assume such an ending.

Ottawa may now dream of a cooperative security NATO, the logical successor to Pearsonian internationalism as Haglund suggests, but it is surely the tonic that excites and not the vessel. NATO, despite taking seriously the need to reinvent itself for the new millennium, remains for some observers more nightmare than dream, a lingering echo of a bygone era whose limited utility (not least in a traditional military sense) continually confounds efforts to demonstrate conclusively its growing international irrelevance. Canadian representatives now give NATO speeches about peacebuilding, human rights, and international criminal tribunals, but virtually none about military security, collective defence, or traditional security challenges. General Naumann's hierarchy of security risks could likely not have been reproduced presently by DFAIT officials, either in order of importance or in anticipated methods of response. The department's infatuation with the new security firmament thus moves Canada ever farther from its alliance moorings, sinking NATO ever so slowly into the dustbin of Canadian diplomatic history. The 1994 Defence White Paper seems fated to lose its running battle with the same champion.

As security itself evolves, so too must the policies and actions of those who operate in its milieu; as NATO has long acknowledged, old organizations will bend or break, at their discretion. But if practitioners guess wrong on the evolution of the international order—and by privileging so completely their own assessment of a brave new world Canadian leaders risk doing precisely that—then the consequences will extend well beyond policy ambiguity and reduced capacity to the detriment of both long-term goals and national credibility. For the present, protestations to the contrary notwithstanding, Canada's occasionally admirable iconoclasm on the security front renders its NATO membership more a contradiction in terms than a valuable adjunct to overall objectives. Spirited oratory and high-sounding rhetoric resist conflation with demonstrable commitment and practical coherence. As Desmond Morton once wrote, Canada remains a NATO ally "more or less," but it no longer luxuriates in splendid ambiguity.[35] The sight of Canadian fighter-bombers flying combat missions alongside allied warplanes in 1999 inexplicably shocked the Canadian conscience. After nearly decades of defence cutbacks and force reductions and, in recent years, endless pronouncements on our new security missions, it seemed terribly out of character.

NOTES

The views expressed in this paper are mine alone and do not necessarily reflect the views or policy of the Canadian War Museum.

1. Roy Rempel, *The Failure of Canada's European Policy, 1955-1995* (Montreal: McGill-Queen's University Press, 1996); Sean M. Maloney, *War Without Battles: Canada's NATO Brigade in Germany, 1951-1993* (Toronto: McGraw-Hill Ryerson, 1997); and Paul Buteux, "NATO and the Evolution of Canadian Defence and Foreign Policy," in *Canada's International Security Policy* eds. David B. Dewitt and David Leyton-Brown (Scarborough, ON: Prentice-Hall, 1995).

2. *NATO Expansion: Two Perspectives*, Occasional Paper, Centre for International Relations, Queen's University (June 1997), "View from a Member State."

3. Privileged platform. Address to the annual meeting of the Atlantic Council of Canada, Department of Foreign Affairs and International Trade, Ottawa, Ontario, November 1996.

4. Canada's actions, according to some observers, led to beneficial changes in the Science Program, which had been widely criticized by other participants. Canada currently contributes about $2.5 million to the program.

5. J.M. Borwein, "CMS Report on NATO Science" (December 1997), at the CMS website <<http://camel.cecm.sfu.ca/CMS/Docs/NATO.html>>.

6. Confidential interview.

7. Confidential interviews with CF and DND personnel, Brussels (June 1997) and Ottawa (January–February 1998 and March 1999).

8. See, for example, Roger Hill, *In Alliance: An Oral History of Canadian Involvement in NATO* (Ottawa: Canadian Institute for International Peace and Security, 1991). The Department of Foreign Affairs and International Trade recently added a section to its website entitled "Canada and NATO" which makes many of the same points. Not surprisingly, it implicitly rejects the notion that Canadian commitment to the alliance has in any way diminished.

9. Confidential interview, Montreal, 27 March 1997.

10. *NATO: The Transatlantic Bargain* (New York: Harper & Row, 1970), p. 6.

11. Confidential interview. Washington, DC, 30 April 1999.

12. David Haglund, "View from a Member State" in *NATO Expansion: Two Perspectives* (Kingston, ON: Queen's University, Centre for International Relations, Occasional Paper 56, June 1997), p. 1.

13. This, of course, was the Trudeau vision of alliance commitments but he was hardly alone. For an earlier iteration of this view, see James M. Minifie, *Peacemaker or Powder Monkey? Canada's Role in a Revolutionary World* (Toronto: McClelland & Stewart, 1960). On the Trudeau period, see especially J.L. Granatstein and Robert Bothwell, *Pirouette: Pierre Trudeau and Canadian Foreign Policy* (Toronto: University of Toronto Press, 1990).

14. Karl Kaiser, "Reforming NATO," *Foreign Policy* 103 (Summer 1996), pp. 128–43.

15. Andrew Cohen, "Security and NATO," in *Canada Among Nations 1993-94: Global Jeopardy*, eds. Christopher J. Maule and Fen Osler Hampson (Ottawa: Carleton University Press, 1993), pp. 260–64.

16. "When It Comes to Canada's Interests, It's the Pork Barrel that Counts," *Globe and Mail*, 31 March 1992.

17. It is also worth noting that the number of senior Canadian officials at NATO headquarters, both military and civilian, has declined precipitously since the early

1990s, leaving few personnel to advance Canadian interests at the highest decision-making levels.

18. For competing perspectives, see *The Enlargement of NATO: Why Adding Poland, Hungary, and the Czech Republic to NATO Strengthens American National Security* (Washington, DC: U.S. Department of State, 1998), and Michael Mandelbaum, "NATO Expansion: A Bridge to the Nineteenth Century," <<http://www.cpss.org/nato/mandel97>> (June 1997).

19. "Canada First to Ratify NATO Enlargement," Reuters wire service, 3 February 1998.

20. House of Commons Standing Committee on Foreign Affairs and International Trade, Evidence, 20 March 1997.

21. In so doing, the minister apparently ignored advice from within his own department and from other government agencies, including sources in the Department of National Defence. Confidential sources.

22. Confidential interviews.

23. "Call For a 'No First Use of Nuclear Weapons' Regime," 24 February 1998, Project Ploughshares website, <<http://watserv1.uwaterloo.ca~plough/nfu.html>>.

24. Confidential sources.

25. Dean F. Oliver, "Canada and NATO Enlargement: A Response to Richard Kugler" (paper delivered to the Canadian Council on International Peace and Security, Ottawa, 2 June 1998).

26. David G. Haglund, "The NATO of Its Dreams? Canada and the Co-operative Security Alliance," *International Security* 52/3 (Summer 1997), pp. 464–82.

27. *Ibid.*, p. 480.

28. See Gerald Porter, *In Retreat: The Canadian Forces in the Trudeau Years* (Montreal: Deneau and Greenberg, nd).

29. For a critique, see Fen Osler Hampson and Dean F. Oliver, "Pulpit Diplomacy: A Critical Assessment of the Axworthy Doctrine," *International Journal* 53/3 (Summer 1998), pp. 379–406.

30. It is perhaps worth noting that Haglund's discussion of "grand strategy" emphasizes the notion of strategy as "principle", saying little about plan or practice, and almost nothing about implementation. This implicitly elevates strategy to the ideational equivalent of "values" and, in effect, strips it of all practical interpretive weight.

31. Text of an address by General Klaus Naumann, CMC, delivered at the Atlantic Council of Canada annual meeting, Ottawa, 27 October 1998. (Because General Naumann was unable to attend the meeting due to the crisis in Kosovo, Admiral John Anderson, Canada's former ambassador to NATO, delivered the address in his place. John Marteinson of the Atlantic Council kindly made a copy available to the author.)

32. While a compelling and provocative assessment, Haglund's interpretation of Canadian-NATO symmetry would also only hold true if it were demonstrably the case that a reformed NATO would pacify the Liberal Party's backroom anti-NATO lobby, which also appears nowhere close to happening.

33. As Mandelbaum has argued with respect to enlargement and associated adjustments, for example, NATO might gain Poland but lose the United States.

34. Carl Cavanaugh Hodge, "Europe as a Great Power: A Work in Progress?" *International Journal* 53/3 (Summer 1998), p. 490.

35. "Canada as an Ally—More or Less," lecture to the Canadian Forces Staff College, Toronto, 9 April 1982.

Future Directions in Canadian Security Policy

From a Marginal Actor at the Centre to a Central Actor at the Margins

DAVID B. DEWITT

Centre for International and Security Studies
York University

Defence and Security

For a considerable period of time, Canadians have not been overly concerned with issues of national defence.[1] We have not felt threatened by imminent invasion; we have not felt that our core values or institutions have been under challenge by some foreign or even domestic force; we have not felt coerced to undertake domestic or foreign policies seen to be inimical to our preferences.[2] In a word, the idea of national defence seems to be of decreasing relevance to most Canadians.

Yet there has been no lack of activity in this sector of public life. Since 1993 there have been a series of government documents emanating from the House, Senate, and the Departments of Foreign Affairs and International Trade (DFAIT) and of National Defence (DND); Parliament has convened hearings; and the informed public has offered their own assessments of foreign and defence policy.[3] In addition to these general documents, we can add the special reports commissioned to address specific concerns, including the Reserves, the Somalia inquiry, maritime and naval issues, UN rapid reaction capability, procurement concerns including fixed wing and helicopter aircraft and nuclear-powered submarines, and the military justice system.

What animates many of these efforts is the need to relocate the Canadian military in the post–Cold War world.

Obviously this is not surprising; indeed, it is the responsible thing to do. Both DFAIT and DND undertook internal studies in the late 1980s in order to assess their own capacities to formulate and implement policies attuned to the dramatic changes that were unfolding during this period, especially around east-west relations. Already some analysts in Ottawa, and colleagues within the Canadian academic community, were keenly aware of the need to rethink their ideas about international security and how foreign and defence policies might address these emerging challenges.[4] Yet even with well-informed reviews and reports, the analyses and sentiments have yet to be codified or consolidated into an overall strategic view of Canada's place in the world of war and peace. While this chapter is not the place to pursue this larger issue, it is worth noting that in spite of much effort by people both within and outside of official circles, it remains difficult to point to a single statement or document that clearly articulates for Canadians what, in fact, it now means to have a professional Canadian Armed Forces (CAF). Why should a significant albeit decreasing proportion of the government's budget and our tax dollars go towards maintaining a military force?[5]

This has not been a particularly quiet time in the world. The use of organized violence seems not to have diminished. From Bosnia to Chechnya, the Great Lakes Region to Sierra Leone, Afghanistan to Sri Lanka, and Algeria to the Gulf, military force has been applied often with tragic consequences. Protracted conflict and violence, both intra- and interstate, is indicative both of the continuing utility and perverse misuse of military force. And yet, it is equally obvious that none of these or, for that matter and to our good fortune, no other examples directly threaten Canada. To the extent any of these affect Canada, they do so because they offend our values and for some, our interests. Canadians and our government make that determination. For reasons ranging from the normative to the instrumental, we decide to represent these activities in ways that link us as Canadians to the event or the outcome. These are not, in and of themselves, national defence concerns though they are issues that are potentially within the mission and mandate of the Canadian Armed Forces.

There are, of course, recent examples where some have perceived palpable threats to Canada or Canadian interests. We have had experiences on both our coasts concerning fish and maritime zones; there remains substantial concern over Arctic issues; questions about the penetration of Canada by non-Canadian cultural forces remain at least as relevant now as thirty years ago; who really controls our economy continues to focus the attention of many; and these very same issues but with their own particular colour inform much of the nationalist debate around Quebec and federalism. In some interesting ways, as both John Ralston Saul and Franklyn Griffiths have argued, these core questions around sovereignty and identity are, in fact, the issues of our national defence.[6] While in many ways they may be quite correct, it is of course striking that by and large the military is not the policy instrument which can address most of these concerns.

Unlike people who reside in countries either with a history of empire or a current position of significant global power and aspirations, we rarely hear Canadians speak of a national security policy or apparatus. When such language is employed, it is often in terms of culture and identity as well as sovereignty, often linking the former two to the third. Canadians express concern about international security, and by that we generally have meant a sense of a preferred world order—what it should be, how it might be achieved, what our roles and responsibilities are.[7] We wish war to be avoided, for disputes to be settled peacefully, and for trade and commerce to occur globally under norms and rules that lead to predictability and stability. Canadians have the good fortune to seek these things from a relatively unencumbered and secure position. Overall, Canadians have accepted the fact that as a highly penetrated country—penetrated by peoples, ideas, finance, capital, technology, culture, etc.—we are influenced quite directly by events worldwide. Moreover, not only is our material well-being inherently connected (and this well before the concerns over globalization), but also we often have personal or historic ties with these places. We have easily assumed a personalized sense of mission concerning bringing peace and, if not that, some respite and sense of hope to troubled places and people. Hence, our sense of identity within the global community has become linked with a compelling need to "do something," whether the now-classic peacekeeping operation or the innovative but more long-term activities of peacebuilding and conflict prevention. This is the conventional wisdom about how Canadians see the world and themselves.[8]

International security, for Canadians, has long meant more than the issue of defence; it has meant engagement and it has assumed that the Canadian state is prepared to allocate its resources through both bilateral and multilateral channels in support of such efforts. Yet, unlike other countries, we have not used the language of national security policy for we have presumed that our understanding is a shared understanding, our concerns are shared concerns, and our sense of challenges to security are reflected in the norms, rules, and institutions that have been with us since the end of the Second World War and continue to evolve as the conditions and context warrant. Moreover, and this perhaps is the fundamental point, unlike many others we have, by conviction and by necessity, been able to differentiate between unilateral and multilateral situations. National defence is a category that anticipates threat to or within national boundaries and hence assumes a policy of preparation, often unilaterally but also in the context of an alliance, in response to this direct threat. International security is a term associated with a more inchoate possibility of challenges to peace and well-being, often indirect and distant, ascribing a situation in which many are or may be affected.

It calls upon a cooperative effort in response to a mutually recognized problem that challenges the interests of many but not necessarily one's own sovereignty, although institutions may be compromised and values undermined.

In the post–Cold War world, however, governments and citizens alike have become increasingly sensitive to issues that do not fit comfortably into the category of national defence nor under the rubric of international security. These are not new factors but rather have taken on a new saliency. Issues such as the illicit movement across national borders of drugs, people, technology, and money are perceived to be threatening to national interest. If we can agree for the moment that a relatively simple but not entirely inappropriate definition of security is the capacity of the government (or those in charge of whatever unit of analysis we might be working with) to control or manage entry or exit across recognized boundaries that define the locus of control—territory, intellectual or cultural space, identity—then it is evident that many of the issues that resonate in Canada as concerns of threats to national interest are indeed security challenges but not necessarily matters of national defence. Some, such as territory, resource, and border management and control, require a relatively narrow aspect of military skills, knowledge, and organization or policing capabilities including surveillance, enforcement, and interdiction techniques. But many others, including some of those alluded to above, require multilateral cooperative action in support of the more classic bilateral activities on which most interstate relations are built. Increasingly, these issues involve a mix of international actors—including those not "sovereignty bound" to borrow from Rosenau's nomenclature—and not simply states or governments. Moreover, the use of armed force whether by the military or even by police often is not the appropriate policy instrument.

International security is a broader idea than national defence, which focuses specifically on direct threats to territory, institutions, and values. It is, to borrow from social constructivists, a subjective assertion that some action or situation is viewed as requiring a response or intervention because our lack of resolve would be dissonant with our sense of identity, commitment, and place in the international community. War, famine, genocide, and the violation of international law all would be candidate categories, although as we well know not all such events or situations stimulate our government to act, or to act in a timely or appropriate fashion. From a national or governmental perspective, a threat to international security does not exist in the abstract but requires the government to make the linkage between the event and national norms and values leading to the allocation of resources. Various statements by Lloyd Axworthy on human security, reflective of the earlier *Agenda for Peace* offered by then Secretary-General Boutros Boutros-Ghali, along with the creation of Canada's peacebuilding fund is an interesting response. Although partially motivated by political instinct, these also were prompted by the minister's own genuine concern with generating more long-term commitment in ways not previously undertaken by the Canadian government.[9]

Over a decade ago, Rod Byers captured one of the enduring problems of the Canadian government in the phrase, commitment-capability gap.[10] Although Byers was referring specifically to the disjuncture between defence policy and defence capabilities and decried the situation where the Department of Finance was more central in effecting defence policy than the Department of National Defence, the problem not only has continued in DND but can be generalized to most sectors of Canada's foreign policy. Our self-defined image is one of liberal internationalism that provides not only a philosophy of interstate relations but also presumes a commitment which reaches far and wide without prejudice. Yet, in practice while our capabilities and resources constrain our actions, we continue to profess global engagements; this at a time when DFAIT, CIDA, IDRC, and DND among others have faced severe budgetary reductions.[11]

In principle, this desire to be globally engaged might not be all that bad. Better to have a country like Canada—reasonably open, pluralist, liberal democratic, multicultural and immigrant-based—pronounce and engage wherever the challenge emerges than to court the dangers of isolationism or leave it to others, especially in light of rampant American triumphalism currently prevalent in Washington. But there is a problem when we are unwilling to face the need to make choices, and that by so doing we not only continue to set expectations (we have them and others have them of us) that cannot be fulfilled but hamper our abilities to make logical choices concerning where, how, and why to commit our scarce resources. This, like most other issues, is not new. Official and unofficial studies and documents alike over the years have noted, time and again, the Canadian preference to be involved wherever, whenever, and however the need arises on matters of international peace and security, including humanitarian issues, but that our reach exceeds our grasp, our desire is greater than our capacity, our commitments are not matched by our capabilities. I am not arguing for what some have called niche diplomacy as a back door into neo-isolationism; rather, for a transparent articulation of criteria for determining priorities for Canadian commitments in the various sectors of international affairs in order to allow us to undertake effective policy.[12]

A Marginal Actor at the Centre (or where we have come from)

I need not go into this assertion in any detail. The story is well known. Our post–World War II commitments included the central pillars of NATO, NORAD, and the United Nations. The first two were intimately linked in doctrine and operations and hence in procurement and deployment. National defence policy and the ethos within the Canadian Forces were informed initially by the allied experiences of the Second World War and then by the shared perceptions concerning the Soviet Union. Others, including some of the authors in this volume, either have written in detail about these years or were participants in the policy-making process. Suffice to note that our desire to be at the table when policies and decisions were debated and made concerning Western security interests required a minimum level of operational commitment and sustained presence visible to all our NATO partners. Though our post-1945 military force was never terribly large, concerns with North America's vulnerability to an over-the-pole Russian attack, the need to protect the North Atlantic sea lanes, NATO interoperability requirements, and domestic economic interests combined to reinforce an already close relationship with the United States armed forces and with key European partners. Canada–U.S. defence production-sharing arrangements and industrial offsets with the United States, providing air force and main battletank-training facilities for our European allies, commitments to Arctic and North Atlantic surveillance, placing troops and equipment in NATO bases in Europe—all ensured that the NATO arena remained the principal focus and priority concern for our defence community.

And yet, it is important to note that throughout this Cold War period, it was the third pillar—UN operations—that confirmed in the minds of Canadians and others our commitment to international security.[13] The story line on this is equally well known: every UN peacekeeping operation through till 1989 involved Canadian troops. Although we are reminded that there have been more and larger operations since the end of the Cold War, the formative years involved protracted conflicts requiring long-term placement of troops, often in a political environment of some instability including the fear of escalation involving one or more of the world's major powers. These operations did not require Canadians, we chose to be there; and they did not require—indeed, did not permit—the deployment of major weapons systems. Canadian troops were valued both because of their training in a modern multipurpose, combat capable force (to use the jargon of the 1994 Defence White Paper), but also because of the political context and role Canada played within the multilateral world of the United Nations and related institutions. These operational commitments enhanced Canada's reputation and professed commitment to, and possibly its influence in, such institutions while also providing an indirect method for Canada to share the larger burdens of international security operations with its NATO partners.

Over the forty years of the Cold War, while our doctrine, policy, and procurement essentially were determined by our NATO and NORAD commitments, it was in the areas of UN and NATO out-of-area operations that Canada made its most significant contributions to international peace and security. In spite of an ad hoc approach to these situations, from Suez to Saigon Canada arguably made a difference. While it is probably correct to argue that from the traditional ideas of national defence and national interest NATO and NORAD were more significant to Canada than becoming involved in these far-flung and intermittent responses to crises, from the perspective of the target and the partner, it also is true that our value was far greater out-of-area than in the North Atlantic. And I think it can be argued that these engagements have contributed in substantial ways to forging a sense of who we are and our place in the international community.

To put it differently, where would Canada's absence have been most costly, and to whom and in what terms? This counterfactual, of course, is not a question unique to Canadians. It can be asked of many countries that are not major powers, for it is a question that really is driven by one's position on the spectrum of those old-fashioned realist concepts, power and influence. Outside those situations which directly challenge one's national sovereignty, bilateral and multilateral relations inherently involve exchanges, and the degree of symmetry or equivalence among the partners has much to do with the outcome and the attendant costs and benefits. The Cold War and notably the North Atlantic theatre provided the crucial incentive structure. Thus, relatively small countries like Canada and the Netherlands could be part of the most important military alliance in the non-communist world, and for comparatively little cost reap the full range of benefits that came with an integrated collective defence arrangement. While it may be too harsh to state, as some have, that Canada has been a free rider in terms of these overarching security arrangements, there is little doubt that in both soft and hard terms, substantial benefits were offset at minimal costs. Furthermore, had our contribution to NATO and NORAD been less or even absent, it is unlikely that this would have had any significant military or strategic impact on the alliance, although there probably would have been some residual political or economic costs. Furthermore, the defence of Canadian territory and sovereignty likely would not have been significantly weakened. What is in little doubt is that the political, economic, and military costs to Canada for its absence would have been enormous. And besides, we were there because for us it was the principled, responsible thing to do; it reflected our values; and it made sense.[14]

During this same period, the opposite exchange relationship existed with our involvement in UN and out-of-area operations. In these residual and usually ad hoc arrangements, the UN Secretary-General and Security Council came to expect and we came to assume if not also desire that Canada would be invited to be a lead member of UN peacekeeping operations.[15] Correctly or not, Canadians adopted the sense that such missions were the pride and indeed right of the Canadian armed forces. The political significance of this close identification cannot be overestimated, for in the midst of Cold War rhetoric and seemingly intractable conflicts, Canadians saw one of their principal missions to assist countries—principally those emerging from postcolonial struggles and the legacies of imperialism—in managing hostilities, pre-empting east/west intrusion, and creating the conditions for non-violent dispute resolution. While NATO and NORAD were essentially static, status quo defence arrangements in which we were minor players, UN operations occurred in situations of uncertainty, where being there made a difference, where Canada's role often was to lead, and where our political as well as economic attributes were significant aspects of our influence. Albeit indirectly, this out-of-area activity was yet another way by which Canada could contribute meaningfully to the overall security interests of its NATO partners.

As with our participation in NATO, our "returns on investment" were substantial. However, unlike NATO, the returns were primarily on the soft side—reputation, status, and influence in international institutions and with those developing countries who valued our location as an advanced Western country without an imperial or colonial legacy but with direct access to the big powers—and in terms of the creation and consolidation of our own image. Being a liberal internationalist within the UN and other multilateral frameworks has been both relatively positive and safe. Moreover, it has provided Canada with venues for the pursuit of specific interests and for the development of coalitions around areas of Canadian priority. This is the perception, perhaps at least part mythology, that the UN in particular has provided the vehicle for the articulation of Canada's place in the international community. Not to discount some of the pointed criticisms of multilateralism in general and the UN in particular, but outside of our bilateral relations with a very few countries—the United States, Britain, France, Germany, Japan, and China—there are probably no more important diplomatic missions to Canada than the UN in New York and in Geneva, along with NATO on the security side. In spite of all this, there is no doubt that throughout the Cold War, UN operations were ad hoc arrangements often grudgingly approved by the P-5 who often viewed these as marginal to international peace and security.

Yet this was the arena in which Canada operated so fluidly and effectively. For these decades, though there is no doubt about the critical importance of NATO and NORAD, Canada was a marginal actor within the central theatre of east-west relations. At the same time, in spite of and at times because of the complications in UN diplomacy introduced by Cold War politics, Canada assumed a position of central importance throughout the more diffuse UN and out-of-area world of north-south relations, including but not limited to participation in peacekeeping missions. In the end, both east-west and north-south arenas brought Canada considerable benefits at relatively low cost.

A Central Actor at the Margins? (or a glimpse into the future)

By now it is a truism to note that the peace dividend was more a political slogan than anything else. Since the end of the Cold War, the number and severity of violent inter- and intrastate conflicts has been substantial. The concomitant number of UN-sponsored missions, more of them at greater financial cost and more complex in mandate and operations, is but one indicator of the stark situation faced by the international community. Again, we face the perverse situation where military force is required to impose order and end violence which whether or not initially created by other militaries has been expressed through the wanton use of organized violence. Moreover, in this decade we have witnessed new atrocities throughout the world, with names such as Bosnia and Chechnya, the Gulf and Algeria, the Great Lakes region and Sierre Leone, Argentina and Colombia, China and North Korea giving us a global sense of the pervasiveness of such activity. With the tit-for-tat nuclear tests by India and Pakistan, we have borne witness to the most profound challenge to the fragile non-proliferation regime that quite possibly will concatenate into the other areas of weapons of mass destruction.

The creation of a new language—of peacebuilding and peacemaking and peace enforcement—to complement that of peacekeeping is one indicator that violent events are no longer viewed simply in terms of peace and war. The two threatening experiences with Iraq since the end of Desert Storm, the aborted attempt to address the complex situation in the Great Lakes Region and the former Zaire, and the uncertain response to the South Asian nuclear testing show the degree to which even the major powers feel constrained not to act unilaterally without at least some pretext of international and regional support under the cloak of law and principles. The interconnectedness of events and actors, and the challenges they pose to norms, principles, and institutions suggest that the so-called marginal areas, the out-of-area regions, are emerging as central to international security.[16]

The spread of weapons of mass destruction coupled with the advanced technologies required for weapons targeting and delivery is highlighting the transformation of periphery to core, or what were the marginal, out-of-area sectors into arenas of central concern. Coupled with the growing chorus around issues of illegal drug trafficking, illicit migration, illegal trade in small arms and in dual-use technologies, the resulting implications for terrorism, economic espionage, and money laundering, it is evident that out-of-area no longer has any meaning in terms of its previous designation of tertiary importance. These diffuse and global challenges to security and, in some instances, to peace are not amenable to the static thinking that dominated the security politics of the Cold War east-west confrontation.

Each of these has the potential of affecting Canada directly or indirectly, and some of this already has occurred. It is evident that if security is, indeed, the capacity to manage exit and entry across the boundaries for which one is responsible, then our security is compromised. To the extent that these trans-boundary activities undermine our public and private sectors, our core values and institutions, and our abilities to manage the shadow of the future, then these security problems are transformed into national threats. What is clear, of course, is that the world of security and threat is now more diffuse and complex, less easy to target, and certainly not easily responded to by military force, or not force alone.[17]

But that is not to state that the role of the military is less important. Today the need for a modern and sophisticated military may be as great as ever though the tasks are more varied and demanding, challenging some of the underlying assumptions of military culture. The multipurpose, combat capable force recommended by government and by some non-governmental commentators may well remain appropriate as a core concept. What is contentious is how that is to be amended to fit the specific demands of particular operations and what that would mean for doctrine, for procurement, for deployment. Furthermore, as in the past, effective foreign policy requires explicit incorporation of security and defence policy, an increasingly daunting challenge in an era when we increasingly erode the standards of sovereignty and non-intervention through multilateral actions for humanitarian as well as peace and security goals. The perceived need to act in pursuit of both the traditional idea of national interests—sovereignty, institutions, values, etc.—and the more opaque but nonetheless material concerns with international or global security places enormous strain on our institutional capacity.

For Canada, in addition to the traditional duties of border defence and aid to the civil power, the military is an aspect of our international identity and our commitment to the politics of peace and security. This most notably has and should continue to include the participation in international arrangements through multilateral institutions and alliances. Furthermore, there is a growing awareness that the long-term project of peacebuilding will require an operational capacity to ensure security and stability within the area of operations. Peacekeeping in both its traditional sense of monitoring ceasefires and lines of disengagement and in its more recent style of active intervention also involving aspects of human security as purported both by the United Nations and the Canadian government is likely to remain a profession in high demand, one where the military might no longer be the only or even the most important element in every operation, but where it likely will remain a necessary and at times critical component.

Though one may despair that we are entering the twenty-first century with military force still an important factor in local, national, and global affairs, it would be foolhardy to pretend otherwise.[18] Yet as Canadians it is evident that we have the luxury of facing few direct military threats, though our security is being profoundly compromised. Moreover, many other issues within Canadian society and abroad call out for a greater commitment of political will and other scarce resources to resolve social inequities and underdevelopment. It therefore is incumbent on the Canadian government to address the very real need to explain the rationale for Canada to maintain a standing professional armed forces. Though this has yet to be done, it need not be difficult. Certainly public opinion favours continued responsible Canadian participation in defence and security matters, and the Canadian government continues to signal its willingness, however ill prepared, to share in the burdens that come with its professed role in global affairs.[19]

Cooperative Security: Moving from the Margins to the Centre

It remains evident that a powerful case can be made to ensure Canadian capacity to confront the very real and substantial security challenges posed by many of the issues noted. There is no doubt that much of the world remains unsafe and that, even granting the importance of critically reassessing the place of internationally organized or sponsored military assistance and intervention, there will continue to be the need for responsible use of armed force. In spite of much justified criticism of aspects of the Canadian military, overall the publicly available evidence indicates a strong belief by Canadians and by their government that Canada must continue to play a responsible part in sharing the burdens of international peace and security, and that along with the full panoply of instruments available to a modern government, this requires a professionally trained and equipped armed forces.[20]

Among the peace and security challenges that have emerged in the first post–Cold War decade, one can identify at least four general categories: weapons proliferation, including but not limited to weapons of mass destruction; civil or internal warfare, often targeted not solely at competing elites but also at mass populations, especially where ethnic or other community differences exist; terrorism; international or transnational crime including drugs, migration, money laundering, technologies especially but not limited to the dual-use variety, and economic espionage. Although most of these activities are state supported, oftentimes non-state actors are able to act independent of state authority.

Aspects of all four areas are relevant to the mandate of the armed forces. All but the first category would have been designated as marginal during the Cold War in terms of the type of threat regardless of geographic location. Now, of course, these are the issues that focus the attention and resources not only of foreign ministries and military headquarters, but also the intelligence community and police well beyond the North Atlantic and European arenas. These are security problems not isolated to one part of the world or another, but are widespread and linked reflecting both the ease of movement and the porousness of borders as well as the market forces of globalization.[21] Moreover, these are issues that cannot be managed, never mind resolved unilaterally, but require coordinated policies undertaken in a cooperative atmosphere. While at times more regionally focused and other times globally, multilateral cooperative security is a required part of any effort to eradicate these challenges to state and human security.

In earlier pieces I've argued in general for the development of a cooperative security approach for the post–Cold War world and, more specifically, for

Canada in this new security environment.[22] More recently, David Haglund has taken this up in terms of NATO as well as Canadian strategic thinking.[23] Without reviewing those arguments, I remain convinced that a cooperative security approach to Canadian—and indeed most state—involvement in international peace and security activities is warranted. Moreover, as Denis Stairs so clearly articulates, Canadian domestic political culture favours the creation of coalitions, the acknowledgment of pluralisms, and the need to seek managed solutions; hence, I would add, creating a natural affinity between how we "do business" at home and how we wish to pursue our interests as well as our responsibilities abroad.[24]

Among other things, cooperative security calls for: an inclusiveness to security politics in both partners and agenda; the initiation and maintaining of "habits of dialogue" as a means to ensure discussion around potentially contentious issues as well as a process to "institutionalize" confidence building and reassurance measures; over time gradually transforming existing institutions or creating and sustaining new institutions with the organizational capacity to address emerging security concerns (i.e., before they reach the level of threat) although in the interim much can be accomplished through ad hoc arrangements unencumbered by the complexities of formal institutions. Cooperative security does not diminish the centrality of bilateral relations; this is a false dichotomy. Rather, it places multilateral instruments as a necessary complement to bilateral relations, enforcing the perception that many if not most of the security challenges we now face require coordination and cooperation among many even when the security problems may not be perceived as a direct threat to one's own specific country or people. Cooperative security, while acknowledging the necessity for leadership and the unique place of major powers, prescribes multilateralism and cooperation over unilateralism and confrontation.

Clearly, aspects of all these factors should resonate among Canadians who so long have lived with the arguments of Pearsonian liberal internationalism. The difference today resides in the complexity of the security challenges in this increasingly diffuse international system. This complexity is both in terms of the issues—the broadening of the security debate previously alluded to—and the actors. Even for those who accept the argument of the "unipolar moment," it is obvious that with more than 185 states which, at one and the same time, jealously guard their sovereignty while also supporting various forms of multilateral actions of intervention for a variety of reasons, state, interstate, and non-governmental organizations are all playing in and affecting the "security game." [25]

So long as Canadians and their government continue to believe in the necessity for Canada to be a responsible actor on matters of international security—that is, to extend beyond the merely defensive posture of territorial and boundary management to a more proactive pursuit of peace and security reflective of Canadian values as well as specific interests—then our preference for multilateral approaches must remain central to our foreign, security, and defence policies. But it is not merely the multilateralism of the post-1945 era, in which collective security was a rhetorical device for UN politics while the real security process was dominated by the collective defence of opposing alliances. Today, there is a need for a realistic multilateralism, again not one that succumbs to the ideology of collective security pundits but rather a process that creates opportunities for cooperative engagement of the issues at hand. While there remains the requirement to bring military and other might to bear, even in the contested areas of interregional boundaries there are opportunities to facilitate coordinated and collaborative management of the process of resolving disputes.[26]

What this means for the Canadian armed forces has not yet been adequately addressed by officials or the government. Multilateral security policy is now more than the standard requirement that we have the capacity to participate in NATO actions or in support of UN missions. Rather, it calls on the government to rethink the role of the military not only in terms of the traditional mandate of the armed forces but also in conjunction with both the broader range of security challenges and other policy instruments available to the modern state. It requires that we begin to address more thoroughly the role of civil society—both our own and the international NGO community—in matters historically assumed to be better left to the soldier. Further, it is incumbent on the leadership of the Canadian armed forces to analyze the full range of challenges to Canada's national defence, to our security, and to international peace and ask quite candidly in which of these does the military have a lead or supporting role, and of those, how might that be carried forth and in coordination with what other domestic and foreign partners?

This is not an argument for transforming the Canadian military into a constabulary force; but nor is it a simple acceptance of "lets be prepared to fight yesterday's war." There is no doubt that citizens and government alike remain convinced that the privileged position of Canada and Canadians comes with an obligation to be a responsible international actor in both situations of peace and of conflict. Discussions also have addressed the proper role of the Canadian armed forces, and whether an "all purpose force" is necessarily the best use of our limited resources. This alone is no longer a sufficiently inclusive analysis. While the debate over the structure and role of our armed forces remains unsettled, more generally we need to examine the extent to which we can best contribute to international peace and security, linked as those goals are with equally broad commitments to development, human rights, good governance, and human security more generally. Yet while each and every one of these is laudable, not all are equally achievable given resources and circumstances. Moreover, as Denis Stairs notes in his contribution to this volume, our instrumentalist foreign policies in the service of social engineering also require careful reconsideration as they come with their own costs and unintended consequences.

The shattered world of 1945 served as the foundation for a reconstructed international system, part divided between two defensive alliances, part united through the ideal of a universal multilateral institution. While the former avoided direct military confrontation, much of the world experienced the spillover from the east-west confrontation, with the United Nations at one and the same time serving as an arena for the more generalized ideological battles yet also facilitating the moderation and management if not resolution of hot conflicts. Canada played various roles in both arenas: a supporting actor of marginal importance at the centre stage of east-west conflict but a lead actor in many of the provincial theatres worldwide. Canadian diplomats became adroit at quietly finding ways to use multilateral processes and special bilateral channels in efforts to bring peace and security, while the Canadian military continually serviced the needs of the United Nations, all the time functioning primarily within a NATO east-west mindset.

Just as NATO's old out-of-area theatres are no longer of peripheral importance to the international community, so Canadian interests, capabilities, and talents honed as part of the Pearsonian legacy of liberal internationalism are now at centre stage. Even the post-Maastricht and NATO-enlarged Europe now faces the types of conflicts in which Canadian experience and expertise has much to offer, while elsewhere in the world, issues of peace and security continue to call for a mix of military and development expertise, including peacebuilding that is increasingly reliant on the services of civil society.[27] While there is no reason to assume that Canada should not play a significant role in this period of post–Cold War uncertainty and turbulence, Canada has not yet addressed the core question of resource allocation and within that, the issue of the Canadian armed forces. Although governments have played politics with defence department budgets and procurement decisions, there has been a noticeable lack of positive analysis concerning how our military at the turn of this century can best contribute to enhancing Canadian interests and values, including peace and security. Moreover, this type of assessment cannot be done in isolation of those many other factors that are part of the new security environment, many of which must be addressed by other, non-military components of governments and international organizations.

As we conclude the first decade since the ending of the Cold War, both peace and prosperity remain elusive goals for the majority of humankind. The Asian miracle of economic growth and performance legitimacy is tarnished if not dissipated; nuclear proliferation has not been contained; "balkanization" has regained its currency as a very real and poignant expression of the politics of identity, nationalism, and barbarity; the legacies of neo-colonialism remain as vivid and dehumanizing as in the past; and the disparities between north and south increase. This is not the description of a world without need, and it is inconceivable that any government of Canada will not be possessed to some extent by values that command it to undertake sustained commitments to assist. However, it is also increasingly evident that sooner or later, by policy or by circumstance, Canada also will face the option of sliding back into the old notion of triage: assess the seriousness of the competing claims on your resources and choose those most likely to be helped by your intervention, leaving aside those who can manage without it as well as those who will succumb even should you try to help. In such a world, one in which we Canadians have not yet had a national debate, how will we determine where we should allocate our military and other security instruments in support of peace and stability? What roles will the military play and what will their connection be to the other security actors increasingly evident in this more complex world?

NOTES

1. Although I recognize and acknowledge—indeed I have been part of—the debate concerning the inclusiveness of the concept of "security," in this paper I will not address in any detail such issues as environmental security or other forms of "nontraditional" security challenges. My primary focus here is the role of the Canadian armed forces in Canada's security and defence policy.

2. The obvious exception has been the perception by some that the movement for Quebec sovereignty is a direct challenge to Canadian security. The Trudeau government's invoking of the *War Measures Act* in response to FLQ terrorism is the most dramatic example of Canada's recent experience with a domestic threat viewed as sufficiently serious to mobilize the armed forces. The Mulroney government's decision to reconvene Parliament in the summer of 1987 in response to the "security challenge" posed by the illegal landing of South Asians on the shores of Nova Scotia foreshadowed the current although still improperly managed issue of the nexus between migration and security.

3. See Douglas L. Bland, ed., *Canada's National Defence, Volume 1, Defence Policy* (Kingston: School of Policy Studies, Queen's University, 1998); *Defence White Paper* (1994); *Canada in the World* (1995); etc. From the public, note *Report on the Review of Canadian Defense Policy* (Committee of 13, Centre Québécois de Relations Internationales, Université Laval, Québec, 1994) and *Canada 21: Canada and Common Security in the Twenty-First Century* (Toronto: Centre for International Studies, University of Toronto 1994).

4. For a modest contribution to the debate on some of these issues, see David B. Dewitt and David Leyton-Brown, eds., *Canada's International Security Policy* (Scarborough, ON: Prentice-Hall, 1995).

5. Some would argue that these issues did receive serious attention and that there were solutions offered. See, for example, *Canada 21* and some of the background studies for this report. Nevertheless, there are others who have serious reservations about the manner of the debate and the recommendations that emerged during the 1993–95 period. See, for example, David Haglund, "Here Comes M. Jourdain: A Canadian Grand Strategy Out of Moliére," *Canadian Defence Quarterly* 27/2 (Spring 1998). While I have my differences with aspects of Haglund's argument, I certainly agree with his overall critical assessment about the ideas of collective and common security and obviously, given my own earlier writing, I am sympathetic to his support for the premises underlying the concept of cooperative security as well as the logical implications for policy and practise.

6. For example, see the extended essay by Franklyn Griffiths, *Strong and Free: Canada and the New Sovereignty* (Toronto: Stoddart, 1996).

7. See, for example, David B. Dewitt and David Leyton-Brown, "Canada's International Security Policy," David G. Haglund, "Changing Concepts and Trends in International Security," and H.P. Klepak, "Changing Realities and Perceptions of Military Threat," in Dewitt and Leyton-Brown, *Canada's International Security Policy*. For further consideration relevant to the larger global context, see Robert W. Cox, "Production and Security," and David V. J. Bell, "Global Communications, Culture, and Values: Implications for Global Security," both in David Dewitt, David Haglund, and John Kirton, eds., *Building a New Global Order* (Toronto: Oxford University Press, 1993).

8. Recent polling data continue to confirm the general tendency of Canadians to view positively Canada's participation in international security activities, including the use of armed force beyond traditional peacekeeping missions. Regular polls

were conducted and assessed by the now defunct Canadian Institute for International Peace and Security, and reported in their magazine, *Peace and Security*. More recent public opinion data can be found on the Internet; for example, at «www.com.compas.ca».

9. Speech by the Hon. Lloyd Axworthy, Minister of Foreign Affairs, at York University, November 1996.

10. See R.B. Byers, *Canadian Security and Defence: The Legacy and the Challenges*, Adelphi Paper No. 214 (London: International Institute for Strategic Studies, 1986). This phrase was a focus for discussion in the *1994 Defence White Paper*; see Bland, *Canada's National Defence*, pp. 281-86.

11. Canada's ODA (Official Development Assistance) slipped by over 40 percent between 1990 and 1996, where it is now at the extraordinarily low level of 0.24 percent of GDP.

12. The companion chapter in this volume by Denis Stairs really sets the tone and much of the content for a serious examination of what our foreign, defence, and security policy must consider in any reformulation.

13. See Jack Granatstein's chapter in this volume for a trenchant critique of Canada's role in peacekeeping.

14. The work of the late John Holmes on Canada in the immediate post-1945 period when we forged new security relationships with the North Atlantic community and with the United States remain among the most insightful.

15. While the 1967 parliamentary debate that led Mitchell Sharp, then Canadian Secretary of State for External Affairs, to articulate a set of criteria for Canada's involvement in UN missions is indicative of a growing concern over "mission creep," it also points out the anticipation as well as pride felt by Canadians about having a privileged claim to participate in peacekeeping activities.

16. One of the notable aspects of the post–Cold War security environment has been not only the continuation of protracted conflicts such as those in the Middle East and in the Mediterranean but how these types of complex conflicts that involve both the displacement of large domestic communities as well as interstate violence seem increasingly prevalent with no evidence as yet of any greater success by the international community in achieving successful resolution.

17. It is increasingly evident to experts both within and outside of Canada that aspects of migration are linked directly to the illicit movement of drugs, money, and provocative technologies. The difficulties of addressing these issues is clear though the answers are not. The United Nations and the European Union have established high-level committees to examine these challenges, while an increasing amount of academic research is underway evident in both mainstream and specialized journals. See also Jeffrey Simpson, "Lack of UN Resolution Gives Refugee Status to Drug Pushers," *Globe and Mail*, 11 June 1998.

18. The palpable lack of an informed and serious debate in much of the West, including Canada and the United States, about NATO enlargement should be of concern regardless of where one stands on this issue. Similarly, the manner by which the India-Pakistan nuclear tests were summarily observed, commented upon, and then forgotten is testimony to the fragile qualities of the public's interest and possibly the government's capacity to sustain a focus on these very large issues of regional and global security.

19. The issue of preparedness continues to be a challenge for those government departments charged with carrying out the government's policies. DFAIT, CIDA, and DND have faced severe budgetary reductions over the past decade and while

current indications suggest some selective recovery, this has yet to be borne out. A recent example of the problems encountered can be seen in the government's desire to participate in NATO air exercises regarding the ongoing repression of ethnic Albanians in Kosovo, but its inability due to the earlier decision to scrap Canada's only air refuelling capability, making it impossible without American assistance to send Canadian fighter planes to Europe in order to participate in the NATO exercise. See Paul Koring, "NATO Flights to Proceed Without Canadian Aircraft," *Globe and Mail*, 15 June 1998. This issue is of sufficient concern that Canadian Forces Command and Staff College chose national mobilization in the face of a war emergency as the theme for their "Exercise Defence Planner" as the concluding assignment for the 1997–98 class.

20. As I've hinted elsewhere in this chapter, there is much debate about the specific criteria used to define "responsible participation," "appropriate military training," doctrine, procurement policies, and so forth. The past decade has been a wake-up call for the military and for Canadians to reassess the armed forces as an institution and what role the military should play in the formulation and delivery of Canadian policy. Nevertheless, there remains an underlying commitment for Canada to be a central actor, at least in the various multilateral institutions, on matters of peace and security, and along with that an acknowledgement that a professional military must be a policy instrument available to Canada.

21. Ecological and environmental "security" is an issue of central relevance but beyond the scope of this discussion.

22. David Dewitt, "Common, Comprehensive, and Cooperative Security," *The Pacific Review* 7/1 (November 1994); with some minor modifications and expanded to address Canadian security policy in Dewitt and Leyton-Brown, *Canada's International Security Policy*. An earlier statement can be found in "Canadian Defence Policy: Regional Conflicts, Peacekeeping and Stability Operations," *Canadian Defence Quarterly* 21/1 (August 1991).

23. David Haglund, "The NATO of Its Dreams? Canada and the Co-Operative Security Alliance," *International Journal* 52 (Summer 1997) and Haglund, "Here Comes M. Jourdain."

24. As well as his contribution to this volume, see Denis Stairs, "The Political Culture of Canadian Foreign Policy," *Canadian Journal of Political Science* 15 (December 1982) and his "Will and Circumstance and the Postwar Study of Canada's Foreign Policy," *International Journal* 50 (Winter 1994–95).

25. One merely need consider a few items currently in the news: humanitarian intervention in the Great Lakes Region; diplomatic and military intervention in the areas of the Former Yugoslavia; the creation of a UN Standing War Crimes court; the international response to the Asian financial crisis; the Ottawa process in support of the anti-personnel landmines convention; the role of both state and non-state (NGO) actors in such places as North Korea, the Great Lakes Region, the Horn of Africa, and Cambodia.

26. Whatever failures one might charge the European and other major powers with over the situation in the Former Yugoslavia and, more generally, the Balkans region, it is remarkable to observe the extent of the cooperation between and among both allies and former adversaries; all the more so when compared with the situation in the Great Lakes Region and the Horn of Africa.

27. See Roland Paris, "Peacebuilding and the Limits of Liberal Internationalism," *International Security* 22 (Fall 1997).

Indigenous Rights in Canada

An International Perspective

KEN COATES

University of New Brunswick
at Saint John

eginning in the late 1960s, demands for the recognition of indigenous rights have been a significant feature on the Canadian political landscape. First Nations' organizations from coast to coast to coast have pressured federal, provincial, and territorial governments to honour existing treaties, negotiate land claims deals where treaties have not previously been signed, recognize the "inherent" right to aboriginal self-government, and otherwise address the legacy of several hundred years of colonialism and paternalism. In justifying these demands and in pressing the case for greater government action, indigenous activists and their supporters have highlighted those aspects of Canada's past that explain the condition of First Nations' people and that support the indigenous positions. Although these pronouncements often make better politics than history, condemnations of the fur trade, residential schools, treaty processes, the Indian Act, legislative efforts to suppress cultural practices and countless other acts of neglect or unwarranted intrusion have figured prominently in Canadian public life.

The final report of the Royal Commission on Aboriginal Peoples, and subsequent efforts to apologize for government actions and to establish a reconciliation process, emphasize the degree to which Canadians, past and present, are responsible for the injustices meted out to the indigenous residents of what is now Canada. Public-minded Canadians are now well versed in the significance of Jay's Treaty, the Royal Proclamation of 1763, the numbered treaties, and the culturally destructive initiatives of the Department of Indian Affairs. In the Canadian public mind, the indigenous rights issue is a Canadian-made problem, with in-country roots and, logically enough, national solutions.

There is considerable merit in approaching the indigenous rights issue in this fashion. The Canadian legal process, which now figures so prominently in the attempts to reconcile aboriginal expectations with the government's limited sense of collective responsibility, turns on the interpretation of Canadian legal precedent and legislation. Recent court decisions, like the Delgamuukw case in British Columbia and the New Brunswick judgment that granted the Micmac the right to harvest trees on Crown lands, arose out of specific Canadian legal and political conflicts and were decided on the basis of a reading of Canadian law and jurisprudence. The indigenous rights struggle is, it seems, a quintessentially national conflict that will be resolved in Canada, within Canadian legal and political structures.

But the indigenous rights movement in Canada did not emerge in isolation. It has, in fact, influenced and been influenced by similar struggles in many other parts of the world. The Canadian indigenous rights struggle developed in an international context, continues to be shaped by actions and decisions in other nations, and is a pivotal element in a global legal and political conflict involving original inhabitants and settler societies. A series of global developments, ranging from the era of colonial expansion to the rise of the United Nations, including the human rights movement and the political activism and radicalism of the American Indian Movement (AIM), and capped in recent years by the emergence of an influential Fourth World movement, have had a significant impact on both the actions of indigenous peoples and the receptiveness of the Canadian population to aboriginal protests.

Consider the current state of the indigenous rights movement around the world. In Yakutia (central Siberia in Russia), politicians worry about finding a compromise between the government's development priorities and the cultural and economic needs of the Small Peoples of the North. The situation is not much different than that facing the Innu in Labrador. Thousands of miles away, in the Amazon River basin, the Yanomami seek to defend their land and their life ways from the incursions of miners and developers, replaying a struggle that was waged in many areas of Canada a century ago. The Tainui people of the Waikato District of New Zealand, in contrast, discuss how they plan to invest the money that they received through their October 1995 settlement with the national government, a similar challenge to that facing the First Nations of the Yukon and the Inuvialuit of the Mackenzie River basin. And so it goes around the globe. In countries as diverse as Indonesia and Sweden, Thailand and Nicaragua, Australia and Botswana, indigenous peoples struggle to assert their right to traditional territories and, using this claim as their base, seek settlements from national and regional governments that will give them the resources, land, and administrative controls necessary for self-determination and cultural survival.[1] And across Canada, the Lubicon Cree attempt to secure a just settlement from the federal and provincial governments, the Micmac fight to hold onto newlyregained harvesting rights, dozens of groups in British Columbia try to settle outstanding land claims, and the Inuit of Nunavut (in the Eastern Arctic) struggle with the challenges and opportunities of regional self-government.

As in Canada, the international rights and land claims process is awash in contradictions and tensions, between the development ambitions of settler populations and the traditional values of First Peoples, between the limited fiscal resources of national governments and the pressing social, financial, and cultural needs of indigenous societies, and between the sustained vigilance of international organizations and supporters and the often hostile opposition of local non-indigenous people to potentially disruptive indigenous rights claims and settlements. There is, as well, conflict inherent in the attempt to merge indigenous culture and contemporary legal systems, for settlements seek not only to resolve outstanding legal entitlements but also to bridge the cultural gap between indigenous and settler societies. The conflicts over land, the guardianship of the environment,[2] land claims settlements, legal debates, and the survival of indigenous societies has emerged over the past forty years as influential global movements. Each country and region seeks to resolve indigenous land claims within a specific national legal, financial, and social context, but the impetus to deal with indigenous rights arises from broad, international pressures and concerns. The battle over indigenous rights, then, represents a classic struggle between the international and the local, and an effort to bring regional realities into line with international sensibilities.

In this conflict, Canada has figured very prominently. Canadian First Nations have been at the forefront in terms of pressing their claims at the international level. Somewhat contradictorily, the Canadian government has also played a significant role in elevating the status of indigenous groups at the United Nations. For the past decade, indigenous leaders from around the world have been pressing the United Nations to adopt a Declaration on the Rights of Indigenous Peoples. The development is unprecedented, for the movement for indigenous rights has brought together hundreds of indigenous groups that, hitherto, were little known outside their traditional territories. In recent years, the Yanomami of Brazil and Venezuela, the Chittagong Hill peoples of Bangladesh, and the Gwitch'in of northern Canada have managed to attract international attention to their struggle for cultural survival, finding support among indigenous and non-indigenous peoples alike. The processes of globalization, which brought hardship and dislocation to indigenous peoples around the world, have more recently provided both the technical capacity, organizational contexts, and the reassessment of Western/ industrial values necessary for indigenous groups to reach beyond their hereditary boundaries in the defense of their life-ways.

There is, as yet, no wide agreement on which groups properly belong under the "indigenous" epistemological umbrella. During the United Nations meetings on the Draft Declaration on the Rights of Indigenous Peoples, the indigenous representatives have insisted on an open-ended conception of indigenous and have relied on self-definition to determine membership. National governments, which often see a distinction between indigenous and ethnic minorities, have great difficulty with this definition. To the degree that the indigenous "label" attracts international attention, there is the possibility that other groups will attach themselves to the movement, potentially lessening the impact of the indigenous protest in the process.

Indigenous peoples (also described, in various academic and popular studies, as tribal, small, aboriginal, or original peoples) are generally defined by a series of internal and external characteristics. Indigenous peoples are noted for their intensely spiritual and cultural attachment to the land. Most definitions focus on the human-land relationship and the cultural belief, shared by many different peoples, that human society is meant to live with the land and not to dominate the natural environment. They tend to be self-contained societies, not seeking to expand to new territories nor to establish dominance over neighbouring groups. Through well-known processes of colonization and foreign domination, indigenous peoples have, with few exceptions, lost political control of their land, enjoy few political rights within the nation-states erected around them, are small minorities with their host countries, and share only marginally in the economic and social benefits of resource development and industrial expansion, much of which has taken place on their territories. One of the most widely accepted definitions is by Martinez Cobo:

> Indigenous communities, peoples and nations are those which, having a historical continuity with pre-invasion and pre-colonial societies that developed on their territories, consider themselves distinct from other sectors of the societies now prevailing in those territories, or parts of them. They form at present non-dominant sectors of society and are determined to preserve, develop and transmit to future generations their ancestral territories, and the ethnic identity, as the basis of their continued existence as peoples, in accordance with their own cultural patterns, social institutions and legal systems.[3]

Indigenous groups, described by anthropologist John Bodley as "victims of progress,"[4] have been profoundly transformed by historic processes of globalization; what First Nations in Canada describe as a "Canadian" process is, in fact, primarily a regional manifestation of a much broader phenomenon. The transformations commenced with the "Columbian exchange," or the biological and epidemiological transfers that accompanied the age of European expansion. This unintentional but profoundly disruptive consequence of exploration and initial settlement brought diseases that ravaged indigenous populations, animals, and plants that competed with local flora and fauna, and a surging migrant population that quickly pushed local inhabitants from their territories. Over subsequent generations, European, Christian, and commercial value systems drove newcomers to push further into indigenous territories, and armed them with the assurance of cultural and religious superiority. Weakened by disease, vulnerable to the military technology of the newcomers, indigenous groups struggled against the incursions. They responded in a variety of ways, from fleeing the settlement zones to staging desperate battles to keep the foreigners out. The indigenous groups experienced occasional success, but generally waged a losing battle against the many-faceted incursions of the newcomer populations.

The world was, between the commencement of the age of exploration and the end of the nineteenth century, blanketed by foreign incursions onto indigenous territories. The newcomers came to farm or to raise livestock, to open mines, to build railways, roads, or canals, to establish a strategic advantage over a European rival, or to locate a cheap source of labour for planned commercial operations. They were armed not only with guns, new technology, and the backing of an empire. They came, too, with the certainty of faith and the support of the expansionist Christian church. Thus supported, they both displaced and then sought to "save" the "heathen," believing that their expansion was as much an act of Christian charity as it was a land grab. By the late nineteenth century, most of the world's accessible agricultural zones had been settled by newcomers. Indigenous peoples in these zones had either been destroyed, displaced, or amalgamated into new colonial societies. Paternalistic attempts at assimilation had much the same consequences as more aggressive measures of land confiscation and government domination. The original inhabitants bore the brunt of a painful transformation, for the loss of their land was typically accompanied by direct assaults on indigenous language, culture, and spirituality.

But many indigenous peoples, including those in extremely difficult situations, held onto their traditional ways. Some, like the Maori of New Zealand, made numerous economic and social accommodations to the incoming population but held onto their language and traditions. In many other lands, indigenous peoples found that the newcomers had limits on their reach. Their interests extended to coastal zones and to the areas of commercially viable agriculture. Although there were occasional exceptions—major mineral discoveries often sparked a flood of economic migrants into a remote region—the outlying districts were generally ignored. Here, in lands dismissed as marginal districts by settler societies, indigenous peoples held onto life-ways developed over many centuries. And with the option of continuing to hunt, fish, and live much as before, indigenous cultures were in a better position to select from the assimilative packages brought to them by missionaries, teachers, military officers, and government officials and to adapt to the new technologies introduced by the newcomers.

The Canadian experience can be easily slotted into this generic overview. The First Nations in the sub-Arctic and Arctic, with the exception of those located near mineral discoveries, had considerable contact with fur traders but much less interaction with others until after World War II. Those peoples located in coastal zones, in the rich agricultural lands of the St. Lawrence valley and the Great Lakes district were swamped and dislocated by early settlers. And the inhabitants of the western plains, their lifestyle disrupted in the mid-nineteenth century by the destruction of the buffalo herds, were shifted to small residential reserves during the prairie settlement boom of the late nineteenth and early twentieth century.[5]

Through the first half of the twentieth century, distance and the absence of agricultural possibilities ensured that huge sections of the globe remained largely in the hands of the original inhabitants. Although Canada, for example, claimed sovereignty over its vast northern territories, it had but a tiny official presence in the area and left the indigenous peoples very much on their own. Such was also the case across the Australian outback, through Papua New Guinea,[6] in the highlands of Central and South America, and across much of Africa. And even where governments made an extensive effort to contact the indigenous peoples, as in the Soviet Union, practicalities ensured that the people remained on the land and generally with sufficient freedom to set their own cultural and linguistic norms.[7] World War II proved to be a major turning point.

During and immediately after the Second World War II, much of the marginal land around the world was quickly and decisively absorbed into the global economy. The war saw the construction of major new transportation routes through the remote regions, and the establishment of dozens of airports in hitherto inaccessible areas. Governments became increasingly sensitive to the needs and opportunities of these regions, and moved in at war's end to ensure that they maintained control. More importantly, the postwar industrial boom demanded a massive increase in the production of raw materials. Demand for timber, minerals, hydro-electric power, oil and gas resulted in one of the most rapid frontier expansions in human history. Within a matter of two decades, literally hundreds of new mines opened up in areas far beyond the settlement zones. Thousands of miles of new roads and railways were driven through mountain ranges, across deserts, and into tribal territories. Complete new towns, designed to mimic those of more urban areas, were dropped into remote districts. New communications and travel systems tied these distant lands directly into metropolitan and industrial societies. This description, which summarizes conditions in the Canadian North, applies equally to such diverse regions as Australia, the former Soviet Union, Brazil, and Scandinavia.

The postwar development brought a rapid clash of technology and indigenous populations, and highlighted the inherent conflict between environmental sustainability and industrial, material views of the world. Christian Bay was writing about the Yanomami, but he could well have been describing dozens of other postwar collisions between indigenous cultures and the development frontier:

> In truth there is a massive war going on today between technology and nature, and nature keeps losing ground. This means that the human species keeps losing ground, too, for we are rooted in nature and are a part of nature, even if most of us are no longer as directly embedded in nature and are not as immediately vulnerable as the still surviving, still relatively unsubjugated peoples, peoples like the Yanomami, who have lived in and have cared so well for their forest habitants for so many centuries. In sharp contrast with the commercial exploiters of our own civilization, the Yanomami have been responsible trustees of nature, for their own future generations, and have learned how to keep their numbers limited. Are they now to be denied a future?[8]

At a pace and with an urgency rarely before seen in history, tens of thousands of square miles of indigenous territory was pulled into the orbit of the modern industrial economy. Lands rejected by newcomers as uninhabitable were now seen to hold highly desirable resources and considerable wealth. Indigenous peoples who had lived apart from (or only tangentially connected to) newcomer, industrial societies now found themselves in the vortex of a worldwide development boom. From the Amazon basin to eastern Siberia, and from the "red centre" of Australia to the highlands of Thailand, the economic and consumptive imperatives of the modern industrial economy were dropped onto tribal peoples. With a few exceptions, these occupations were relatively peaceable, at least in terms of the absence of overt military action. But indigenous groups lacked the authority, political or otherwise, to block the development thrust. In most instances, massive projects were lauded as signs of "progress," and celebrated as providing an opportunity to bring the isolated, land-based peoples of the remote regions "into the twentieth century." The loss of hunting lands or access to a favoured fishing river was deemed a minimal cost when weighed against the numerous "benefits" that would invariably follow industrial expansion. As Jason Clay has argued:

> The past century of "progress" and "civilization" provides good evidence that more indigenous cultures have disappeared than during any previous 100 year period. Although more laws, treaties, and

entions protect human rights and outlaw genocide than ever
e, it is arguable that the most violations occur today as well.[9]

.... Canadian experience, which brought considerable cultural dislocation, social disruptions, and economic turmoil, had Canadian actors, operated within the context of Canadian policy, and proceeded according to a
Canadian timetable. But it did not stand apart, in any substantive way, from
developments that were proceeding apace in other quarters of the world. The
Canadian expansion was muted by a paternalistic bent that was not evident,
for example, in much of the postwar development thrust in Brazil (but was
similar to that in Scandinavia).[10] It was intrusive, but not perhaps as intrusive
as the physical and cultural relocations implemented in Siberia. The point
simply is that Canadian developments fit within a general pattern and thus
reflected the prevalent concerns of that era: resource development, the "open-
ing" of frontier districts, and a general desire to integrate indigenous peoples
in national regimes.

In Canada and elsewhere, indigenous groups resented and resisted the
incursions into their territories.[11] Initially, few people outside the region paid
much attention. Those who did, saw the protests, much as outsider observers
conceptualized aboriginal uprisings in the nineteenth century, as the last desperate attempts of pre-industrial peoples to delay the inevitable advance of
industrial society. For indigenous groups, the struggle was of fundamental
importance; it was about their choice of a future. Indigenous peoples rarely
rejected the industrial system out of hand, and rarely pushed away all of the
technological, spiritual, and cultural trappings of the newcomer societies.
More often than not, they accepted many elements of the new order, tolerated some, and rejected others. As indigenous groups had done over many
centuries, they attempted to adapt and respond to new conditions, but they
tried to do so on the basis of their value system and their way of living. The
post–World War II developments—fast-moving, supported by governments
and industrial corporations, well-financed, and backed by the newcomer populations—presented very little time for contemplation and offered the indigenous peoples little opportunity to react.

The post–World War II era, then, witnessed the coming together of two
streams of indigenous protest: the anger and frustrations of long-marginal-
ized indigenous peoples living in the settlement areas, and the often panic-
stricken reaction of indigenous groups in the new development zones, who
faced the imminent loss of their land, resources, and way of life. The
processes of economic globalization, multinational resource development,
and settler society assumptions about remote regions had combined in less
then two decades to bring about the rapid occupation of vast swathes of
indigenous territory. In the past, the occupation of indigenous lands had
resulted in readily ignored indigenous protests and only tiny voices of support from the settler societies. Before World War II, indigenous protests about

the despoliation of tribal lands and the destruction of traditional cultures attracted minimal attention, beyond occasional sighs of sorrow for the demise of once-proud peoples that were deemed to be the "inevitable" victims of modernization. No longer would these verities hold. For changing political conditions, a re-conceptualization of the role, vitality, and worth of indigenous societies, and the emergence of an international protest movement of and about indigenous rights would create new conditions for the debate over the crises in indigenous societies.

Although the global aspects of the indigenous rights struggle are now well known, it took many years for the protests to coalesce in an international fashion. The early struggles were typically fought—and conceptualized—in national terms. Indigenous groups and their supporters criticized national governments and demanded political or economic action to address the identified problems. While some critics, particularly those associated with left-wing organizations, recognized the often-present hand of multinational corporations, the general consensus was that the problems were national in origin and content and could best be dealt with in a national political context. Indigenous rights advocates could and did use international pressure and international comparisons to advance their case, but the focus for their campaigns remained on national governments.

As a consequence, each country currently seeking to address indigenous rights tended to see the matter within the context of its national history. In Canada, for instance, legal scholars pointed to the Royal Proclamation of 1763 and subsequent government actions and legislation as the foundation for the government's commitment to settle unresolved First Nations land claims. Australia long held that the national legal doctrine of *terra nullis* obviated the need for special attention to indigenous land claims (but had this position turned on its head with the 1992 Mabo decision).[12] New Zealand had the Treaty of Waitangi, the United States its history of signing treaties before settlement and development,[13] Scandinavia its historic pattern of seeking to incorporate the Sami into nation-states, the former Soviet Union a lengthy attempt at Russification and communal organization of the Small Peoples of the North, and Brazil a long period of neglect of the indigenous peoples of the interior. Similar patterns can be seen in other countries. As rights and land claims emerged as a matter of national political importance, each nation turned to its past and to its legal system as a source for both an explanation for participation (or non-participation) and for a solution to a difficult and sensitive political matter.

The Re-Conceptualization of Indigenous Cultures

The emphasis on local developments, however, missed an essential point: the indigenous rights movement was founded on a major shift in international legal and social thinking. While national conditions and realities matter, and matter a great deal, much of the impetus for settling indigenous demands rests with a fundamental, post–World War II shift in the conception of First Peoples, their future and their rights. Before World War II, few countries paid much heed to the idea that indigenous societies had special rights or privileges. In countries with sizable settler populations, indigenous peoples had either been pushed aside, often onto legal reserves or into remote regions, or efforts had been made to incorporate them into the nation. Such legal rights as existed under the laws of the state largely stood in abeyance, overridden by discriminatory legislation or ignored by governments intent on economic development and incorporation.[14]

In the decade after World War II, the situation changed dramatically. The decades-old belief in the importance of assimilating indigenous people was stripped away in the face of aboriginal resistance and determination. Indigenous peoples, at first regionally and nationally and then through an international network of contacts and organizations, pressed openly and with considerable success for attention to their needs and aspirations. Non-indigenous supporters, from churches and environmental organizations to groups set up specifically to advance First Peoples' interests, lined up behind the indigenous protesters. The United Nations, through its International Declaration on Human Rights and subsequent specific initiatives dealing with indigenous peoples, provided a vital international forum for the debate over the future of indigenous societies. The conjunction of growing national and international awareness of indigenous issues, rights and claims ensured that a matter previously relegated to the political background in countries around the world now moved closer to centre stage.[15]

The changing international political scene developed in an interconnected fashion with shifting societal attitudes toward indigenous peoples. In the first half of the twentieth century, most people (to the extent that they considered indigenous societies) viewed the First Peoples as "dying" cultures, struggling in the unavoidable face of development and modernization. Few, save for a handful of humanitarians, social activists, and academics, saw much of value in the traditions and life-ways of people who, by objective, material standards, lived what was readily defined as a "primitive" lifestyle. However, growing concern about the sustainability of Western, industrial societies, coupled with increasing interest in indigenous spirituality, environmental knowledge, and cultural wisdom, altered this social equation. Peoples once relegated to the margins of human thought, considered only as a living remnant of a collapsing social order, were increasingly viewed with admiration and respect.[16] Outsiders sought now to learn from indigenous peoples, and to gain access to the wisdom of the ages contained within the language, worldviews and environmental sensitivities of traditional societies.[17] On top of this, non-indigenous peoples were challenged by the economic poverty and social distress evident in those indigenous communities in contact with settler populations. The combination of liberal concern and growing cultural respect proved to be a potent international force for change, intersecting with a growing awareness of the legal, political, and moral rights of indigenous peoples to a more equitable share of the land, resources, and administrative powers of the modern states within which they resided.[18] There were limits, however. As other movements (women's rights and environmental) discovered, resistance developed when the indigenous rights campaigns appeared to be gathering strength.[19]

Indigenous Rights in International Law and Politics

The establishment of the United Nations in the aftermath of World War II, a process to which Canada made a significant contribution, marked a watershed for minority peoples around the world. The United Nations Declaration on Human Rights, with its strong support for the right of self-determination, was an extremely valuable symbol of the growing international recognition that years of imperial and domestic expansion had displaced numerous minorities and had created innumerable hardships for vulnerable cultural groups. Even more significant, perhaps, than the creation of international law surrounding this issue was the global recognition that campaigns of cultural destruction would no longer be tolerated and that the world community would become ever more vigilant in identifying those countries that ignored the fundamental rights of their cultural minorities.[20]

The rights of indigenous peoples, as a distinct set of demands and requirements separate from those of other minority groups, did not emerge as a significant international political issue for some time. At the first World Conference on Human Rights, held by the United Nations in 1968, indigenous concerns did not emerge as a separate issue. In 1993, at the Second World Conference on Human Rights, indigenous peoples showed up in large numbers and petitioned for special recognition of their unique circumstances and needs. Much has changed in twenty-five years.[21] In the post–World War II period, very few indigenous groups—Canadian First Nations, the Maori in New Zealand, and the Indians in the United States being the major exceptions—had much of a national political presence. And internationally, the culture and aspirations of indigenous groups were shrouded in stereotypes and hidden in domestic self-interest. Governments sought to develop resources in remote regions and generally saw such economic expansion as meeting national needs and felt that these activities would enrich and empower indigenous peoples.

Through the 1950s, concern for indigenous peoples manifested itself in paternalism—assimilationist educational policies, resettlement programs, health care measures—and not in attempts to support the cultural aspirations of the indigenous societies. The first major international political instrument on indigenous rights—the International Labor Organization's Convention 107 of 1957—captured the spirit of the age very nicely. The document called for increased attention to the social, economic, and health needs of indigenous peoples, and urged governments to pay attention to their special needs.

But ILO Convention 107 was strongly assimilationist in its assumptions; indigenous peoples, its drafters agreed, would inevitably be assimilated into the nation-state. And like all of the major documents relating to the theme at this time, the convention was prepared with little input from indigenous peoples.

Indigenous peoples were not quickly deterred, however. The emergence of several powerful and influential groups gave new international prominence to the indigenous rights movement. These were of two major types: international support groups made up of individuals and organizations that wished to stand in solidarity with indigenous peoples and organizations of indigenous peoples. In the first instance, the political radicalism of the 1960s, combined with the rapid development of indigenous lands, convinced numerous non-indigenous peoples to throw their support behind the indigenous rights cause. Some, like the mainstream Christian denominations, made the shift in large measure due to the "discovery" of the impact of their assimilationist policies over the preceding decades.[22] Others, particularly those associated with anticolonial, social, or environmental movements, reacted to the evident despoliation of indigenous cultures and tribal territories. In fairly rapid order, groups like the International Work Group for Indigenous Affairs (1968), Survival International (1969), and Cultural Survival (1972) came into existence and offered their support for indigenous groups in crisis. Most of these organizations focused on non-industrial world issues and areas; Canadian issues did not figure all that prominently in their protests, although they were not reticent about supporting First Nations complaints and actions. These organizations were sharp in their condemnation of western, industrial, and imperial societies (and, initially at least, less vigilant about the destruction of indigenous cultures by the actions of non-Western governments) and provided tremendous assistance in bringing the indigenous cause to the attention of the global media.[23]

Indigenous peoples themselves were organizing internationally.[24] The American Indian Movement, a radical, aggressive and confrontational organization most noted for its violent conflict with the United States government, had a strong sovereigntist message that it shared very broadly. AIM developed particularly strong ties with English-speaking countries, and helped indigenous organizations in Canada and New Zealand change the nature of the debate away from the rights of indigenous groups as poor people to their rights as indigenous societies. John Trudell, cofounder of AIM, addressed the Survival Gathering of indigenous groups in 1980, arguing that:

> We must not become confused. We must not become confused and deceived by their illusions. There is no such thing as military power; there is only military terrorism. There is no such thing as economic power; there is only economic exploitation. That is all that it is. All they know how to do is act in a repressive, brutal way. The Power. We

are a natural part of the Earth. We are an extension of the Earth; we are not separate from it. We are a part of it. The Earth is our Mother. The Earth is a spirit, and we are an extension of that Spirit. We are Spirit. We are Power. ...They want to separate us from our Power. They want to separate us from who we are—genocide.[25]

There were, as well, intellectual and often personal connections between indigenous groups and anticolonial movements, particularly the socialist revolutionary organizations in Central America. Governments reacted unfavourably to such developments, and disparaged indigenous protests as the work of "foreign" agitators. That Georges Erasmus openly displayed his interest in the life and work of Che Guevera, for example, made it easy for many Canadian observers to doubt the aboriginality of his protests. This assumption, however, missed the growing sense of solidarity amongst indigenous groups around the world. (The "radical" or sovereigntist argument, which asserts that indigenous peoples were and are the true owners of traditional territories and that the claims of settler governments lack moral validity, has attracted considerable, albeit minority, attention among many indigenous groups, particularly in the industrialized world.)[26]

By the late 1960s, the Fourth World movement was gathering considerable momentum. International organizations brought indigenous groups together and heightened understanding of transnational conditions and similarities. Canadian First Nations, particularly George Manuel of British Columbia, were instrumental in drawing the groups together and creating an international indigenous (as opposed to international supporters) movement. In 1975, fifty-two delegates arrived in Port Alberni, British Columbia, to attend the founding meeting of the World Council of Indigenous Peoples. Though most of the representatives were from the Americas, indigenous groups from Australia, New Zealand, Scandinavia, and Greenland were represented. (In order to protect several delegates from oppressive dictatorships in Central America, much of the meeting was held in camera—a necessity that shocked many of the Canadian participants.) [27]

A series of political organizations—Fourth World, Inuit Circumpolar Conference, Sami Council, International Indian Treaty Council, Consejo Indo Sud America (CISA)—provided indigenous groups with increased international experience and with support groups that, in fairly short order, spanned the globe. Canadian indigenous leaders played major roles in the Fourth World and Inuit Circumpolar Conference initiatives, and maintained considerable ties with American Indian activists. Intrusions on indigenous territories, peoples or cultures that hitherto would have attracted only scant domestic interest were now assured of a considerable international audience. These organizations, in turn, became adept at capitalizing on media interest and emerging technologies to ensure that the message secured wide circulation. In the midst of the Yanomami struggle for their Amazon homelands, the support of rock star Sting proved of pivotal importance in attracting media attention.[28] In recent years, indigenous organizations have been very effective in their use of the Internet as a means of securing support for indigenous rights protests and to ensure that indigenous groups are kept well informed of developments in other jurisdictions.[29] For some groups, protests meant high-profile media events; for others, it required armed struggle with government troops.

The indigenous protest was not to be deterred. Gaining national and international experience, the indigenous organizations (particularly in the industrial world) became more adept at working with governments and the media; others, in more desperate circumstances, took up arms. As one scholar, summarizing the situation in Central America wrote:

> Worldwide, the self-determination genie is out of the bottle and can't be strained by state-sanctifying rules that shut our Fourth World indigenous nations. ...A second wave of self-determination is encircling the globe. The first broke the back of overseas white colonialism and led to the proliferation of Third World states. Many of these became brown or black colonial powers that invaded or continued the occupation of unconsenting indigenous nations. Now, scores of internationally unrecognized nations—the Fourth World— are at war as a result and must base their self-determination on ambushes rather than treaties.[30]

Several indigenous groups, particularly the Inuit Circumpolar Conference,[31] were soon well-known for their administrative competence and their ability to work with governments on their terms. While, in the main, the indigenous groups remained largely focused on protest and on criticizing national governments, they became increasingly potent advocates for international action. The more outspoken groups, coming mainly from Canada, the United States, and New Zealand but with an increasingly visible group from Scandinavia, lobbied effectively for national and international recognition. And, gradually and grudgingly, it came. Indigenous groups were initially involved in the work of the United Nations through their participation in the Special NGO Conference on Indigenous Peoples of the Americas, held in 1977. In 1982, the United Nations took a decisive step toward the recognition of indigenous rights. The Sub-Commission on Prevention of Discrimination and Protection of Minorities set up a Working Group on Indigenous Populations in 1982.[32] The Working Group was charged with preparing a Draft Declaration on the Rights of Indigenous Peoples. The meetings of the Working Group, which initially involved only national governments and a small number of indigenous organizations, soon became the world's most prominent forum for the gathering of indigenous peoples. National governments lost control of much of the agenda, much to their chagrin, as indigenous leaders pressed for a strong and definitive declaration in support of indigenous rights. The International Labor Organization, through Convention 169 of 1991, removed the assimilationist and paternalistic elements of the earlier statement on indigenous rights. The new convention, however, attracted the support of only a handful of countries.[33] The highlight point in international recognition of indigenous rights came with the naming of 1993 as the United Nations Year of Indigenous Peoples.

Debate about the Draft Declaration continues, and has gained increasing support from indigenous organizations. At the same time, however, national governments have become less interested and are not anxious to push the issue through the United Nations' political structures. While it is incorrect to describe the current situation as an impasse, the nature of the discussion reveals a sizable gap between what governments are prepared to accept and what indigenous groups consider to be an appropriate level of support for their rights and claims. The Canadian government has figured prominently in the discussions surrounding the Draft Declaration—and is one of those countries, as a strong supporter of the United Nations, that is most concerned about the prospect of the document, in its current form, coming forward for attempted ratification. Although wishing to be seen as a supporter of both the United Nations and indigenous rights, the Canadian government would be hard-pressed to accept the document as written.

Although forecasts of the demise of the nation-state abound, national governments remain of fundamental importance.[34] The pressure to address First Peoples' rights emerged from broad international social and political forces; the resolution of indigenous land claims and rights will rest within specific regional and national cultures. The search for solutions will invariably reflect the cultural, social, and political restrictions of the individual nations. The Canadian solution of First Nations claims will be markedly different from Venezuela's resolution of Yanomami rights and aspirations.[35] Australian Aborigines will, of necessity, find a resolution of their legal and moral claims through the Australian judicial and political systems. And efforts by the Ainu to find a measure of social and cultural justice will focus on the Japanese system. In each instance, the international community (through the United Nations, Indigenous Rights International, church groups, and other interested parties) will keep a watching brief on national developments and will, on occasion, intercede in an attempt to press the issue forward. Throughout this process, however, it is vital to remember that behind the national and regional desire to settle land claims rests an ideology and infrastructure of international pressure that has, since World War II, given the indigenous land-claims movement much of its authority, power, and determination.

The Past is No Prologue

The field of indigenous rights is suffused with whiggish and optimistic notions about the inevitability of the attainment of national and international recognition of indigenous rights, and Canada has not been immune to this. Recent court decisions—celebrated as major victories but actually of uncertain consequences—in New Brunswick (relating to the right to harvest trees on Crown land) and British Columbia (the Delgamuukw decision) have increased indigenous expectations, while simultaneously adding to non-indigenous uncertainty. The seeming advance of the UN Draft Declaration on the Rights of Indigenous Peoples has not been tempered with the realization that the declaration remains incomplete and that most national governments, though loathe to voice their concerns publicly, are highly unlikely to adopt a declaration that is anything close to the sweeping, empowering document that is currently being developed. Further, the "rights-based" efforts of indigenous leaders over the past thirty years have achieved some notable benchmarks—from the Canadian land-claims process through to the Mabo Aboriginal rights "victory" in Australia—but have not been matched by appreciable improvements in the material, cultural, or social realities of indigenous life.

Many of the legal achievements have been Pyrrhic at best, as non-indigenous means have found administrative or other means of deflecting the impact of legal decisions.[36] In other instances, the mere suggestion of an advance for indigenous peoples has been greeted with howls of protest from the non-aboriginal minority and to more difficult political conditions for indigenous leaders. That violence and confrontations have erupted in the wake of the false or partial victories achieved through the courts is hardly surprising. After years in the political wilderness, indigenous groups have worked with remarkable dedication to exploit the window of cultural opportunity and to press for political advantage. The assumption has emerged that the passage of time will bring about significant change in the condition of indigenous peoples and that their legal rights and legitimate aspirations will be recognized. But the realities of political life often bear scant resemblance to the separate necessities of non-indigenous economic, social, and political needs.[37] Even in the liberal democracies—Canada,[38] the United States,[39] Australia,[40] and New Zealand[41]—where the political and legal achievements have been the most pronounced—there is ample evidence of a growing and increasingly vocal backlash against indigenous rights. And cynical observers, who seemingly expect indigenous leaders to attain a record of success in public investments that has escaped non-indigenous governments, have been quick to point out failures among the newly empowered aboriginal organizations. There is no easy path ahead, and no assurance that the increased sympathies toward indigenous peoples that have emerged over the past thirty years will continue in the future.

As indigenous groups continue their efforts to press for international recognition of rights and for political and constitutional changes that respect and acknowledge their existence, they have also discovered that theirs is a large, at times unwieldy, alliance. While indigenous groups share a great deal in common—particularly a powerful relationship to their traditional territories—their social, economic, and political conditions vary dramatically. First World indigenous groups (Canada, Australia, New Zealand, Scandinavia, the United States) experience a level of public recognition, government acknowledgment, financial resources, and administrative freedom that other indigenous groups still aspire to achieve. This has resulted, at times, in significant breeches in indigenous solidarity. Ironically, the First World indigenous groups have often been more demanding, more sovereigntist in their approach, insisting that governments move quickly to address their political and constitutional aspirations. Indigenous groups from poorer regions typically have more pragmatic short-term goals: stopping genocidal campaigns, providing the basic necessities of life, or securing the most fundamental of human rights. The gap between "rich" and "poor" that has long bedevilled international organizations has, perhaps not surprisingly, hastened the development of cracks in the indigenous rights movement.[42]

Indigenous politicians, buffeted between reactionary demands from the settler societies and expectations of rapid improvements from their communities, find themselves walking a very difficult line. The growing realization that national governments are loathe to move beyond symbolic recognition of indigenous rights and that there is little likelihood of a truly international initiative to help protect indigenous cultures has heightened the radicalism of many indigenous leaders. At the 1997 meetings on the Draft Declaration on the Rights of Indigenous Peoples, for example, indigenous groups staged a prolonged walk-out to protest the refusal of government representatives to accept the Draft Declaration without further discussion. The simple political reality that very few national governments—primarily those without indigenous populations within their borders—are prepared to support the document as it currently stands is scarcely a satisfactory explanation for indigenous peoples who have faced generations of occupation, dislocation, and attempted cultural destruction. The warning issued in 1994 by Julian Burger and Paul Hunt has particular resonance as the Draft Declaration runs afoul of political realities:

> As the draft declaration is considered in the months ahead, it must not be forgotten that the instrument's moral and political content is a response to centuries of exploitation and deceit. The draft reflects many of the aspirations of the indigenous peoples—among the most oppressed communities on earth. It would be a tragic irony if a draft on indigenous peoples' rights became a victim of protracted negotiations between states. If this is its fate, the international community will be acting in a manner consistent with the conduct of numerous states over the last 500 years.[43]

Indigenous peoples and their supporters around the globe have accomplished a great deal over the past thirty years. These cultural groups had been marginalized and their values, worldviews, and means of living attacked through a combination of economic intervention, government policies, and well-intentioned First World paternalism. The transformation has been profound. Indigenous peoples can, and often do, command the world's attention when their lives or life-ways are threatened—albeit often only when non-indigenous spokespeople or organizations stand with them. They have capitalized on the development of international organizations, the opportunities presented by the emergence of global media coverage, and the promise held within the digital revolution to build global networks, support local, regional, and national campaigns, and to press for greater public recognition of their needs and aspirations. And, to a dramatic degree, the effort has worked. Corporate developers realize that indigenous protests can slow resource projects and governments know that their actions will be held up before the world of international public opinion.

Has it all made a difference? The answer, while still unclear, is far from comforting. Non-indigenous organizations, particularly evangelical Protestant churches, continue their efforts to introduce indigenous peoples to Western thoughts and value systems. The development frontier has slowed and at times has been diverted from indigenous territories, but these victories have been at best partial and often only temporary. Living conditions for most indigenous peoples are little, if any, better than thirty years ago, and patterns of internal social disintegration remain strong. Language loss and the attendant decline in traditional cultures has scarcely abated, as the impact of radio, television, and other intrusive forms of mass media continue to expand across the world. As T'Boil-Ubo-Manobo-Visayan wrote to President Marcos of the Philippines, in 1984, "You must understand that we are in anguish over that (sic) appears to us to be an attempt to wrest our ancestral lands from us, destroy our culture, and endanger our very survival. While we have breath in us we can never give up this struggle."[44] While there is no doubt but that the vigilance and intervention of indigenous groups and their supporters has created a vastly different political reality, there is only spotty evidence that indigenous peoples have regained the control, cultural freedom, and independence that they have been seeking.

In Canada as in many nations, the major indigenous thrust of the past three decades has been on the legal/constitutional front. Indigenous groups banded together to convince the United Nations to recognize universal indigenous rights—and their representatives quite routinely claim that the achievements to date represent a significant advance (even though not a single national government nor the United Nations has endorsed the Draft Declaration).[45] On the regional and national front, indigenous groups have invested their financial and human resources in lengthy struggles over the recognition of legal rights. While there have been victories in the court room, they have seldom matched the supporters' expectations nor have they resulted in dramatic shifts in the circumstances of indigenous groups. Indigenous groups and their supporters have placed enormous faith in these legal campaigns and have assumed that legal victories would force governments and non-indigenous populations to recognize the legitimacy of the aboriginal cause. The rights movement, ironically, is another Western import, and the supporters of the legalistic approach bear some resemblance to the missionaries and other agents of Western thought and values who previously offered indigenous peoples a "solution" to their social, economic, and cultural crises.

Indigenous peoples were never without a voice, but for many decades, they were without an audience. The forces of globalization had, since the early years of European expansion, rolled over indigenous groups like successive tidal waves. Those who lived in temperate zones and in readily accessible territories typically found themselves displaced and dispossessed. For those in isolated, remote regions, harsh environments and distance protected them until the global resource boom of the 1950s and 1960s brought developers into the most far-flung corners of the world. Indigenous peoples were quickly swept up in the human rights furor of the postwar era, and found themselves the focus for First World–based attempts to protect and save them from further dislocation. This effort, founded on a widening sense of Liberal guilt combined with a sincere and growing interest in the nature and values of indigenous cultures, helped create a global support network that moved swiftly into action when the often small, isolated and historically long-ignored indigenous cultures were threatened. Through their work with these international networks, indigenous peoples made their own Fourth World networks and gained the administrative and organizational expertise necessary to forge international links of considerable political potency. Indigenous peoples, though small in number and typically geographically isolated, have created for themselves a seat at the table of international politics.

In several countries, particularly the United States of America and, to a lesser extent, Canada, New Zealand, Australia, and the Scandinavian countries, there are reasons for optimism. [46] For the first time in decades, if not generations, indigenous groups have a prominent place on the political agenda and have, through various legal and political means, gained some measure of control over their destiny. Consider the strength and confidence of the remarks by Douglas Endreson, an Indian lawyer from the United States:

> From the time that the Europeans arrived, tribes were forced to defend themselves, their rights and their people. At stake was their sovereign right to govern themselves and to make their own choices. Tribal powers are now well established in federal law. The battle for the recognition of sovereignty has been won. The new battles will center on the exercise of sovereignty as tribes struggle to achieve economic, political, social, and religious objectives. The Indian future now depends not on the federal government, but on the choices that tribes make in the exercise of their sovereignty. Tribes are no longer on the defensive—they are on the offensive. [47]

But only, realistically, in a very few nations, Canada among them. These conditions, ultimately, are attainable only in those nations with sufficient respect for the rule of law, clear historical obligations to indigenous peoples, and sufficient wealth to divert attention and resources to the poorest citizens in their land.[48] Few indigenous groups have such options.

There is another, darker consideration that needs to be considered. The development of an international indigenous political presence and the emergence of considerable public, non-indigenous support for indigenous rights has done little to arrest the social, economic, and cultural crises that have become endemic among the indigenous population of the world. Global awareness has not, to date, offset the impact of global economic and political forces. Indigenous peoples struggle to maintain an approach to the environment and therefore to their lives that is substantially at odds with that maintained by the majority of the world's people, who have opted for a more materialistic, more ecologically dominant approach.[49] The major "victories" for indigenous peoples consist in the main of limited government recognition of the rights of indigenous groups and of the establishment of small territorial enclaves—a tiny fraction of traditional territories. There is little evidence, after centuries of hardship and several decades of concerted international political action, that the protests of the indigenous peoples have been heard. There may be room, in the development-oriented, expansionist, and materialist global order of the late twentieth century, for the limited recognition of the political and legal rights for indigenous peoples. There may not be room in a globalized economy and society of the twenty-first century for the life-ways, cultural norms, and environmentally sustainable lifestyles of the indigenous peoples of the world.[50]

Two recent situations, both involving the Council for Yukon Indians, illustrate the continuing connections—multiple, complicated, and contradictory—between the indigenous rights struggle in Canada and broader, international developments. During a weeklong 1996 gathering in Whitehorse, Yukon, Canadian and Yukon First Nations had an unusual opportunity to learn from and to contribute to the international indigenous land rights process. The United Nations hosted a gathering to discuss "practical experiences" of land claims, and invited indigenous, government, and NGO representatives from around the world. The indigenous organizations from Canada and the United States, the former already angered by some administrative difficulties in the months leading up to the conference, used the occasion to launch a systematic critique of government actions and ideologies. The local First Nations capitalized on the opportunity to criticize the local territorial government and to accuse the federal government of bad faith in its policy and treaty-making. Ovid Mercredi, Grand Chief of the Assembly of First Nations, was furious at not being formally invited to the conference; he came to Whitehorse, determined to hold an "alternative" conference during which time he promised to expose the "racism" of the Canadian government and the United Nations. Negotiations and concessions resulted in a less dramatic but nonetheless hostile speech by Mercredi.

While the North American representatives were, by outward appearances, pleased with their impact on the meeting, indigenous groups from other parts of the world were unimpressed. Many stopped coming to the sessions, which typically involved prolonged discussions of Canadian policy, long discourses on Yukon-specific grievances, and lengthy public exchanges between Canadian officials and Canadian First Nations; by the final session, most of the non–North American delegates were only occasionally attending the sessions. The First World indigenous organizations paid little attention to the appeals from representatives from poor countries—and were not swayed by several pointed commentaries by these individuals, who asked the First Nations if they wished to change places. Far from demonstrating or developing international indigenous solidarity, the event seemed to re-enforce the very large gap between indigenous groups in wealthier nations—where debates focused on multimillion-dollar land-claims settlements, self-government agreements, and political representation—and poor countries—where the issues centred on group survival, government oppression, and destruction of traditional life-ways.

The following year, in 1997, an unrelated development saw a delegation from the Council for Yukon Indians visit Eastern Siberia. The Canadian, Yukon and Northwest Territories governments had been working for some time on a variety of exchanges and joint projects. The tour by the Council for Yukon Indians was designed to bring northern First Nations into contact with various indigenous groups—generally referred to as the Small Peoples of the North—through the republic. The visit to a series of isolated villages shocked the Yukon First Nations representatives, who were appalled at the poor living conditions, the absence of basic amenities, and the lack of government attention. Mike Smith, Vice-Chair of the Council of Yukon Indians, expressed dismay at the situation and commented that Canadian First Nations had fewer grounds for complaints than he had realized. More importantly, the Canadian delegation expressed their commitment to work with the indigenous peoples of Eastern Siberia, to assist them with their approaches to government and to provide direct support whenever possible.

Canadian First Nations—and Canadian indigenous issues—figure prominently on the international stage. Canadian officials, indigenous or non-indigenous, have not always been aware of the international implications of national actions, nor is there a great deal of understanding of the degree to which international developments have influenced Canadian situations. In the field of indigenous rights, as with so many political, social, cultural, and economic movements over the generations, Canada does not stand alone. It is, instead, closely connected to the broader world order, and generally works within the limits set by prevailing values and assumptions in the industrialized world. The political theatre that is the indigenous rights movement is, ironically, less indigenous than Canadians typically assumed. It is, instead, part of a much more complex international phenomenon, one with its roots firmly in the struggle between commercial/settler societies and the harvesting-based cultures that inhabited so much of the world before the expansion of Europe.

Governments and First Nations will resolve—or fail to resolve—indigenous rights protests within the confines and structures of the Canadian state. Canadian courts, Canadian politicians, and First Nations groups in Canada will argue, debate, negotiate, and, in some instances, settle the age-old grievances that have driven such a sharp divide between Canadians in all corners of the country. But the broader parameters of these discussions will, in substantial measure, be set by the prevailing values of the industrialized world, by the struggle between the liberal impulse that influences much of Western political life and the desire for control of land, resources and legal certainty that underlies the capitalist system. These influences have, in recent years, combined with the rhetoric and passion of the human rights movement, the uneven and unreliable non-indigenous fascination with aboriginal culture and spirituality, and a thin veneer of historical guilt that animates much of the public reaction to indigenous protests. Together, and reaching beyond and around Canadian political decisions and legal precedents, these international influences have had a profound impact on the nature, timing, and public response to the indigenous rights protests in Canada. And Canadian developments in this field have, in turn, inspired and triggered indigenous rights protests in other parts of the world, an initiative now strengthened by the growing sense among some First Nations of an obligation to assist other indigenous groups with their political struggles.

The founding declaration of the World Council of Indigenous Peoples, an event strongly influenced by Canadian First Nations and held on Vancouver Island, provides a poetic summary of the unique combination of the local, national and global influences that have long surrounded the indigenous rights movement: [51]

> Now, we come from the four corners of the earth,
> we protest before the concert of nations
> that, we are the Indigenous Peoples, we who
> have a consciousness of culture and peoplehood
> on the edge of each country's borders and
> marginal to each country's citizenship.
> And rising up after centuries of oppression,
> evoking the greatness of our ancestors,
> in the memory of our Indigenous martyrs,
> and in homage to the counsel of our wise elders:

We vow to control again our own destiny and
recover our complete humanity and
pride in being Indigenous People.

In Canada, First Nations have asserted their pride and determination and managed some impressive political and legal gains. But they, like indigenous peoples in many other quarters of the world, still feel the complicated pressures of social, political, economic, and legal change. And while Canadian First Nations, appropriately, seek to resolve their demands within the context of the Canadian political and legal systems, they are increasingly aware that their struggle is a part of a much broader global conflict and contest, between the original inhabitants and newcomer populations. In the field of indigenous rights, as in so many other elements of contemporary Canadian life, Canada sits clearly within a complex and influential world order.

NOTES

1. There is a small, but growing literature that considers the development of indigenous rights and land settlements in an international context. See, for example, Julian Burger, *The Report from the Frontier: The State of the World's Indigenous Peoples* (London: Zed Books, 1987); Julian Burger, *The Gaia Atlas for First Peoples: A Future for the Indigenous World* (New York: Doubleday, 1990); Steve Pollock, *The Atlas of Endangered Peoples* (New York: Facts on File, 1995); John Bodley, *Victims of Progress* Third Edition (Mountain View, CA: Mayfield, 1990); John Bodley, ed. *Tribal Peoples and Development Issues: A Global Overview* (Mountain View, CA: Mayfield, 1988). See also W. Kymlicka, ed., *The Rights of Minority Cultures* (Oxford: Oxford University Press, 1995); P. Thornberry, *Minorities and Human Rights* (London: Minority Rights Group, 1991); Ken Coates and John Taylor, eds., *Indigenous Peoples in Remote Regions: A Comparative Perspective* (Thunder Bay: Centre for Northern Studies, 1995), particularly the article by John Bodley, "Indigenous Peoples Versus the State," pp. 6–29 and Ken Coates and Brenda Clark, "Indigenous Peoples in Peripheral Areas and Their Struggle for Land," pp. 385–414; Gordon Bennett, *Aboriginal Rights in International Law*, Occasional Paper No. 17 (London: Royal Anthropological Institute, 1978); Independent Commission on International Humanitarian Issues, *Indigenous Peoples: A Global Quest for Justice* (London: Zed Press, 1987); J. Brosted et al., *Native Power: The Quest for Autonomy and Nationhood of Indigenous Peoples* (Bergen: Universitets Forlaget, 1985); I. Brownlie, *Treaties and Indigenous Peoples* (Oxford: Clarendon Press, 1992).

2. For a strongly worded statement on this relationship, see Elizabeth Kemf, *Indigenous Peoples and Protected Areas: The Law of Mother Earth* (London: Earthscan, 1993).

3. Martinez Cobo, *Study of the Problem of Discrimination Against Indigenous Peoples*, vol. 5, paragraph 379.

4. Bodley, *Victims of Progress*.

5. The best surveys of Native history in Canada are J.R. Miller, *Skyscrapers Hide the Heavens* (Toronto: University of Toronto Press, 1988) and Olive Dickason, *Canada's First Nations* (Toronto: Macmillan, 1990).

6. See, as this relates to Western Papua, Anti-Slavery Society, *West Papau: Plunder in Paradise* (London: Anti-Slavery Society, 1990) and TAPOL, *West Papua: The Obliteration of a People* (London: TAPOL, 1983).

7. See Yuri Slezkine, *Arctic Mirrors: Russia and the Small Peoples of the North* (Ithaca: Cornell University Press, 1994).

8. Christian Bay, "Human Rights on the Periphery: No Room in the Ark for the Yanomami?" in Bodley, *Tribal Peoples*, p. 268.

9. Jason Clay, "Looking Back to Go Forward: Predicting and Preventing Human Rights Violations," in Marc Miller, ed., *State of the Peoples: A Global Human Rights Report on Societies in Danger (Boston: Beacon Press, 1993)*, p. 66.

10. Peter Jull, *The Politics of Northern Frontiers: In Australia, Canada and the Other "First World" Countries* (Darwin: North Australia Research Unit, 1991).

11. An excellent source book, drawing on examples of indigenous protest from around the world and over the past five centuries, is Roger Moody, ed., *The Indigenous Voice: Visions and Realities*, 2 vols. (London: Zed, 1988).

12. An excellent historical analysis of the doctrine of terra nullius, and a strong argument for Aboriginal rights, can be found in Henry Reynolds, *The Law of the Land* (Penguin: Melbourne, 1987) and Henry Reynolds, *Fate of a Free People* (Melbourne: Penguin, 1995).

13. There is a vast literature on American policy towards indigenous peoples. The best survey—a serious, systematic and non-polemical piece—is Francis Paul Prucha, *The Great Father: The United States Government and the American Indians* (Lincoln: University of Nebraska Press, 1984). As this relates to more recent developments, see Donald Parman, *Indians in the American West in the Twentieth Century* (Bloomington: Indiana University Press, 1995).

14. For a short overview of the evolution of indigenous rights in international law, see R. Thompson, *The Rights of Indigenous People in International Law* (Saskatoon: University of Saskatchewan, 1987). For a very good study of the historical roots of indigenous law, see L.C. Green and Olive Dickason, *The Law of Nations and the New World* (Edmonton: University of Alberta Press, 1989).

15. As this development relates to the evolution of international law, see D. Sanders, "The Re-emergence of Indigenous Questions in International Law," *Canadian Human Rights Yearbook* (1983), pp. 3–30. See also P. Thornberry, "Self-determination, minorities, human rights," *International and Comparative Law Quarterly 38* (1989), pp. 867–89.

16. This, in turn, has resulted in considerable tourist interest in indigenous cultures and the development of a sizable international cultural tourism industry. See Pierre Rossel, *Tourism: Manufacturing the Exotic* (Copenhagen: IWGIA, 1988).

17. One indication of the degree to which this assumption about indigenous relationships with the environment has seeped into the wider international consciousness came in the United Nations Conference and Environment and Development (the Rio de Janeiro Earth Summit) held in 1992. Chapter 26 of Agenda 21, the official communiqué from the meeting includes a major statement on the importance of the indigenous-environment relationship.

18. For a very interesting study of the intellectual currents underlying this transformation, see John and Jean Comaroff, *Ethnography and the Historical Imagination* (Boulder, CO: Westview Press, 1992).

19. One of the more engaging studies of the process of re-imagining indigenous peoples—and of indigenous peoples reconstructing their realities—is Fergus Bordewich, *Killing the White Man's Indian: Reinventing Native Americans at the End of the Twentieth Century* (New York: Doubleday, 1996).

20. On the connection between human rights and indigenous rights, see IWGIA, Indigenous Peoples and Human Rights (Copenhagen: IWGIA, 1987).

21. Julian Berger, "An International Agenda," in Miller, *State of the Peoples.*

22. World Council of Churches, *Justice for Aboriginal Australians* (Sydney: ACC, 1981); W. Dostal, ed., *The Situation of the Indian in South America* (Geneva: World Council of Churches, 1972).

23. Lydia van de Fliert, *Indigenous Peoples and Indigenous Organization* (Nottingham: Spokesman, 1994). See also Y. Dinstein and M. Tabory, eds., *The Protection of Minorities and Human Rights* (Dordrecht: Nijhoff, 1992).

24. E.A. Povinelli, *Labour's Lost: The Power, History and Culture of Aboriginal Action* (Chicago: University of Chicago Press, 1993).

25. Moody, *The Indigenous Voice*, vol. 2, p. 300.

26. While the "radical" sovereigntists spare few words of criticism in their analysis of the dominant society, they are extremely critical of "sell-outs" who advocate a more limited, pragmatic agenda. Russell Means, one of the more outspoken American Indian activists, wrote, "In fact, our first priority, if we are to move forward to a brighter future rather than toward final oblivion, should be to clean up our own nest. Then we can proceed in unity to do what we must do. In other words, we

must eliminate the element of traitors, sell-outs and other scum from amongst ourselves, the sooner, the better. You might even say it's long past time to get the job done." Russell Means, "Preface: Notes for an Upcoming Speech at Alfred University," in Ward Churchill, ed., *Critical Issues in Native North America*, vol. 2, IWGIA Document 68 (Copenhagen: IWGIA, 1991), p. iv.

27. See D. Saunders, *The Formation of the World Council of Indigenous Peoples*, IWGIA Document 29 (Copenhagen: IWGIA, 1977).

28. This, in turn, highlighted the important point that the rights of indigenous peoples on their own were still rarely capable to draw a media crowd. The Yanomami have attracted continued interest over the years; groups facing similar difficulties in Indonesia, Malaysia, and Papua New Guinea have had much greater trouble securing an audience. See, for example, M. Colcester, *Pirates, Squatters and Poachers: The Political Ecology of Dispossession of the Native Peoples of Sarawak* (Malaysia: Survival International, 1989).

29. One of the best examples of this is the Fourth World Documentation Project, which provides Internet access to major treaties and indigenous-government agreements. Organizations like the Centre for World Indigenous Studies, likewise, play an active role in sharing information on international developments.

30. Bernard Nietschmann, "Miskito and Kuna Struggle for Nation Autonomy," in Bodley, p. 280.

31. For a very useful study that places the work of the Inuit Circumpolar Conference in broader perspective, see Peter Jull, *The Politics of Northern Frontiers* (Darwin: North Australia Research Unit, 1991).

32. Previously, indigenous groups had participated in some of the meetings of the Economic and Social Council, commencing in 1977.

33. Signatories to ILO Convention 169 by 1994 included only Bolivia, Colombia, Costa Rica, Norway, Mexico, and Paraguay. The recent struggles between the Mexican government and the Chiapas people provide an indication of the domestic significance of such international conventions.

34. David Elkins, *Beyond Sovereignty: Territory and Political Economy in the Twenty-First Century* (Toronto: University of Toronto Press, 1995).

35. For an overview of Yanomami rights, see Leslie Sponsel, "The Yanomami Crisis in Amazonia: The Immorality of Greed Versus the Morality of Human Rights," in Coates and Taylor, *Indigenous Peoples*.

36. Many active, knowledgeable scholars support the emphasis on international rights and believe that accomplishments in these areas will support the indigenous rights movement. See Catherine Brolmann et al., *Peoples and Minorities in International Law* (London: Martinus Nijhoff, 1993); J. Crawford, *The Rights of Peoples* (Oxford: Claredon, 1988). For a concise overview, see Indian Law Resource Centre, *Indian Rights, Human Rights: Handbook for Indians on International Human Rights Complaint Procedures* (Washington: Indian Law Resource Centre, 1984).

37. For a similar cautionary note, see Roger Plant, "Addressing Indigenous Land Rights and Claims: The Role of International Technical Assistance" (paper presented at the United Nations Expert Seminar on Practical Experiences Regarding Indigenous Land Rights and Claims, 1996).

38. The 1992 Constitutional referendum, while focused largely on the attempt to accommodate Quebec, included major commitments to aboriginal self-government. The referendum was defeated and in sizable areas of the country, concern over self-government played a significant role in the result. It is important to note that, while many non-Natives voted against the constitutional proposals because

they went too far on the matter of aboriginal rights, the majority of Native votes also voted against the proposals, largely because they did not go far enough. For a major critique of Canadian Indian policy, see Melvin Smith, *Our Home or Native Land? What Governments' Aboriginal Policy is Doing to Canada* (Victoria: Crown Western, 1995).

39. Because of the small and largely isolated nature of the Indian population in the United States, public reaction to indigenous rights has been relatively muted. There has been considerable reaction against the proliferation of casinos run on Indian reservations, many of which have been returning very substantial profits to the tribes. The strongest reaction to indigenous rights has been in Alaska, where the relatively recent (early 1970s) settlement of outstanding aboriginal claims to the land and resources has collided with the non-indigenous population's image of self-reliant frontier dwellers. The collective rights granted to the indigenous peoples and the special access accorded them to hunting and fishing resources does not sit well with the state's non-indigenous majority.

40. Australia provides perhaps the best example of this development. Queensland Member of Parliament Pauline Hansen has been uttering strong, often inflammatory condemnations of the government's Aboriginal policies and has managed to slow the government's planned response to Aboriginal legal victories. There has been a sizable pro-Aboriginal response, but this group has tended to underestimate the extent of support for Ms. Hansen's position.

41. The signing of treaties with Maori groups since 1995 has not eliminated, and in fact has fed, an undercurrent of hostility to Maori entitlements and claims. A self-published, historically-inaccurate, and unrepentant diatribe against Maori rights, D. Scott's *The Travesty of Waitangi*, was one of the top-selling books in the country when it was published.

42. A week-long 1996 gathering in Whitehorse, Yukon, Canada provided a striking illustration of this point. The United Nations hosted a gathering to discuss "practical experiences" of land claims, and invited indigenous, government and NGO representatives from around the world. The indigenous organizations from Canada and the United States, the former already angered by some administrative difficulties in the months leading up to the conference, used the occasion to launch a systematic critique of government actions and ideologies. The local First Nations capitalized on the opportunity to criticize the local territorial government and to accuse the federal government of bad faith in its policy and treaty-making. While the North American representatives were, by outward appearances, pleased with their impact on the meeting, indigenous groups from other parts of the world were unimpressed (several stopped coming to the sessions, which typically involved prolonged discussions of Canadian policy). The First World indigenous organizations paid little attention to the appeals from representatives from poor countries—and were not swayed by several pointed commentaries by these individuals, who asked the First Nations if they wished to change places. Far from demonstrating or developing international indigenous solidarity, the event seemed to re-enforce the very large gap between indigenous groups in wealthier nations—where debates focused on multi-million dollar land claims settlements, self-government agreements, and political representation—and poor countries—where the issues centred on group survival, government oppression, and destruction of traditional life-ways.

43. Julian Burger and Paul Hunt, "Towards the International Protection of Indigenous Peoples' Rights," *Netherlands Quarterly of Human Rights*, vol. 4 (1994), p. 423.

44. Moody, *The Indigenous Voice*, vol. 1, p. 390.

45. Indigenous leaders and their supporters have, time and time again, cited the Draft Declaration on the Rights of Indigenous Peoples or ILO Convention 169 as though these documents have the force of international law. Neither has such status and the continued reference to them has often left indigenous peoples with the impression that the international political community has accepted their political rights and status.

46. The situation that is most favourable for indigenous peoples is probably that in Greenland, where indigenous peoples control a largely self-governing (but not self-sustaining) political jurisdiction. See Per Langgaard, "Greenland: Colony! Home Rule! State!" in Coates and Taylor, *Indigenous Peoples*.

47. Bordewich, Killing the White Man's Indian, p. 336.

48. The Maori in New Zealand have achieved a strong accommodation with the Pakeha society. In Canada, legal recognition of indigenous rights is relatively strong, but social, economic, and cultural conditions remain in considerable difficulty. Australian Aborigines have won several major legal struggles in recent years, but have then faced an outburst of anti-indigenous hostility led by ranchers and mining interests. The Sami of Scandinavia have received considerable recognition of their unique political situation and do not face the cultural hardships of indigenous peoples in many other parts of the world. In most other nations, distance from settlement zones and the absence of marketable resources are the prime determinants of indigenous autonomy, self-reliance, and cultural stability.

49. Jack Weatherford, *Savages and Civilization: Who Will Survive?* (Crown: New York, 1994).

50. On the connections between indigenous peoples and the development ethos of the modern age, see G.H. Brundtland, et al., *Our Common Future: The Report of the World Commission on Environment and Development* (Oxford: Oxford University Press, 1987), particularly pp. 114–16.

51. The declaration is produced in full in D. Saunders, *The Formation of the World Council of Indigenous Peoples*.

Regionalism, Postcolonialism, and Western Canadian Arts

Orientalism and Indigeneity

FRANCES W. KAYE

University of Nebraska-Lincoln

A fter the Second World War, Canada, especially through the agency of Lester Pearson, took a leadership role in forming the United Nations as an organization for the imperial powers as well as for countries that were shaking off colonialism. This is not surprising. Canada had a long history of internationalism within its own borders, and perhaps in no place more than the Prairies. Despite being landlocked, the Prairies were heavily influenced by international ways of thought—both by the ideas of empire imported from Europe and by the cultural traditions of indigenous peoples, whose borders never included the forty-ninth parallel. To understand the dynamics of these relationships, especially as they are expressed in the arts, it is useful to examine Prairie history through the lens of various intellectual movements such as *post*-modernism and *post*-colonialism. In this study, I have focused on the period when a largely European-derived cosmology replaced an indigenous one as the dominant mode for the majority of people living on the Prairies. Moments of crisis tend to reveal fault lines that redefine cultures.

Intellectual movements are rooted in the economic and political conditions of their and in the explicit and implicit cosmologies that shape a society's understanding of its material and intellectual circumstances. Postmodernism is a reaction to modernism, which itself was a reaction to realism and romanticism, which were answers to classicism, and so on, back down the line. Postmodernism was initially a European movement arising to address the condition of meaninglessness engendered by the Second World War and its upheavals. Postcolonialism, although it draws upon postmodern theorists like Foucault and Barthes as well as nineteenth-century figures such as Marx and Nietszche, has arisen primarily in those geographic areas that had been European colonies, the group that Pearson saw Canada as leading. In fact, the term *postcolonial literature* has largely superceded the earlier term for the same phenomenon, *Commonwealth literature;* that is, literatures written in English but originating outside the United Kingdom and United States. Postcolonialism is most powerful where it deals with the conflict between indigenous, or captured, peoples and colonizers. All of these terms—along with the one I have avoided—Third World—are problematic, but they do provide some ways of focusing our attention.

European peoples are not the only ones to have colonized tribes or nations other than their own. Most of what archaeologists and historians can glean about long-term cultures on all inhabited continents except Australia suggests that warfare and territorial aggression were characteristic of most places at some time during the past, while the prelude to the Second World War included imperial behaviour on the part of Japan. The extent to which Europe, especially Spain, France, and England, colonized the rest of the globe beginning in the fifteenth century is extraordinary. The European conquest of Asia, Africa, Australia, and the Americas depended on technology, on ideology, and especially in the Americas, on disease. Asia, Africa, and South America were relatively heavily populated by sedentary, hierarchical civilizations. In their colonies on these continents, European strategy evolved into a practice of subjugating the indigenous peoples to the task of exploiting their own territory for the use of their European masters. In America north of Mexico, and in Australia, New Zealand, and some parts of South Africa, however, the indigenous populations were far less dense than those in Europe, usually relatively mobile within a defined region, and not possessed of the gold or spices that Europeans found in South America or Asia. Canada, for instance, rendered to the empire wealth in the form of furs and fish.

What the North American peoples had, however, was land—without any title Europeans felt bound to respect. At the point of sustained mass contact between Canada and Europe—say John Cabot's 1497 "discovery" of Newfoundland—European technology was not definitely better than American technology. Bows and arrows were considerably more accurate and swifter than blunderbusses; indigenous clothing gave better protection against the weather than did European clothing; and indigenous diets were better balanced and healthier than those of most Europeans in Europe—let alone of men crowded on tiny ships for months on end before landing on an unfamiliar shore. What tipped the balance was disease and ideology. North Americans ate well and lived relatively disease-free lives. Dogs were their only domesticated animals, whereas Europeans, Asians, and Africans, living in close quarters with a number of different kinds of livestock, were prey to strains of bacteria that had mutated and gained strength by swapping back and forth from one species to the other. By the time Europeans hit North America, they carried not only their own diseases but also strains hybridized by contact with Asian and African bacteria. These plagues ran rampant among indigenous North Americans with no natural resistance. They not only killed large numbers of people outright but also disorganized societies and in many cases damaged human fertility so that groups could not rebuild their numbers. Such devastation played neatly into European ideology. Early settlers in what would later be called Massachusetts, for example, thanked their god for a smallpox that killed Native people, because it gave the Europeans room to establish their own settlements.

Patterns of warfare in North America before 1492 are not entirely clear in either the oral or the archaeological record, but they do not seem to have included mass annihilation and territorial conquest. Native cosmologies included origin stories for particular nations that acknowledged the people of that nation as distinctive and often as the first people, but they were neither proselytizing nor exclusive. Almost always they featured the ideas of both balance and creative disequilibrium, usually represented by a Trickster figure. An ideology of subjugation, annihilation, and absolute good and evil, such as that promoted by fifteenth-century versions of settlement Christianity, was foreign to indigenous North Americans, as was the kind of warfare and "peace" that it produced. Ideals of balance and sharing are of little use in the face of what must have appeared to Native peoples as monomaniacal killers.

When Columbus sailed west to find the East, most European scholars and navigators knew well enough that the earth was a globe but assumed that Europeans, sailing ships with relatively small cargo capacity, would die of thirst or hunger before they reached the Indies—as Columbus would have done had he not reached Hispaniola. When it became quite clear that Columbus's landfall was something quite different from Asia, Europeans did not change their ideology toward these newfound lands. Columbus called the people he met "Indios," and Europeans proceeded to treat them in essentially the same fashion that the Spanish had treated the Moors and the Jews. As "infidels" the Indios were subject to murder, expulsion, slavery, and forced assimilation. The stereotypes of the Noble Savage and the fiend intent on spilling Christian blood were conveniently to hand in Orientalism. As France and England became the colonial masters of Canada as well as of the East, the intellectual development of Orientalism could be fitted as easily to North America as to Asia, especially, as Edward Said has shown, since Orientalism as an ideology was unaffected by the Orientalists' encounters with Asian peoples. Many of the pronouncements by Orientalists that Said cites could have been proclaimed against Native North American nations, and no one would have noticed any incongruity, since Orientalism does not acknowledge the distinctiveness of the cultures with which it comes in contact.[1]

Postcolonialism, as I use the term, is an intellectual tool that applies some of the ideas of postmodernism to the conscious scrutiny of Orientalism and its attendant ideologies in an attempt to reverse the ideology and "read" the culture and assumptions of the colonized peoples. It accepts the premise that indigenous cultures existed before colonialism, maintained their own development during the colonial period, and continue to function and adapt. Postcolonial criticism, however, is concerned with the intersection between indigenous and colonial cultures—otherwise it would be indigenous or colonial culture. Thus, it addresses two partially overlapping audiences—peoples of indigenous cultural heritage and peoples of colonial cultural heritage—with different intellectual needs. For the most part, postcolonialism as an intellectual movement has looked more at Asia and Africa than at North America, but it has also been used to some extent for Canada, Australia, and New Zealand.

Canada, however, differs greatly from Asia and Africa in two ways. Asian and African societies are truly postcolonial. However much of their social fabrics may have been deformed by colonialism and however much their current rulers may be Native elites who have internalized Orientalism, they have returned to majority rule. Even South Africa and Hong Kong now "belong" to the people of their own continents rather than to British or settler rulers. Canadian indigenous peoples, as either communities or individuals, continue to be denied sovereignty or meaningful collective representation in political and economic power. Much of what self-government they have achieved is based on the principles of the liberal Western European state rather than relational tribal society. Indian Country is occupied territory. This does not imply that Native people are always going around thinking about the occupying forces, but it does mean that the polemical arguments raised by indigenous political leaders, scholars, and artists are framed, in large part, in opposition to the constraints of a continuing colonial relationship to government and the dominant society. Canada's *post*-colonial society is actually a settler society. But indigenous and settler cultures in the postcolonial world overlap. Even had Europe never "discovered" India, the subcontinent would be vastly different in the twentieth century from what it had been in the fifteenth. Despite the assumption of Orientalism, borrowed by nineteenth-century anthropologists, that Oriental (or Native North American) peoples are essentially static, they are constantly changing. As it has happened, the changes involved colonization, and, as far as the everyday lives of people on any continent are concerned, they are powered less by the cataclysms of conquest than the technological changes and the global aggregations of capital—as opposed to wealth—that resulted from conquest and colonization. Vine Deloria, Jr., points out how the results of this kind of expropriation are glossed to neutrality by the "Contributions" school of American history, but the alternative is to see the contemporary technological world imposed on indigenous peoples as helpless victims. [2] Nineteenth-century Europeans did not have computers or refrigerators or automobiles or blue jeans, and the technology that led to these products is not the child of European intellectual superiority but of the mineral, vegetable, and human wealth plundered from the non-European world and concentrated for the use of the European and European-settler societies. The search in postcolonial art, especially that produced from within an indigenous culture or on the increasingly wide margins of overlap between settler and indigenous culture, is for an ideology in which indigenous values and beliefs can be returned to the centre, colonial culture beliefs be either "othered" or assimilated, and material conditions of contemporary life understood in relation to retained, rediscovered, or sometimes, of necessity, reinvented cultural values.

Canada is, however, a settler society, now more than ninety-five percent non-Native. For the settler society, the postcolonial goal is to establish an identity separate from the mother country, either without an acknowledgment of an indigenous culture or with its acknowledgment in the form of cultural appropriation, in which the indigenous culture becomes the "universal" heritage of all Canadians, without requiring any obligation on the part of settler heirs to the living inheritors of the indigenous culture. In Canada, this differentiation from the mother countries must be carried out at the same time that the settler culture avoids being subsumed by its powerful neighbour to the south—both the first settler colony to gain independent status and an imperial power in its own right. The United States has established its identity in several ways—as the City on the Hill, the Shrine of Liberty, the Wild Frontier, Nature's Domain, and the Universal Guarantor of Democracy, among others. This leaves us with the comforting myths of the Mosaic, Not the Melting Pot, and Indian policy that avoided at least the appearance of wars of annihilation and Trails of Tears—not to mention beavers, Mounties, Quebec, and an eternal search *for* an identity. While the essence of postcolonial definition is differentiation from the metropolitan centre, Canada's struggle for identity is complicated by having the United States on its doorstep.

In talking about the Canadian West, however, we are talking about region, not nation, and regional definition, because it is not primarily political, is even harder to establish than is national identity. In addition, "the metropolis" against which western Canada is to define itself is more than a little vague. Toronto? Which Toronto? The Family Compact? The West Indian community? Vancouver? New York? Montreal? London? Multinational corporations? Mozart's Salzburg? John Wayne's Hollywood? Jean Chrétien's Ottawa?

To a large extent, of course, the answer is determined by who is asking the question. For Said, Orientalism is not the construct of a particular geographic metropolis. In its most literal meaning, it is a body of work created by scholars who are self-consciously removed from "the Orient" but who see

rtue of their textual studies and their travels in Asia, as the
pable of explaining the "exotic" Orient to the "normal" Occi-
sion, Orientalists are those colonial administrators and West-
such as Flaubert, who more or less unconsciously accept
n and put it into effect in the political or creative realms. Finally
sm becomes the joint property of the European, and, later, Euro-
North American, populace who are familiar with the work of the administrators and artists and thus give their consent to the colonialism authorized by
Orientalism. Orientalism remains as a kind of "white noise" that normalizes
Euro-Canadian perceptions and cannot understand how "anyone" could be
offended by such events as the Glenbow Museum's 1988 "Spirit Sings" exhibition of indigenous North American arts or the Royal Ontario Museum's
1990 exhibition of the Africa brought home by Canadian missionaries.

The Subaltern Studies group locates the metropolis as the place from
which the voice of command comes to the subaltern. The focus of Subaltern
Studies is neither on colonial discourse nor on indigenous discourse but on
the point where indigenous discourse has been suppressed by colonial discourse. Even postcolonial studies focused on the Americas do not necessarily define the metropolis. David Stannard in *American Holocaust* makes little
distinction of either place or time in metropolitan speech regarding indigenous Americans. Thus Columbus, Cortes, Custer, and even L. Frank Baum
and W.D. Howells are caught making almost identical justifications for anni-
hilating either one particular group or the whole "race" of "Indians."[3] Since
the essence of both Orientalism and Indian hating is "othering," rendering
the Asian or Native North American person not human, their diction is a
mirror image of what the Orientalist or Indian hater wants to be and thus
tends to rely on descriptors such as savage, brutal, low, cunning, treacher-
ous, inhuman, and the like, words that do not contrast one human culture
with another but human with (putatively) non-human. Only when words
like un-Christian or infidel enter the mix is there any cultural content, and
even that is so vague as to be essentially meaningless. As centuries of religious wars in Europe have established, there exists no single standard definition of Christian.

For an indigenous culture, resistance to the metropolis is resistance to
whatever force—soldiers, administrators, missionaries, teachers, bankers,
assimilated Native governors—the empire sets up against it. Resistance is also
the deceptively simple act of living one's own life on indigenous terms, negotiating the material world of colonialization without internalizing the corro-
sive racism of the colonizer. If living well is the best revenge, living
unself-consciously may be the best resistance. One might find examples of
this kind of resistance in Harry Robinson's Okanagan stories or the narrative
of the girl Owl in Ruby Slipperjack's *Honour the Sun*.[4]

For the settler culture, the relation of resistance is much more difficult.
For western Canadians of British descent, there is a relation to the homeland

that one has, with whatever misgivings, chosen to leave. For western Canadians who are of neither indigenous nor British origins, one has a relation to one's homeland as well as to the British origins of the culture one has chosen, with whatever misgivings, to join. British culture includes an unexamined white privilege—European descent is tacitly understood to be the room temperature from which everything else is a deviation—but beyond that, British culture is not necessarily homogeneous nor finite nor even British. Neither Jesus, Rembrandt, Mozart, nor Michelangelo was British, but they all inhabit and to one degree or another define the "British" culture that was transplanted to western Canada.

For Said, religion, scholarship, art, and colonial policy are all one seamless web of Orientalism. For settler society in western Canada, however, a "fundamentalist" Christian point of view may be anti-intellectual, prefer Hollywood-produced mass art to either "high" culture or a regionally based culture, and claim that Canada is a Christian, English-speaking culture with no reason to treat Native peoples or francophones any differently than any other Canadians (who are, by default, Christian and English-speaking). On the other hand, a liberal "mainstream" Christian point of view may accept all religions as valid for their own believers, favour Mozart and Michelangelo over both American and Canadian products, and believe Native religious ceremonies deserve specific legal protection. Someone from a secular background or who has consciously rejected an ancestral, usually Christian, faith may find all spiritual beliefs, Christian, indigenous, or otherwise, hooey, and prefer science to any of the arts.

Once we look at a settler culture, the monolith of metropolitan culture dissolves like a sand castle—leaving only the somewhat lumpy notion of whiteness. Furthermore, while most postcolonial critics are looking at a colonial period against which they may define themselves, settler society in Western Canada appears only at the very tail end of the nineteenth century. Not only are there many metropolitan centres, but the opposite of regional culture is no longer the metropolis but rather a multinational commercial mass culture that, as Stan Rogers has seen as well as anyone, depends on the interchangeability of both people and places. A McDonalds is the same whether it be in Moscow or Washington or Toronto or Saskatoon or Drumheller—or Sackville. So is a Mozart CD or a Rembrandt reproduction or a Saturday afternoon broadcast from the Metropolitan Opera, a rather frightening notion for anyone who thinks of "high" culture as totally different from the McCulture of the Golden Arches.

Although regional culture in the West still rests on the assumption of white privilege, the idea of regional culture, like that of indigenous culture, implies that both art and soul are distinctive, that contemporary life is not reducible to interchangeable strip malls. The idea of the metropolis, that one is more successful in Calgary than in High River, more successful in Toronto than in Calgary, more successful in Los Angeles than in Toronto, and so on is one of the most seductive tales of the industrial revolution and one that our schools have been feeding us for the past hundred years. Implicit in any study of region, however, is the idea that this metropolitan bias is not the whole story, that it is important to know where one is from—and at least to contemplate staying there.

If the identity of the settler culture of the American West is built on suppressing Indians and settling on their "unused" land, the settler culture of Canada's West is considerably more complicated. Canada takes pride in having avoided the Indian wars and trails of broken treaties south of the border. However, that was largely because, except for the Selkirk settlers, Euro-Canadians only moved into the West en masse after the largely American destruction of the buffalo; also, the decimation of the Blackfoot and Cree peoples by smallpox had rendered military resistance futile for Native plains peoples and had compelled them to accept reserves far smaller than those originally promised indigenous peoples of the United States, but later broken up. Starvation, the outlawing of Native religious ceremonies, and the forced assimilation of boarding schools are also forms of violence, as January of 1998's non-apology has somewhat grudgingly conceded. In constructing for themselves an "original relation" with the place of western Canada,[5] Euro-Canadian settlers brought European art with them and redefined it in terms of a new landscape. On one level, they created white privilege by laying down an imaginative understanding of the land based on Eurocentric art forms. They suppressed Native peoples then appropriated their culture, fitting it into both explicitly malign and seemingly benign European paradigms of Native culture from the "murdering redskin" to the "Noble Savage," both echoing and repudiating what had happened in the United States. They brought all kinds of Christianity and they brought secularism as well.

A regional culture does not exist just because a few artists or arts institutions sit down to create it. Without an audience that is involved and committed either to or against the work, there can be no regional art. For the most part, I have focused on the settler culture. Scholars from within Native communities are working to define, internally, indigenous strategies of resistance and revival. My job as a non-Native scholar is, I believe, "cleaning up the debris colonizers have left" by examining how settler strategies of suppression, appropriation, discovery, and naturalization create not only a seemingly value-neutral regional art society but also a background of white privilege, of Eurocentrism, as the norm. [6]

As Said shows in his study of Flaubert and others, art serves effectively as the handmaiden of ideology, colonial or otherwise. Let us look for awhile at some of the ways art functioned in both the settler societies and the indigenous societies during the mid-1870s—the period between 1873, when the "Law in a Red Coat" marched West symbolizing imperial order, and 1876, when the negotiations for and conclusion of Treaty 7 marked the imperial transformation of an indigenous society to a settler society.

When the Mounties marched West, one of their number was sixteen-year-old Fred Bagley, the bugler.[7] Since the North-West Mounted Police were impossibly few in number to patrol the hundreds of miles of border with the United States and to eject the American whiskey traders, not to mention over-awing the indigenous nations of the Canadian plains, the Mounties needed to rely on symbolism.[8] Their scarlet tunics were the most obvious devices, but the bugle was not far behind. It symbolized order and a clear chain of command, going all the way back to the Queen. It stood in opposition to what the Mounties perceived as the disorder of aboriginal life. Both the scarlet uniforms and the precision inherent in bugle calls were strategies the British had developed to impress the "Natives" of India and Africa.

Although Euro–Canadians had been engaged in the fur trade with various Native nations for hundreds of years, and although a sizable and prosperous mixed-blood and mixed culture society flourished throughout the Prairies, the average Euro–Canadian—to the extent there was any such being—still viewed Native peoples through the stereotypes of savage and child, inherited from the Orientalism accepted without question by the white Fathers of Confederation. For the indigenous plains peoples themselves, however, the 1870s were the last years of a cultural golden age that, however beset, seemed as likely as not to endure forever. The high plains culture of the nineteenth century, the bison, Sun Dance, horse culture that existed in some guise from the Laurentian Shield and the Missouri River to the Rockies and from the North Saskatchewan to the Rio Grande, was itself a hybrid, dependent upon the reintroduction of the horse to the grasslands of North American whence it had evolved, and to a lesser extent on the introduction of European guns, steel, and other trade goods. The freedom of the horse culture allowed people to make full use of the migratory buffalo herds, and the prosperous buffalo economy granted the people the time for art, which is, of course, more plentiful in hunter-gatherer societies than agricultural-technological societies. These were culturally mixed societies, an aggregation not only of European and Native but of many Native groups, including people of woodlands origins, such as the Blackfeet, Crees, and Dakotas, who learned the Sun Dance from resident groups as they moved out onto the Plains.

Not only were the horse, the gun, and steel tools of European origin, but so were glass beads, floral beading styles, ledger books and coloured pencils, and even many of the pigments for dying porcupine quills. The arts of the Plains cultural renaissance were European-influenced as far as materials went, but their cosmology, their principles of social organization, and their ideas about the relationships of human beings to the rest of the universe were all deeply rooted in existing indigenous philosophies. War, like art a cultural pursuit enabled by leisure and abundance and stimulated by wide-ranging cultural contact, was probably more European-influenced than art, however, in its emphasis on killing and on control of territory. A Blackfoot legend collected at the beginning of this century tells of the introduction of death to warfare, suggesting that this was a relatively recent change. [9] The use of the horse for buffalo hunting was a significant pull factor of people onto the prairies, while the encroachment of Euro–North American settlers from the east, and especially from the southeast, was an equally significant push factor. As population in the area increased, especially toward the end of the period of Native control, as the bison herds decreased, warfare changed from a pursuit of individual honour and the capture of horses and humans to bloody territorial defence, patterned, perhaps, on European styles of warfare and European attitudes toward land "ownership." Introduced scourges such as smallpox and the whiskey trade also affected issues of war and peace. So many people were dying of smallpox that the Blackfoot Many Buffalo Stones Woman effected a peace between her people and the Crees. Neither group could afford more deaths.[10] Whiskey traders, like smallpox, were also destabilizing forces, and their depredations influenced people like the respected Blood chief Crowfoot to accept both the North-West Mounted Police and Treaty 7.[11]

That the society of the Great Plains in the nineteenth century was a cultural mixture should not, however, obscure the fact that its organizing principles were firmly centred within time-honoured Native traditions. The English and French languages, Christianity, and Western materialism were present among the Metis but otherwise existed only on the fringes—if at all—of plains society. Glass beads and German silver augmented but did not replace elk's teeth and bone as ornamentation, and even though beads did largely replace porcupine quills, they served the same material and cultural function. Ledger book art was an extension of hide painting, not an outgrowth of European art traditions. The Sun Dance remained the central ceremony of almost all Plains tribes (even during and after its suppression for several generations in both Canada and the United States). Clans and medicine societies determined tribal organization during the golden age. Reciprocal gift-giving and large ceremonial giveaways remained the standard in plains societies until nearly the end of the nineteenth century, and even after these ceremonies, like the West Coast potlatches, were banned by governments and missionaries, they remained the desirable norm, in marked distinction to the hoarding propensities of Euro–North American cultures. Land, in the nineteenth century, despite conventions regarding sacred places, traditional hunting areas, and accustomed gathering and horticultural sites, was not governed by a system that even remotely resembled European ownership conventions. Sacred and secular were rarely easily separated, and all the arts partook in some sense of the sacred, whether in terms of the beadwork designs on a cradleboard or the significance in music of the drum (the heartbeat) and the eaglebone whistle (the connection to sky).

Euro–Canadian agricultural and urban settlers who came into what are now called Alberta, Saskatchewan, and Manitoba starting in the late nineteenth century believed that they were entering "unnamed country" or "virgin land," but they were actually entering the cultural homeland of a vigorous, successful polyglot civilization in which a variety of religious and artistic practices thrived and developed. Just as the square survey, fences, ploughs, and later coal, oil, and gas extraction blurred but did not obliterate the curves of the land and the native vegetation, so Euro-Canadian settlement and culture could not clear the slate of the indigenous culture that the indomitable Blackfoot, Cree, Assiniboin, Dakota, and other plains peoples continued to practice and remember. When the bugle met the Plains, it did impress the Indians—though as much with the stupidity of announcing to potential enemies that all the garrison was going to bed as with any respect for order. Satanta, of the Kiowas in the southern Plains, learned bugle calls on a captured army instrument and used them to disorient U.S. troops in battle.[12] The bugle was much more useful in comforting the Mounties and other Euro–Canadians than it was in awing the Native peoples. As for the whiskey traders, whom the Mounties had been sent to subdue, they may not have stayed long enough to hear the bugle—Fort Whoop-Up, their most notorious stronghold, was empty when the law in the red coats marched in. Perhaps not surprisingly, Fred Bagley, who ended up staying in Calgary, turned his hand to a more complex musical style, that of the wind band. For nearly fifty years, he founded and conducted bands, both military and civilian, in the Calgary area, his audience by then firmly defined as Euro–Canadian.[13] Bands provided cheap public entertainment and popularized the airs of opera and operetta, reassured homesick listeners with medleys based on British folk songs, and kept alive the sense of empire with patriotic and martial airs. The wind bands were a staple of empire from India to Alberta. Unlike the Sun Dance songs, developed in the land of enormous skies, where the linkage of sun and deity seems undeniable, the music of the bands defied place, homogenized Calgary and the metropolis, be it the home counties of England or the towns of Ontario, or the actual metropolis where most of the sheet music was published and disseminated, London.

If the Sun Dance is seen as syndoche of indigenous plains culture, the wind band concert can symbolize the settler culture, though its lack of sacrality distinguishes it from the Sun Dance and illustrates the difficulty of comparing indigenous and settler art forms. The role of audience is different as well. Although relatively few people take part in a Sun Dance as dancers, singers, or sponsors, no one is merely a spectator. Everyone is a participant, because the success of the Sun Dance presages the success of the people throughout the year to come. At a band concert, however, the distinction between audience and performers is clear, with the exception of those who danced the two-step to marches at the end of the last century and of occasional sing-along numbers and small children dancing spontaneously on the grass or in the aisles.

In a postcolonial culture, however, the distinctions between settler and indigenous are much less clear, and the hybridization that goes on tends to be dominated by the terms of the settler rather than the indigenous culture, despite significant, successful resistance on the part of indigenous communities. The great flowering of the buffalo, Sun Dance, horse culture in the Canadian Prairies was relatively short, approximately a century from the acquisition of viable horse herds to the destruction of the free-ranging buffalos and the negotiation of Treaties 4, 6, and 7 in the 1870s. Another two decades elapsed before the mass immigration of European and Euro-Canadian settlers, beginning in the 1890s and peaking just before World War I. A truly colonial period exists from Confederation in 1867and the cession of territory (without the consent or even notification of its inhabitants) from the jurisdiction of the Hudson's Bay Company to Canada, to the end of the land rush in about 1913. It is marked by two wars of resistance, the Red River in 1869–70 and the North West in 1884–85, both led by the Metis prophet Louis Riel and both put down by Imperial and Canadian troops. Cree leaders Big Bear, Poundmaker, and Piapot and their young men, as well as relatively few other Indian combatants, also joined in the 1885 warfare. For the most part, however, the conquest of the prairies was carried out by the ravages of smallpox, the destruction of the buffalo, and the negotiation (free or coerced) of the treaties. The settlers' influx, marked by the creation of the provinces of Alberta and Saskatchewan in 1905, defines the second half of what I am calling the colonial period. It is the settlers' attempts to salve their sense of "not-at-homeness" by the importation and re-establishment of culture, with wind bands, amateur theatricals, parlor organs, newspaper verse, and the like that lays down the first tissue of European culture in the region. These attempts grew slowly during the two wars and the interwar years, and then accelerated with the growing prosperity, leisure, and population base of the area after World War II. It is at this point of growing self-confidence and regional identity that we begin to see a "postcolonial" point of view in which the object of art is no longer to recreate English culture, as the bands had done, but to define a Canadian prairie culture that is "universal" but distinct from that of the "motherland" of England; the Canadian hearth of many settlers from Ontario, the Maritimes, and to a lesser extent, Quebec; and from the United States. A settler culture begins to be postcolonial when it claims to be different from, not the same as, its metropolitan culture. This is a distinct process from that of an indigenous culture, especially indigenous cultures like those in Canada, which are still politically and economically colonized. I am here dealing primarily with the attempts of the settler culture to define itself and to come to terms with ideas of indigenousness, both those that assimilate and those that exclude Native peoples and cultures.

In the aftermath of World War I Canada as a whole was trying to invent and discover a culture, something that would unify its vast land mass, heavily populated only in a thin band along the U.S. border, and differentiate it from its two colonial parents, Britain and France, as well as from the potent and dynamic, if often materialistic and vapid, power to the south. This process was interrupted by the Depression and World War II but accelerated in the prosperity that came in the late 1940s. The Canadian Broadcasting Corporation and the National Film Board were two early culture-defining entities, but the watershed of a self-consciously developed Canadian culture comes with the Massey Commission, officially the "Royal Commission of National Development in the Arts, Letters and Sciences," which was empaneled in 1949 and reported in 1951. The "Report of the Royal Commission" is both a snapshot of arts and arts institutions and a portrait of the idea of the arts as national definition, crafted by a group chaired and dominated by Vincent Massey, a figure emblematic both of Canadian self-definition and arts as noblesse oblige. The scion of a wealthy industrial family making agricultural implements—including many of the ploughs that broke the prairies—Massey was well educated in both Canada and England, had served as Canadian High Commissioner in London during World War II, and eventually became the first Canadian-born Governor General in 1952. A patron of the arts and brother of actor Raymond Massey, Vincent Massey endowed the commission with prestige and credibility. Among the other four commissioners was University of Saskatchewan history professor Hilda Neatby, who represented the voice of the Prairies.[14]

The Royal Commission and its report served to document on a national scale an artistic tradition that was self-generated and self-sustaining but that relied almost exclusively for imports in its performing arts and remained derivative in its creative arts. The report provided a detailed set of snapshots of "Music, The Theatre, Ballet, Painting, Sculpture, Architecture and Town Planning, Literature, Folklore, Handicrafts, [and] Indian Arts," as well as of "Voluntary Societies, Galleries, Museums, Libraries, Archives, [and] Historic Sites and Monuments" as the topics were listed in the report's table of contents.[15] Yet encyclopedic as the report was, it was also restrictive. Although, as Massey later wrote, the commission tried to avoid the word "culture," which in English "produces an uncomfortable self-consciousness,"[16] the implied definition of "culture" was both elite and cosmopolitan. Even in the creation of a separate section on "Indian Arts cultural forms. The section on music, for instance, talked about symphony orchestras, competitions for young musicians, and even the folk traditions of European immigrant communities but never mentioned jazz or the Big Band tradition in full swing in Canada at the time or traditions such as Chinese opera or other arts imported by Asian immigrants.

Large public arts institutions in western Europe and North America are based in the upper and upper middle classes and focus on European traditions. They operate tacitly within the framework of white privilege, and they represent the most effective way to blend conspicuous consumption with "good taste" and to launder new industrial fortunes of the taint of the nouveau riche. From Henry James's Christopher Newman to Vincent Massey's grandfather and from the founders of the New York Metropolitan Museum of

Art to Eric Harvie and the Glenbow Foundation, support for what the Massey Commission called "serious" music and other arts involves a very complex negotiation among wealth, taste, and community standing. This relationship is further complicated by the recognition that "serious" art does come from a tradition that values complexity, technical virtuosity, and, in the twentieth century, even a certain emotional ambivalence as capable of evoking a rich intellectual response, compared to "popular" art forms that may favour accessibility and sentimentality or sensationalism. *Crime and Punishment* versus Mickey Spillane; Glenn Gould versus Les Brown and His Band of Renown. Although the Canada Council, the institutional embodiment of the Massey Commission, which had called for such a body with such a name, had, like its British counterparts, been willing to fund commercial arts adventures, it has stayed in the "high arts" tradition. The prairie institutions I examine have been funded by private philanthropists, by government bodies, or by middle-class and professional-class patrons. The resulting institutions are not elitist in the sense that they intend to bar "lower-class" audiences—on the contrary, they have often gone out of their way to be accessible to and hence to assimilate everyone—but rather they are elitist in their assumption that they will educate the entire population—urban and rural; upper, lower or middle class; of any ethnicity—"up" to "serious" art. This attitude comes from the unquestioned assumption that "my art is better than your art" but also from the carefully reasoned and felt belief that an appreciation of complexity makes one a better member of an arts audience as well as of a society with a national and regional identity.

Beyond class, however, is the problem of trying to decide how to distinguish when settler art becomes different from metropolitan art and to try to see how the complexity of high art itself becomes homogenizing. The bands that Bagley founded, and their successors, were British bands. Their point was to make Calgary comfortably like home for British settlers. The diffusion of art in indigenous North America resembled a web of interlocking points. While ceremonies like the Sun Dance diffused widely, each nation, band, and family introduced its own ceremonies and art work and spiritual traditions that might or might not be picked up by others. Some cultures valued tradition and repeated formulas over individual innovation, while other cultures reversed these proportions. There were not, however, definable cultural centres and peripheries.

For British culture, however, the pattern was that of a central point surrounded by rays. British band music, played on British-made instruments by British-trained musicians playing off scores printed in Britain sounded the same whether they played in Calcutta or Khartoum or Calgary. A settler culture or regional culture only begins to develop when regional variations occur, and a mass culture, dependent upon technology and literacy, develops a regional identity far more slowly than an oral and handiwork culture, since the centre of production remains in the metropolis. There are still no makers of brass instruments, for instance, in the Great Plains region and very little music publishing. The problem is not that mass culture, whether "high" or "low," is in some way inferior to or inimical to regional or indigenous culture, but that reliance on the metropolitan culture alone fosters a homogeneity and a concomitant sense that the local is inferior and that art, people, and places are interchangeable. Innovation, thus, can come only from the metropolis.

Orientalism only works as a controlling ideology if a metropolitan centre—in this case Europe as a whole—is conceded artistic and intellectual supremacy. Despite considerable cultural pride, no one could have said (or could say) that a Cree Sun Dance was more or less authentic than a Blackfoot Sun Dance or a Dakota Sun Dance. Said's critique of Orientalism as an intellectual construct is that it holds as a major tenet that Christianity is authentic and Islam not only inauthentic but mendacious. Given that premise, it was easy for European settler cultures worldwide to replace Islam with the indigenous culture or cultures and end up with the same Eurocentric assumptions. The fact that the indigenous cultures are many and vary among themselves at least as much as the Mediterranean Judaic, Christian, and Islamic cultures vary from each other is not relevant to the "white noise" of European supremacy that makes up Orientalism. Once one has divided the world into "self" and "other" there can be no individuation in the "other" category. At the same time the settler cultures appropriated elements of the respective indigenous cultures to naturalize themselves. Regional culture, then, developed out of a complex and often largely unconscious negotiation among the metropolitan cultures, the indigenous cultures, and the settler cultures, in which each changes each. The resulting plurality of cultures includes both the distinctiveness of indigeneity, the complexities of technology and literacy, and the particularities of a specific landscape, climate, flora, fauna, and human histories.

The point is neither that the particular is "better" than the universal—or vice versa—nor even that we need to combine both. In some respects, we have no alternative to combination; in many others, an alternative is both possible and desirable. One can also make the philosophical argument—and I would make it—that indigeneity is a particular value that deserves the protection of governments and peoples who in their imperialist guise have attempted for centuries to suppress it. What we face is choice, and all choice involves exclusion. Light, physicists tell us, is both a wave and a particle, *but it can never be a wave and a particle at the same time*. No structure can adequately protect the rights of the individual and the rights of the community. Metropolitan, technological society cannot simply accept indigenous values. Mozart *is* sometimes McCulture.

As a university professor and a grandchild of four sturdy arts pioneers in World War I–era Calgary, I hold the bias, the belief, that "high" art is "better" than "popular" art because it sustains a more complex and thus a more probing relationship between the intellect and the emotions of the audience. Although I would define the break between "serious" and "mass" arts somewhat differently than did the Massey Commission—including jazz, for instance, and local brass bands in the serious category, defining Native arts as high in their complexity (but not simply assimilating them into the national grab bag), and in fact finding more of a gradation than a sharp line between categories, even those as traditionally disjunct as verse in a little magazine and in a greeting card—I share the perception that there is a distinction. It is not the distinction suggested by recent attempts to define "cultural literacy," which tend to define non-European material, but it is important. Human beings need an art that requires that attention be paid. Art is our most potent tool for knowing ourselves and for changing ourselves. Stories do define us, and they can be transcendent or limiting. At the same time I am aware that the arts I am discussing—and valorizing simply by the seriousness with which I am discussing them—are both colonialist and class-based and that I have chosen to focus more on imperialism than on class. To the extent that objectivity is a noble goal—and not just a chimera that denies that human perception includes emotion even though human brains are hardwired for emotion—it can be approached not through mythical value-neutral observation but through an attempt to recognize and state one's biases, even if "subjectivity" be as elusive as "objectivity."

Given these biases, then, I am suggesting a few institutions and artifacts that confront the metropolis and emblematize the settler culture's varied attempts to create an art that was commensurate to the prairies. Native traditions of hunting and gathering allowed for considerable "leisure" that could be employed in various art forms that were essential to the culture, from quilling exquisite cradle boards to painting war exploits and spirit helpers on tipi covers to learning and replicating complicated spiritual ceremonies. The Metis fiddler was a Prairie conjunction of a number of European folk traditions as well as Native traditions of music and dance. For Euro-American settlers, however, whether dispersed on homesteads or hoping in little grasshopper towns or building what would eventually become regional metropoles, there was far less leisure time. Pieced quilts and sampler embroidery were mostly from earlier or later periods. Still, fiddlers for dances, band concerts in the park, and piano and choir in church on Sundays; amateur theatricals, amateur watercolours, poetry, or at least doggerel, in the local papers; vestments and silver for Catholic churches, stained glass windows, more restrained decorations for Protestant altars, onion-domed Ukrainian churches—all were part of the collective life of Prairie settlers, though many there were who would not have deemed them necessities.

The importance of performing subsistence activities in a sacred manner that seems to have been crucial to the tribal peoples of the Prairies was not as obvious in the eyes of most of the technological peoples who displaced them. One heritage of both American Puritanism and North American Social

Darwinism was a suspicion of any activity that did not plainly induce to empire building. Religion was acceptable. One needed to observe enough proprieties to mollify any putative deity, but art was at best recreation, the pause that refreshes before one returns to "subduing the wilderness." As Sinclair Ross shows in his writings, a community could fall into arrears on the preacher's salary or even the teacher's, but not on the doctor's nor the banker's. And no one in the little town of Horizon thought of buying paintings, though a citizen with artistic skill was handy to be volunteered for making posters for the Ladies Aid Bazaar. Yet despite the values of a boomer society, art remained a basic human necessity and, perhaps more striking in a self-consciously "new" society, an indicator of class more accurate than wealth. Canada's adherence to at least the suggestion of a non-materialistic class system has led both to pious hypocrisy and the Red Tory tradition of noblesse oblige, but it has led as well to the social viability of art and of arts institutions. But art audiences remain tenuous. In *As for Me and My House*, the Bentleys are poor, but Mrs. Bentley's piano playing as well as Philip's drawing and his apparently learned sermons help validate their social primacy as the preacher and his wife. Nonetheless, Mrs. Bentley finds her truest artistic expression not in her public piano playing but in her journal, the one medium in which the artist is, by convention, her own and only audience.

Once settler societies get beyond borrowing from their metropoles, they begin to look for ways to define themselves as distinct. Difference from the homeland often means the discovery of the indigenous. That can be landscape and wildlife painting, or the borrowing of Native cultural forms or the appropriation of Native culture itself—as when Canada hosts an Olympics or Commonwealth Games, for instance, and showcases a Spirit Sings collection of Native artifacts or performances by a Native dance troupe to represent "Canada" as a whole. It can also mean a focus on non-British and non-French immigrant strains or, in opposition to the culture of the United States, "the mosaic, not the melting pot." According to Gayatri Spivak, Subaltern Studies, one of the major intellectual strains of postcolonial theory and criticism, offers a new way of considering change in colonized societies by proposing:

> first, that the moment(s) of change be pluralized and plotted as confrontations rather than transition...and, secondly, that such changes are signalled or marked by a functional change in sign-systems.[17]

Spivak sees the instrumentality of such as the subaltern, the subjugated class that manages to exert itself against both the colonialized elite and the native bourgeoisie that extends elite rule. It is less easy to define the subaltern class in a settler society than on the Indian subcontinent upon which the Subaltern Studies group has focused its work. Class in the settler society is a far greater variable than in the purely colonial society, while class in the far smaller indigenous society is concomitantly compressed. Transformative confrontations in Canadian society may arise between various groups within the settler society or between the settler society and its European or United States metropoles as well as between indigenous and settler societies. The struggle to become indigenous to this place, to the prairie provinces, requires a dialogue with the indigenous cultures that long predate Euro-Canadian occupation of the Plains; but the other element in the cultural cartography is the metropoles in Europe and the United States, as well as central Canada. Settler colonies make art about difference from the metropolitan centre, and distance can be defined and imaged as both the land itself and as the pre-existing culture. But settler colonies also continue to practise the metropolitan culture, and the struggle to naturalize it on an international level of skill and sophistication is also part of the picture.

In a longer study, I have tried to trace out some of the implications of the kinds of internationalisms I have suggested above. In the present context, however, I wish to conclude that the Prairies have been involved in a complex international arts dialogue from the moment that European materials proceeded their makers through the trade routes that had for thousands of years crossed what are now international borders in the Western hemisphere. As we look at Canada in global and continental terms, it is worth remembering that we have always been the home of international and global cultures.

NOTES

1. In my discussion of the "discovery" of the western hemisphere, I have drawn upon Tsevetan Todorov, *The Conquest of America: The Question of the Other*, trans. Richard, Howard (New York: Harper and Row, 1984) and David Stannard, *American Holocaust: The Conquest of the New World* (New York: Oxford University Press, 1992); for Orientalism, I am using Edward Said, *Orientalism* (New York: Pantheon, 1978).

2. Vine Deloria, Jr., *We Talk, You Listen: New Tribes, New Turf* (New York: Macmillan, 1970), pp. 40–41.

3. Stannard, *American Holocaust*, cf. pp. 70–71, 76–79, 126, 245.

4. See Thomas King, "Godzilla vs. Post-Colonial," in *New Contexts of Canadian Criticism*, eds. Ajay Heble, Donna Palmateer Pennee, and J.R. (Tim) Struthers (Peterborough, ON: Broadview Press, 1997), pp. 241–48.

5. Bill Ashcroft, Gareth Griffiths, and Helen Tiffin, *The Empire Writes Back: Theory and Practice in Post-colonial Literatures* (London: Routledge, 1989), p. 135.

6. Emma La Rocque, "Preface; or Here Are Our Voices—Who Will Hear" in *Writing the Circle: Native Women of Western Canada*, eds. Jeanne Perrault and Sylvia Vance (Edmonton: NeWest, 1990), p. xxv.

7. Fred Bagley, "Journal," Glenbow Alberta Institute Archives; additional material from Norman Draper, *Bands by the Bow: A History of Band Music in Calgary* (Calgary: Century Calgary Publications, 1975), pp. 5–14.

8. Treaty 7 Elders and Tribal Council, *The True Spirit and Original Intent of Treaty 7* (Montreal: McGill-Queens University Press, 1996), p. 270.

9. "The Young Man and the Beavers: Another Version" in *A New Series of Blackfoot Texts from the Southern Peigans Blackfoot Reservation, Teton County Montana, with the help of Joseph Tatsey*, ed. and trans. C.C. Uhlenbeck (Amsterdam: J. Muller, 1912), p. 88.

10. Hugh Dempsey, *Calgary: Spirit of the West* (Calgary and Saskatoon: Glenbow and Fifth House, 1994), pp. 8–9; Hugh Dempsey, *The Amazing Death of Calf Shirt and Other Blackfoot Stories* (Saskatoon: Fifth House, 1994), pp. 67–79.

11. Treaty 7 Elders, *True Spirit and Original Intent*, pp. 74–77.

12. Matthew Jones, class lecture, University of Nebraska-Lincoln, February 1998.

13. Draper, *Bands by the Bow*, pp. 5–14.

14. Vincent Massey, *What's Past Is Prologue: The Memoirs of Vincent Massey* (New York: St. Martin's Press, 1964); Royal Commission on National Development in the Arts, Letters and Sciences, 1949–51, *Report* (Ottawa: Edmond Cloutier, 1951).

15. Royal Commission, *ibid.*, pp. v–vi.

16. Massey, *What's Past Is Prologue*, p. 452.

17. Gayatri Chakravorty Spivak, "Subaltern Studies: Deconstructing Historiography" in *Selected Subaltern Studies* eds. Ranajit Guha and Gayatri Chakravorty Spivak (New York: Oxford University Press, 1988), p. 5.

Reflections on the Tenth Anniversary of the Canada-U.S. Free Trade Agreement
What Has the FTA Meant for Canada?

GEORGE J. DE BENEDETTI

Department of Economics
Mount Allison University

January 1, 1999, marked the tenth anniversary of the Free Trade Agreement between Canada and the United States. This occasion invites us to reflect on why Canada entered into freer trading arrangements, and on the effects of freer trade on the pattern of Canadian exports and imports, on employment and wages, and on the openness of the Canadian economy.

Why Free Trade?

The problems of increasing structural unemployment and low-productivity growth in the Canadian economy were among the concerns of the Royal Commission on the Economic Union and Development Prospects for Canada, chaired by a former Liberal finance minister, Donald S. Macdonald. One of the recommendations of the commission, which reported in 1985, was that Canada should liberalize its trading arrangements through worldwide tariff reductions. However, the commission did not specifically recommend a free trade agreement with the United States. The Conservative Government, elected in 1984 under the leadership of Brian Mulroney, had set out to instill confidence in the Canadian economy by convincing Canadians that a Conservative government would manage the Canadian economy better than its Liberal predecessors. The new prime minister, who had opposed free trade while a candidate for the leadership of his party in 1983, reversed his position in office, and on the occasion of the so-called Shamrock Summit with President Ronald Reagan in March 1985, declared his support for freer trade with the United States. It is difficult to know precisely what factors made the prime minister change his mind. An account by a senior minister of Mulroney's Cabinet suggests the two events, the report of the Macdonald Commission and the Shamrock Summit, seemed to have influenced the prime minister's decision to pursue free trade with the United States.[1] After signing the Free Trade Agreement with the United States (FTA) in 1989, the Mulroney government entered into the North American Free Trade Agreement (NAFTA) in 1994, and took an active role in the preparatory negotiations leading to the formation of the World Trade Organization (WTO) in 1995 as successor to the General Agreement on Tariffs and Trade (GATT).

Another important actor in setting the economic agenda of the day was the finance minister, Michael Wilson. A Bay Street professional, he brought to Parliament and the Cabinet a conviction that there was too much spending in the public sector.[2] He and his policy advisors would set a Conservative course designed to raise the level of saving in Canada through a combination of policies in the 1980s and 1990s.[3] Through efficient financial markets, the additional saving in the private sector would result in more investment, which in turn would lead to a larger capital stock and higher long-term economic growth. The success of such policies would address the short-term problems of inflation and deficit reduction, and would partially address the longer-term problems of lagging labour growth productivity and international indebtedness. Free trade was part of this agenda.

The Conservative Economic Plan

Tax reform, deficit reduction, inflation reduction, and free trade were the pillars of the plan.[4] Each was designed to contribute to a higher level of national saving. Underlying tax reform was the principle of moving away from income taxes toward sales taxes as a basis of taxation.[5] The introduction of the GST, a consumption tax, would discourage spending, increase saving in the private sector, and contribute to higher government revenues. The lowering of taxes on saving by introducing a capital gains tax exemption and higher RRSP contribution limits would use the Income Tax Act as well to motivate saving in the private sector. Deficit reduction measures, especially through cuts in government spending and increased revenue from consumption taxes, would increase saving in the public sector.[6] Overall saving, the sum of private and public sector saving, would be affected as well, since economists define national saving as the excess of private saving over the government budget deficit.[7] Any reduction in the government deficit would therefore increase national saving. Although the efforts to reduce inflation through restrictive monetary policy would raise interest rates in the short term, achievement of a lower inflation rate would bring about lower interest rates in the longer run. Lower interest rates would increase saving in the private sector through lower interest income taxes, where the Canadian tax system assesses nominal interest income and not real interest income (nominal interest income discounted by the rate of inflation). As well, lower interest rates would increase saving in the public sector through lower interest payments on government debt. Free trade would reduce Canada's trade deficit because lower tariffs would cause an increase in exports and reduce the cost of imports. Reducing the trade deficit in goods and services would reduce the need to borrow abroad to finance that deficit, and thus reduce future international indebtedness. In this respect, free trade was to contribute to increased national saving. Another aspect of the free trade agreement would encourage more direct foreign investment in Canada, and thus increase the future international indebtedness and reduce the level of national saving.[8] Which opposing force would dominate, no one knew. The adoption of the free trade agreement as policy contained a hopeful assumption that the positive effects of an improved trade balance on the national saving rate would outweigh the negative effects of more foreign investment.

The plan was not entirely successful. Although, inflation reduction was attained, neither deficit reduction nor a lessening of international indebtedness materialized during the Mulroney years. The GST did not raise as much revenue as expected in the earlier years. The $500,000 capital gains tax exemption introduced in 1985 was reduced to $100,000 in 1988 (and subsequently eliminated in 1994).[9] Government deficits increased over the Mulroney era. Canada's current account deficit (its negative balance of trade in goods and services) did not decrease appreciably, and the rate of foreign indebtedness was not decreased. The overall result was that the intended increase in the level of national saving did not materialize, and consequently, the price of the Canadian dollar remained higher in the late 1980s and early 1990s than had been anticipated, because of the capital inflows required by higher than anticipated foreign borrowing. Although lower tariffs were to reduce the price of Canadian exports to foreigners, the higher-priced Canadian dollar offset some of these cost reductions to foreigners.

Having described some aspects of the political and economic climate under which free trade was introduced in Canada, let us now examine some national and regional effects of the Canada–U.S. Free Trade Agreement on Canada's trade pattern, and the agreement's impact on employment and wages.

Canada's Changing Trade Pattern

Canada's trade pattern changed drastically in the 1980s and 1990s. If we examine Figure 1, we see that there was a large increase in Canada's volume of exports and imports. We also see that a very large component of this increasing volume of trade was with the United States. The share of exports

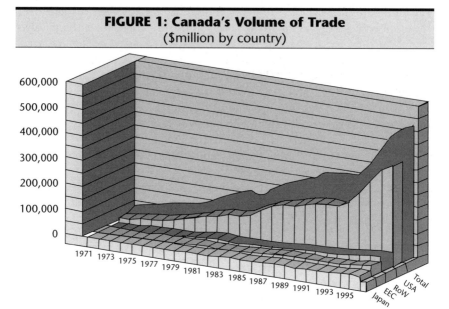

FIGURE 1: Canada's Volume of Trade
($million by country)

SOURCE: Compiled by the author from various Statistics Canada CANSIM series. Export/Import data are in nominal terms and on a Balance of Payments basis.

to the United States grew from approximately sixty-nine percent in 1971 to approximately seventy-eight percent in 1996. As well, we see that the U.S. share was increasing in the immediate years before the signing of the FTA. This in large part reflects that most of Canada's trade with the United States is concentrated in the automobile industry. The increasing share of exports and imports to the United States ensued as a result of Canada's trade having increased at a much faster rate than its increase in trade with the European Community, Japan, and the Rest of the World (see Figure 2). Canada's trade diversion in the direction of the United States, especially between 1988 and 1995, occurred despite the purchasing power of the United States dollar increasing relatively less than other world currencies against the Canadian dollar.[10]

To help determine to what extend the FTA was responsible for the rapid increase in the volume of merchandise trade between Canada and the United States, Daniel Schwanen compared changes in Canada's exports and imports in those sectors where the agreement liberalized trade (i.e., those sectors where tariffs fell) with changes in those sectors where the agreement did not liberalize trade (i.e., those sectors where tariffs did not fall because trade had long been free).[11] He concluded that bilateral growth in trade in sectors liberalized by the FTA considerably outpaced growth in other sectors not liberalized by free trade.[12] Furthermore, the study concluded that industries such as food products, chemicals, steel, clothing, furniture and furnishings

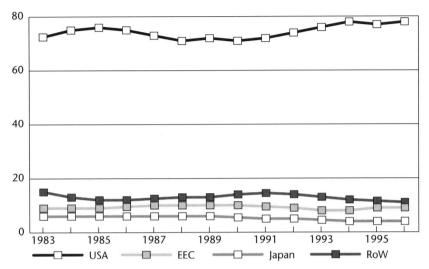

FIGURE 2: Canada's Volume of Trade
(% of exports and imports by country)

SOURCE: Compiled by the author from various Statistics Canada CANSIM series. Export/Import data are in nominal terms and on a Balance of Payments basis.

experienced fast two-way growth, suggesting an increased degree of intra-industry specialization within North America.[13] This conclusion of increased intra-industry specialization, especially in those manufacturing industries where economies of scale are large, is supported by other studies.[14]

The effects of the FTA on trade in services are opposite to that of merchandise trade. The Schwanen study concluded not only that growth in bilateral trade in services slowed down after the introduction of the FTA, but that this slowdown was more pronounced in sectors "liberalized" by the agreement than those sectors not directly affected by the FTA. Two factors may have been at work here. One was that although the FTA included future commitments to freer trade in services, the agreement only marginally freed trade in services. The second factor was that many countries opened services to foreign competition to a greater degree than they did for goods. Consequently, Canada increased its share of trade in services in the liberalized sectors with other countries in the world.[15]

In Figure 3, we see that the importance of trade for Canada in terms of its GDP increased. The volume of trade (the total value of exports and imports) as a proportion of the level of economic activity (GDP) doubled from approximately thirty-eight percent in 1970 to approximately seventy-six percent in 1995. This was especially true in 1995 when domestic demand was sluggish and most of the growth in GDP was externally driven.

FIGURE 3: Canada's Trade as a Percentage of GDP

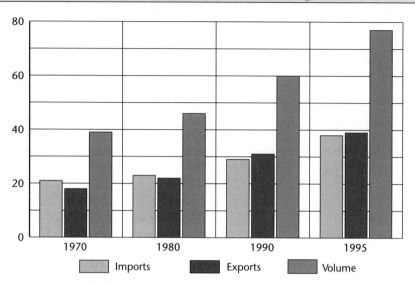

SOURCE: Compiled by the author from various Statistics Canada CANSIM series. Export/Import nominal data are in nominal terms and on a National Accounts basis.

Regional Effects of Free Trade

Although Canada as a whole increased its trade both in absolute and relative terms with the United States, especially since the signing of the FTA, the regional effects of this increased trade were not homogeneous. Pierre-Marcel Desjardins, using a modification of shift-share analysis, examined the relative importance of three shift-share subcomponents (USA trade shift component, non-USA trade shift component, and domestic demand shift component) to the economic growth of the provinces.[16] In his study, Desjardins examined the relative importance of these sources of growth in the provincial GDPs over two periods: 1985–89 (pre-FTA) and 1989–93 (post-FTA). His results, summarized in Table 1, show that six provinces (New Brunswick, Quebec, Ontario, Saskatchewan, Alberta, British Columbia) had the relative growth importance of their USA trade shift component increase in the post-FTA period compared with the pre-FTA period. As well, six provinces (Newfoundland, New Brunswick, Quebec, Ontario, Alberta, British Columbia) had the relative importance of their non-USA trade shift component increase between the two periods.[17]

Four provinces (Quebec, Ontario, British Columbia, and New Brunswick) had a decrease in the post-FTA period in the relative importance of growth from the domestic demand shift component.[18] This suggests that these four provincial economies have become more open. However, for Quebec,

	TABLE 1		
Province	USA Trade Shift Component	Non-USA Trade Shift Component	Domestic Demand Shift Component
Newfoundland	–	–	+
Prince Edward Island	–	–	+
Nova Scotia	–	–	+
New Brunswick	+	+	–
Quebec	+	+	–
Ontario	+	+	–
Manitoba	–	–	+
Saskatchewan	+	–	+
Alberta	+	+	+
British Columbia	+	+	–

SOURCE: A summary compilation by the author of Tables 11.8 and 11.9 (pp. 229–32) of the Desjardins study.

Ontario, and British Columbia, the displacement of domestic demand between the two periods was more attributable to the increasing value in the USA trade shift component, whereas for New Brunswick, the displacement of domestic demand between the two periods was more attributable to the increasing value in the non-USA trade shift component.[19] The decreasing importance of the domestic demand component relative to the increasing importance of trade with the United States as a source of economic growth in three of Canada's largest provincial economies suggests that the FTA has produced stronger north-south links through increasing international trade and weaker east-west links through a reduction in interprovincial trade.

Employment Effects

The impact of the FTA alone on employment and wages is not easily measurable. The period since the introduction of the FTA has also seen effects on employment and wages resulting from a continued shift of employment from the manufacturing to the service sectors, technological change requiring more skilled workers and fewer unskilled workers, restrictive fiscal and monetary policies, the recession of the early 1990s, exchange rate movements, and labour-cost competition from beyond the Canada-United States trade zone. In other words, we are not able to analyze the effects of the free trade agreement from a stable set of other coincident factors.

Despite this wide array of factors changing the economic climate, some proponents of free trade are ready to claim that the FTA had beneficial effects on employment, and some opponents of free trade are ready to claim job losses due to the FTA.[20] One difficulty in looking at anecdotal evidence is we can more easily see the obvious large job losses concentrated in those firms that shut down as a consequence of free trade, and less easily see any job gains spread widely across many firms and industries as a result of free trade. The C.D. Howe study by Schwanen found that the non-liberalized sectors, where trade was already essentially free, had the best relative performance in maintaining jobs and raising manufacturing wages. Growth in wages in the liberalized sectors, those newly exposed to increased competition through the FTA, did not fare as well. In those sectors where intra-industry trade increased and where one would expect higher labour productivity gains due to increased specialization and higher remuneration, wages were fairly stable. Another conclusion of the study was that there was no significant difference between the shrinkage in manufacturing employment in both the liberalized and non-liberalized sectors relative to total employment since the signing of the FTA.[21] (One would expect that if the FTA had a negative impact on employment, that the employment reduction in the industries liberalized by the agreement would be proportionately higher than that in the non-liberalized sectors.)

The recently published Gaston-Tefler study confirms the employment and wage results of the Schwanen study.[22] Gaston and Tefler concluded that 390,600 manufacturing jobs were lost in Canada between the implementation date of the FTA, January 1, 1989, and 1993, but free trade was not responsible for all the job losses. In the United States, 1,661,500 manufacturing jobs were lost.[23] The pattern of job losses is similar across manufacturing industries on both sides of the border, with some exceptions: Canadian job losses have been accompanied by American job gains in food and beverages, chemicals, rubber and plastics, and metal mining, and the United States experienced smaller job losses than did Canada in paper, petroleum, and coal products. These latter industries in Canada seemed to have suffered from free trade.[24] As well, the heavily unionized industries were concentrated in the non-liberalized sectors, and it was these sectors that lost a disproportionate number of jobs. Other "losers" include those industries that were sensitive to a Canadian–U.S. interest rate spread, and to a strong Canadian dollar.[25] Of the total jobs lost in Canada between 1989 and 1993, the authors concluded that tariff reductions were responsible for no more than fifteen percent of those manufacturing job losses, and eighty-five percent are attributable to other factors such as the Bank of Canada's fight against inflation, and increasing labour costs in Canada relative to the United States.[26] With labour productivity not increasing as fast in Canada, and the maintenance of a wide positive interest rate differential by the Bank of Canada to fight inflation, the Canadian dollar did not fall, and so there was little offset to the higher labour costs embodied in Canadian exports. Future studies based on more recent data will be needed to sort out the specific effects of free trade from the overall trend of shrinking employment in the manufacturing sector, and other factors such as recessions, inflation fighting, and labour costs and productivity.

Conclusion

We saw that Canada entered the Free Trade Agreement with the United States as a means of solving structural unemployment and long-term productivity problems addressed in the Macdonald Commission. Free trade was part of a four-point plan to increase the national level of saving that evolved in the Mulroney years. Following the implementation of the FTA ten years ago, Canada increased its trade with the United States in nominal terms. This effect was evident both in absolute volume and the United States' relative share of Canada's total trade. The relative importance of trade to Gross Domestic Product rose significantly for Canada. The growth in merchandise trade in the liberalized sectors outpaced that of the non-liberalized sectors. As well, intra-industry specialization increased more in the liberalized sectors.

We saw that the effects on employment were more difficult to measure because so many other factors were changing, even as tariff reductions under the FTA took effect gradually. These included the recession of the early 1990s, which was a primary cause of drastic shrinkage in manufacturing employment. Paradoxically, however, the non-liberalized sectors showed the best relative performance in employment and wage remuneration. In some liberalized sectors, especially where economies of scale were important, job losses in Canada seemed to correspond with job gains in the United States. Of the total jobs lost in manufacturing in Canada between 1989 and 1993, approximately fifteen percent could be attributed to the lowering of tariffs under the FTA. Many of the lost jobs were unionized jobs. Other factors such as the recession, and restrictive monetary policy, high labour costs, and a high Canadian dollar were responsible for the remainder. For bilateral trade in services, growth actually slowed down, but more so in the sectors liberalized by the FTA. This performance in services is disappointing since it was expected that the FTA would produce some momentum in the growth of dynamic (high value) service exports.

Although it has been ten years since the signing of the FTA, the data in the studies cited in this paper at best explore only the first six years of the agreement. One difficulty with an early phase of any free trade arrangement is the restructuring of output and employment that ensues. Jobs lost in an early phase may be gained at a later stage. As time passes, we will have the advantage of more recent manufacturing data, and better data collection methods for services, which can help us shed more light on all the issues.

We also saw that the effects of the FTA on the regions of Canada were not similar. The economies of New Brunswick, Quebec, Ontario, and British Columbia became more open (i.e., less dependent on the domestic economy and more dependent on world markets). The shift to greater linkages with the

United States was more pronounced for Quebec, Ontario, and British Columbia than it was for New Brunswick, which seemed to increase its trade even more with the rest of the world. The greater integration of the large economies of British Columbia, Ontario, and Quebec with the United States suggests that the FTA has yielded more continental linkages, rather than a global pattern, to Canada's economy.

NOTES

1. John C. Crosbie with Geoffrey Stevens, *No Holds Barred: My Life in Politics* (Toronto: McClelland & Stewart, 1997), p. 307.

2. See Donald J. Savoie, *The Politics of Public Spending in Canada* (Toronto: University of Toronto Press), 1990.

3. G.N. Mankiw and W. Scarth, *Macroeconomics: Canadian Edition* (New York, Harcourt Brace, 1995). pp. 209–10. See also, Frank Strain and Hugh Grant, "The Social Structure of Accumulation in Canada, 1945–1988," *Journal of Canadian Studies* 26/4, pp. 75–93 where the authors argue that social, political, and economic development in the 1960s and 1970s weakened the position of business in society, and made it more difficult to earn a profit. In the 1980s, business fought back and attempted to create a social environment more conducive to profit taking. Deregulation, restrictive monetary policy and its accompanying high rates of unemployment, reduction in government spending (net of interest payments) back to early 1950 levels, and free trade were all part of this small "c" conservative pro-business agenda. The large "C" Conservative plan outlined in this paper based on Mankiw and Scarth's account is consistent with the Strain/Grant thesis.

4. Mankiw and Scarth, *Macroeconomics*, p. 209.

5. *Ibid.*

6. Some economists thought that there was too much of a consumption component and not enough of an investment component to public spending. Therefore, by definition, cuts in government spending would result in decreased consumption and increased saving.

7. Economists will recognize this as the problem of the "twin deficits." A government budget deficit plus the excess of private investment over private saving creates a trade deficit in national income accounting terms.

8. Mankiw and Scarth, *Macroeconomics*, p. 210.

9. On March 23, 1985, the Mulroney government introduced a $500,000 lifetime capital gains tax exemption beginning with $100,000 in 1985, and then increasing to $500,000 over a five-year period. The exemption rate was fifty percent. In 1988, they reduced the lifetime exemption to $100,000, but increased the exemption rate to sixty-six point six percent. In the 1990–94 period, the exemption rate was increased to seventy-five percent, but the lifetime limit of $100,000 was maintained. In 1994, the $100,000 capital gains tax exemption was eliminated for the vast majority of Canadians under the Liberal government. Nevertheless, the $500,000 exemption still remains for farm property and small business shares.

10. Daniel Schwanen, *Trading Up: The Impact of Increased Continental integration on Trade, Investment, and Jobs in Canada* (Toronto: C.D. Howe Institute Commentary, 26/3/97), p. 6.

11. The liberalized sectors include: meat and dairy products; fresh fruits and vegetables; processed food, beverages; crude materials; textile materials; chemicals; petroleum products; steel; basic fabricated metals; other fabricated materials; industrial machinery; transport equipment, excluding autos; office and telecommunications equipment; other equipment; clothing; furniture and furnishings; other household goods; and other end products. See Schwanen study, Table 3, p. 11.

    The non-liberalized sectors include: crude oil; automobiles and parts; crude food and feed; other crude materials; fabricated products; industrial machinery; agricultural machinery; aircraft; medical and safety equipment; printed materials; and other transactions. See Schwanen study, Table 3, p. 11.

12. Schwanen, *Trading Up*, p. 6.

13. *Ibid*, p. 10.

14. See, for example, the study by Ravichandran Munira Thinam, Mary A. Marchant, and Michael R. Reed entitled, "The Canada U.S. Free Trade Agreement: Competitive Tradeoffs Between Foreign Direct Investment and Trade," *International Advances in Economic Research* 3/3, pp. 312–24. See also J. Holmes, "The Continental Integration of the North American Automobile Industry: From the Auto Pact to the FTA and Beyond," *Environment and Planning*, vol. 24, pp. 95–119.

15. Schwanen, *Trading Up*, pp. 10–11.

16. The traditional shift-share approach disaggregates growth into three (shift-share) components. The first component (national growth) corresponds to the rate of growth that would have occurred, if the provincial economy grew at the same rate as the national economy. The second component (the industrial mix) represents the difference between the rate of growth for a particular industry or sector nationally and the average growth for all industries or sectors nationally. The third component (competitive share) accounts for the fact that a particular industry or sector in a particular province is growing at a rate different from the national average of all provinces for that particular industry or sector. The Desjardin analysis adds three subcomponents (USA trade shift, non-USA trade shift, and domestic demand shift) to each of the three traditional shift-share components. Pierre-Marcel Desjardin, "Trade Liberalization and Sub-National Regions: With Evidence from Atlantic Canada" (Ph.D. diss., University of Texas at Austin 1997).

17. *Ibid.* p. 235.

18. *Ibid.* p. 238.

19. The study also concludes that "Prince Edward Island, Nova Scotia, and Manitoba may not be benefiting directly from trade liberalization" (Desjardin, "Trade Liberalization," p. 241).

20. See, for example, the Fraser Institute study by Marc T. Law and Fazil Mihlar, "Debunking the Myths: A Review of the Canada-US Free Trade Agreement and the North American Free Trade Agreement," *Public Policy Sources Document, No. 11* (Vancouver: The Fraser Institute, 1998) and the Canadian Council for Policy Alternatives study by Bruce Campbell, "Free Trade: Destroyer of Jobs," (October 1993). The study concludes that "while it is not possible to determine the precise number of job loss attributable to the FTA or anticipated with NAFTA, it is clear that they destroy far more jobs than they create."

21. Schwanen, *Trading Up*, pp. 21–22.

22. Noel Gaston and Daniel Trefler, "The Labour Market Consequences of the Canada–U.S. Free Trade Agreement," *Canadian Journal of Economics* 30/1, pp. 18–41.

23. *Ibid.*, p. 24.

24. *Ibid.*, p. 25.

25. *Ibid.*, p. 27.

26. *Ibid.*, p. 18.

The Changing World Order and Quebec's International Relations

An Analysis of Two Salient Environments

Louis Bélanger

Department of Political Science
Université Laval

For almost forty years now, the Quebec state and its governments have sought some kind of political recognition on the international scene, a recognition considered essential to the preservation and development of Quebec's distinct identity. Basically, successive governments have tried to implement what has often been described as one of the most activist international policies conducted by any federated unit. In accordance with this policy, they have promoted the idea that the Quebec state is capable and legally qualified to act as the ultimate international interlocutor for the Quebec people in all areas either within its constitutional jurisdiction or relating to what makes Quebec a distinct sociocultural entity within Canada[1]. If governments in Québec City have been relatively successful in the past in their efforts to develop international relations and forge an international personality for Quebec, it is because their agenda was matched by a tolerant—and sometimes quite receptive—international environment. In the following pages, I would like to examine the changes that have taken place or are taking place in this environment and try to understand their implications for Quebec's international relations by focusing on two particularly salient environments for Quebec: *La Francophonie* and North America.

The problem of finding a way for Quebec to express its distinctiveness in international affairs while remaining part of the Canadian federation cannot be separated from the more dramatic issue of the eventual recognition of Quebec as a new sovereign state. This is especially true now in light of the strong YES vote in the 1995 referendum, the current political climate in Canada, the willingness of the current government in Québec City to call a third referendum if reelected, and the importance given not to international law per se, but to international monitoring, in the recent Supreme Court opinion relating to Quebec secession. Here again, the receptivity of the international community, and particularly of francophone and North American partners, is crucial for the realization of the sovereigntists' ambitions. Therefore, my discussion of the significance of the ongoing evolution of each international environment for Quebec international relations begins with the question of Quebec's international personality as a provincial state—referred to here as paradiplomacy—and then continues with the delicate problems linked to an eventual attempt by Quebec to be recognized internationally as a sovereign state—referred to here as protodiplomacy.[2]

Quebec As a Paradiplomatic and Protodiplomatic Actor: An Overview

Quebec's political evolution since the Quiet Revolution of the 1960s cannot be understood without reference to the way in which Quebec opened outwards to the world during this period. The state has played a major role in this area, as it has in many others. Straining and sometimes breaking the limits of diplomatic convention, thus leaving federated states with very little room for manoeuvre, Quebec has succeeded in weaving an impressive network of international ties at various levels. With the help of a number of allies, particularly France, Quebec has forged itself a fragile, but nonetheless real, international personality.[3]

The importance of Quebec's international activities cannot be underestimated. Indeed, until recently, Quebec, especially through its Ministry of International Relations, devoted greater resources to its international activity than all fifty American states combined.[4] Despite major budget cuts, Quebec's network of foreign delegations has no equivalent within the Canadian federation,[5] especially since Ontario decided to close its outofcountry offices in 1993.[6] As regards the formality of those relations, Quebec had signed 410 official agreements with various foreign partners by the end of 1995.[7] A study of the 292 agreements signed prior to 1993[8] showed that over half were with governments or government organizations representing sovereign states.[9] This is significantly more than the other Canadian provinces. With its partners in the Frenchspeaking world, Quebec has also succeeded, albeit not without difficulty, in securing a kind of special status that gives it a distinct identity and allows it to play an active and remarkably autonomous role within francophone international organizations. Quebec sits as a "participating government" on the Francophonie agency and is a regular participant at the Francophone summits where it takes part in discussions with other francophone heads of state and governments on terms that vary according to the politics of the issues being debated.[10] This status has enabled Quebec to participate in major international cooperation projects such as the international French-speaking TV consortium, TV5.

The Quebec state has been able to take advantage of the Canadian constitution's lack of explicit provisions regarding the central government's foreign policy prerogatives in order to give its own constitutional demands international scope. However, behind the politicalconstitutional question lies a perhaps more fundamental issue, that of the definition of the terms of Quebec's identity and the mode of legitimization of the Quebec state. Two opposing perspectives have dominated this debate in the past. For the Parti Québécois, an independent international policy is legitimized by the need for Quebec to be a state and for Quebecers to be a people so as to have a voice in the international community of peoples and nations. At the end of its second term in office in 1985, the PQ Government released an international policy statement that effectively portrayed Quebec's international activities as the expression of the interests and values of Quebecers as a people.[11] Back in office in 1994, the deputy premier of the current PQ government renewed this interpretation, this time with reference to the concept of the nation-state. In its contemporary, elective guise as the "place where democracy is exercised, where social arbitration takes place and where citizens have the greatest chance of being involved in the decisions that concern them," the nationstate is seen as the basic unit of international politics according to this new nationalist perspective.[12] And as Quebec is considered to fit this description of the nationstate, the Quebec state is therefore called upon to act in its own name internationally.

In contrast, the Quebec Liberal Party's vision of Quebec diplomacy is more "functionalist" or "sectorial" in nature. The most recent Liberal government proposed that Quebec's foreign policy sphere be defined as "international affairs," as "distinct from foreign policy."[13] The latter is confined to a "formal framework" within which questions of strategic equilibrium, security, and defence are dealt with through recourse to international law. Issues related to the economy, health, agriculture, tourism, aviation, transportation, research, culture, telecommunications, etc., are seen to have "become what can be appropriately termed international affairs," i.e., issues evolving outside the "formal framework" of foreign policy.[14] The logic of government action in this sphere is related to the logic "of provinces and regions." Its legitimacy is rooted in the internationalization of Quebec's sectorial, economic, and social missions rather than in the existence of a distinct political identity.

Quebec's international policy may vary with the different degrees of interventionism and nationalism that characterize the two main parties that alternate in office in Québec City. Yet, it remains a fundamental instrument for the construction of Quebec's political identity and the very foundations of its legitimacy as a state. This is unlikely to change, no matter how Canada's constitutional framework evolves. In fact, none of the major constitutional reforms discussed in recent years has sought to reduce Quebec's current ability to intervene on the international stage, and Quebec will attempt to express its constitutional powers and identity internationally whatever its future status. What can and does change however, as will be seen in the following pages, is how this attempt fits within the international context: what possible interpretation of this context can be used to legitimize paradiplomacy and how is it perceived by foreign interlocutors?

Before examining the specifics of our two salient environments, some general observations about how the changing world order affects the conditions in which Quebec paradiplomacy is conducted should be made. For example, international law has evolved. After having shown some flexibility in order to accommodate federated states—through actual federal clauses in treaties or specific proposals to amend the law in treaties—the architects of international law appear to be increasingly intolerant of states whose political systems seem to prevent them from fully respecting their obligations.[15] The momentum for paradiplomacy has changed. What appeared in the 1970s to be irreversible growth in the involvement of regional governments in international affairs, solidly grounded in the transnationalization of world politics, can be seen today as a somewhat more contingent phenomenon.[16] In recent years, activities abroad by federated states in North America and Australia have reached a ceiling or, in many cases, have drastically declined, while European leaders of paradiplomacy, like Bavaria and Catalonia, appear to remain heavily dependent on political personalities and circumstances.[17] The withdrawal has been quite drastic in Canada, first with Ontario going as far as closing all of its foreign bureaus, followed by Quebec's elimination of two-thirds of its network.[18] Finally, compared to the context of the 1960s when Quebec emerged as a paradiplomatic actor, the post–Cold War context of the 1990s has proved to be more sensitive to aspirations which, if encouraged, could fuel what is perceived as a general movement toward the political dismemberment of existing states.[19] Thus, it is increasingly difficult to legitimize Quebec's international activities as being part of a global trend of interdependence affecting all federated states.

In any case, the permanence of the sovereigntist option in Quebec has always made it difficult for the Quebec state to be seen as an ordinary paradiplomacist. And now more than ever, it is certainly difficult to disentangle Quebec paradiplomacy from its protodiplomacy: Quebec cannot ignore the need to pave the way for eventual foreign recognition when dealing with partners abroad and, at the same time, foreign governments cannot overlook Quebec's political context when cooperating with the province. It is not only the close results of the last referendum that link the government's international agenda so directly to the question of sovereignty. More importantly, it is the specific procedure envisioned by the PQ government to secede that creates this situation. Unlike the 1980 referendum, the 1995 vote did not seek a mandate to negotiate an agreement on "sovereigntyassociation" with the federal government, an agreement that would have ultimately been submitted to the public for ratification.[20] The 1995 referendum asked voters to approve a bill providing for a unilateral declaration of independence in the event that the Quebec government was unable to agree with Ottawa within a year on the terms of Quebec's accession to the status of a sovereign state.[21] A "yes" victory would have immediately set the sovereignty process in motion, including the search for international support and, eventually, the quest for official international recognition.

Given the evolution of political positions in Canada since October 1995, the Quebec government can be expected to seek a similar mandate in the next referendum, allowing for a unilateral declaration of sovereignty or independence, if and when necessary. I would also suggest that the immediate relevance of the international community for the actors involved in the political dispute over Quebec's status has been highlighted in the recent opinion of the Supreme Court. In its answer to the first question posed by the federal government on the constitutionality of an act of secession by Quebec, the Court clearly identified the international community as the ultimate judge of the conduct of both the governments of Canada and Quebec during the negotiation that would follow a referendum giving Quebec a mandate to negotiate secession.[22]

Quebec in La Francophonie

After the end of the Cold War, when many voices were demanding that the multilateral organizations that still reflect the post–World War II balance of power be restructured, France attempted to redefine her role in the international order and preserve her status as a great power. Having stretched the postcolonialism resources to the maximum, Paris decided to once again use its privileged status as a former metropolis to come forward as the leader of the francophone world.

This change of image and strategy was of paramount importance for Quebec. Politically, Quebec had greatly benefited from its inclusion by France in the cooperation networks that followed decolonization and within which diplomatic patronage was a common practice. Thus, in 1968, at Gabon's invitation but France's suggestion, Quebec attended in its own right the meeting of the Conference of National Education Ministers (CONFÉMEN) in Libreville. Since then, the Francophonie has been the preferred battleground for the QuebecCanada conflict over Quebec's international personality. Thus, a practice was instituted allowing Quebec to engage in a number of cooperation activities abroad, in fields that come under its constitutional jurisdiction. This was accomplished without either Canada or Quebec overtly renouncing their incompatible interpretations of their respective prerogatives in foreign policy matters.

In 1971, a first compromise between Quebec and Ottawa enabled Quebec to work within the Agency for Cultural and Technical Cooperation (ACCT) as a "participating government," after this status became part of the agency's charter. A second compromise was worked out in 1985, when the governments of Canada and Quebec agreed on a formula allowing Quebec to participate in the new Summits of Francophone Heads of State and Government. The 1985 agreement gave Quebec the same status as it had within the ACCT when cooperation and development issues were being examined during summits. In return, Quebec agreed to recognize the federal government's authority in international political and economic issues. In concrete terms, the text of the agreement is as follows:

> On matters related to the international political situation, the Premier of Quebec is present and acts as an interested observer. On matters related to the international economic situation, the Premier of Quebec will be in a position, after concertation and with the express agreement of the Prime Minister of Canada, to intervene on what is of interest to Quebec ... [On matters related to cooperation and development] the Government of Quebec participates in the debates and deliberations as a full member, according to the modes and practice of the Agency for Cultural and Technical Co-operation (ACCT).[23]

This compromise was negotiated at a time when the area of cooperation held a dominant place in the deliberations of the francophone organization. However, already in the first few summits, the question of politics was becoming increasingly predominant, often on the fringe of official discussions. Canada significantly contributed to this development when, under Brian Mulroney's leadership, it proposed that the protection and promotion of human rights become part of the Francophonie's mission. France, once it decided to use the organization in a strategy of post–Cold War repositioning, sought to institutionalize this overstepping of the francophone institution's original mandate, which had been centred on cooperation. At the summit held at Chaillot, France succeeded in requiring that, between summits, the ACCT's political control be reinforced through the creation of a ministerial conference and a permanent council of the Francophonie.[24] Then, at the Cotonou summit, its proposal to create a position of secretarygeneral of the Francophonie to be named at the 1997 summit in Hanoi, was adopted. The establishment of a "spokesperson, arbitrator and conciliator" of the Francophonie as well as a "senior official" of the agency, was aimed not only at increasing the Francophonie's visibility and capacity to intervene on the international scene, but also at linking intergovernmental cooperation—carried out under the auspices of the ACCT in the cultural and technical fields—with the movement's new political ambitions.[25]

Canada was also clearly pushing for a similar politicization of the Francophonie. For example, at the summit held in Cotonou, it proposed that the francophone organization undertake to prevent conflicts, while actively taking part in preparing the resolution to reform the institutions concerned.[26] Quebec's initial reaction was to mistrust this trend since the liberal government was openly against both the creation of new permanent institutions by the Conference of Heads of States and Government as well as the extension of cooperation activities beyond sectors traditionally covered by the agency. It was also against introducing political issues that could be debated within other forums into the agenda of the multilateral Francophonie.[27] However, for reasons related to the sovereignty question, the current government is not in a position to oppose the French aims too overtly. Nevertheless, prior to Cotonou, during negotiations with Paris, Ottawa, Quebec, and Brussels over the reform of institutions, Quebec had requested that the changes in structures not weaken Quebec's status.[28] Fearing a fresh assault on the ACCT by France, the government even publicly expressed its fears on the eve of the ministerial conference in Marrakech in December 1996.[29]

Even if Quebec's status remains unchanged, the politicization of the Francophonie will nevertheless have undermined its real significance. Quebec will continue to participate in the new Agence de la Francophonie and in the summits on the basis of the tacitly renewed agreement on its participation, at the first meeting of heads of states and government in 1986. However, the agenda of the summits and organizations that follow up on the work between the summits might be increasingly dominated by political issues and, consequently, Quebec's voice will be heard less and less. Furthermore, if the agency, by force of circumstances, ended up with more and more political mandates, Ottawa might be strongly tempted to call for a review of the modes of participation of "participating governments." Ultimately, it would not be beyond the realms of possibility for Ottawa to cite changes in the nature of francophone institutions as grounds for a reconsideration of past agreements concluded with New Brunswick and Quebec.

In this respect, Boutros Boutros-Ghali's last visit to Canada in autumn 1998 speaks volumes. Stressing the fact that the Francophonie Secretary-General is a higherlevel political figure than previous leaders of the Francophonie, Ottawa refused to let Quebec be in charge of his security during the Quebec portion of his trip. Because the incident was seen as a breach of previous agreements and also probably as Ottawa's first attempt to use the pretext of the elevated status of the Organization of the Francophonie to challenge what Quebec had achieved, the PQ government reacted firmly. The SecretaryGeneral did come to Quebec but all his meetings with government representatives and other public authorities were cancelled.

In fact, the Quebec government is now facing the same situation as that which prevailed in the late 1970s, when the initial proposal for a francophone summit was examined.[30] It justifiably fears that greater politicization would have the effect of marginalizing its participation in francophone institutions, which ultimately depends on the relative weight of cultural and technical cooperation versus the big issues of economic and international policies. However, this time the difference is that Quebec City cannot entirely rely on France's strategic alliance to reopen its agreement with Ottawa on the modes of its participation in the restructured organizations of the Francophonie. Originally, France was concerned that a highly political content might make people suspect a vague desire for neocolonialism on its part. Similarly, it was worried that a highly institutionalized multilateralism would cause the network of bilateral relations established with its former colonies to be called into question. As we said, it has since radically changed perspective and it would certainly no longer risk compromising its plan for a political Francophonie by supporting Quebec's cause. At most, France would be in a position to guarantee Quebec its current status.

Moreover, the current Quebec government would not risk alienating Paris, its principal ally on the protodiplomatic front, by pushing too hard on the paradiplomatic front. Thus, once again a sovereigntist government cannot escape from the strategic protodiplomatic perspective, if only because it knows that its behaviour should arouse sympathy which will eventually translate into support when the time comes and, at the same time, because Quebec's interlocutors are concerned about the significance of their relations with Quebec. In its protodiplomatic strategy, the government must grant a prominent place to the Francophonie and its member countries, among which France obviously ranks first. In the strategic space structured by the protodiplomatic issue, France is in fact the positive pole that counterbalances the United States' hostile attitude.

Even if France, which is fundamentally republican, also pursues a conservative foreign policy as regards recognition and even if it would also undoubtedly prefer a constitutional solution to the Canadian political crisis, it nevertheless remains the only country capable of eventually counterbalancing the United States' attitude.[31] Several French political figures, including the current president, have let it be known in the past that France "would accompany" Quebec on its democratically chosen path. During Premier Parizeau's official visit to France in early 1995, Jacques Chirac, then a presidential candidate, even hinted at the ripple effect that France's recognition of Quebec would have on the other member countries of the Francophonie.[32] Although these declarations do not allow us to judge what might effectively be France's reaction to a unilateral declaration of sovereignty (UDI), they nevertheless indicate an entirely unique and rare openmindedness.

In the Péquiste scenario, soon after Quebec's declaration of independence, France would initiate a more or less orchestrated movement of international recognition, coming chiefly from the francophone world, which would be difficult to resist.[33] This momentum strategy was at the centre of Jacques Parizeau's "grand jeu."[34] After a positive referendum, Quebec's current status within the institutional Francophonie could effectively turn out to be a valuable asset in its quest for international recognition. Depending on the circumstances, this status might provide Quebec with an excellent forum in which to announce its intentions to eventually declare independence. Subsequently, an attempt would be made to have Quebec's status within the agency and summits naturally change from that of a "participating government" to that of a "full member."[35] Thus, with these scenarios well in mind, the Quebec government is taking advantage of the opportunities provided through its participation in the various organizations of the Francophonie to spread its protodiplomatic message quite directly.

Quebec in North America: The Quest for the Missing Political Link

In many ways, North America is Quebec's natural gateway to the world. Geographically, economically, historically, and even culturally, Quebecers, like other Canadians, are and feel fundamentally North American. However, this reality has never been expressed in political terms. It may seem paradoxical that Quebec has had to go far beyond the confines of its own backyard—to Europe mostly, but also to Africa—in search of sometimes ambiguous but nevertheless tangible support for its claim for international status. As for the question of sovereignty, North America appears particularly unreceptive to attempts by the present Quebec government to advance its cause.

In the following pages, to understand this situation and possible prospects for the future, I would like to situate Quebec's para- and protodiplomacies in the evolving North American context, broken down here into three components: the United States, Mexico, and the integrated North American economic zone created by NAFTA.

The United States

We will begin with the United States. To put it mildly, the American political class has never been very receptive to Quebec's efforts to project its own political personality outside Canada's borders. Quebec has never succeeded in establishing truly direct relations with the U.S. government. Attempts to set up a permanent delegation in Washington similar to those Quebec already operates in six other American cities and some twenty other countries around the world have been systematically resisted by Ottawa. Moreover, although in 1978 Quebec opened a Washington tourist office, which has since served as a kind of political outpost, it has done so in violation of the Canadian federal government's rule forbidding any of the provinces to have advisors staying regularly or maintaining a residence—even a permanent one—in the U.S. capital.[36] Moreover, although Quebec had signed 166 cooperation agreements with the central authorities of a variety of foreign countries by 1993, only two of them were with the United States.[37] One of these two was a cooperation agreement on social security signed in the aftermath of the Canada–U.S. Free Trade Agreement. In this case, Quebec was forced to accept the mention of a treaty between the two central governments in the preamble of the memorandum, a decision that ran counter to Quebec doctrine in this area.

One of the reasons for the weakness of Quebec's relations with the U.S. federal government could be the availability of other choice partners on the American side, the federated states. At first glance, stateprovince relations would appear to provide Quebec with a promising avenue for political cooperation. On closer investigation, however, it is clear that Quebec did not make the kind of headway it had sought in this area. Although Quebec did establish formal relations with virtually all the states of the Union, they were in areas of technical cooperation such as transport vehicle licencing. Quebec also had high hopes for such cross-border and regional cooperation forums as the Conference of New England Governors and Eastern Canadian Premiers, but this kind of cooperation never went beyond relatively specific economic issues, particularly in the energy field. It would appear, then, that the weakness of Quebec's relations with Washington cannot be attributed to the richness and success of its relations at the subnational level.

So how can this problem be explained? Some people, including Jean-François Lisée, current advisor to the Bouchard government, claim that governments in Québec City have simply practised a kind of selfcensorship in the face of the American giant and argue that this must explain their inability to penetrate the very open American political class. But it is precisely when Quebec officials have shed their timidity that they have experienced their worst setbacks, probably because they do so when their actions are inspired by separatist aims. When the Parti Québécois Government regained power in 1994, it seemed anxious to gain a foothold in the U.S. capital with a view to the approaching referendum.[38] A new person was chosen within the upper ranks of the party to run the office in Washington, the deputy premier travelled to the U.S. capital to test the air, and a close watch was kept on the comings and goings of Canadian Ambassador Raymond Chrétien. However, the whole approach proved to be too loud and aggressive. The Canadian embassy ended up accusing Quebec's representatives of contravening the principle of unity in Canadian diplomatic representation. This resulted in an embarrassed reaction from the State Department and Jacques Parizeau's visit to Washington was shifted to New York.[39]

This leads us to conclude that, in the case of Quebec, the American government simply applied a policy of strict respect for the unity of Canadian foreign representation. It did so both in response to Canadian pressure and because it felt that this policy was consistent with the goal of maintaining Canadian unity, which will be discussed below.

Washington has always reacted negatively to the prospect of Quebec sovereignty for two reasons, one strategic and the other related to doctrine.[40] The first is distinct to the Canadian situation: the United States has made it clear in the past that it would prefer to remain neighbours with a united Canada, given the close relations between the two countries.[41] However, I believe that the U.S. policy reaction to the situation in Quebec is based more on the broader problem of recognition of new states than on an understanding of the Canadian dynamic itself.[42] This is because Americans are paying close attention to the rise in secessionist claims around the world.[43] Americans associate this phenomenon with a form of "tribalism," for which they have no sympathy.[44] Even those American specialists who are open to dealing with secessionist claims on their individual merits insist that a consistent policy must be followed in this matter.[45] The United States has always resisted secessionist claims and would not want its attitude toward Quebec to be interpreted elsewhere as a sign of increased permissiveness.[46]

The current Quebec government is sensitive to the risk of having its claims lumped together by American decisionmakers with those of ethnic separatist movements responsible for recent violent conflict in various parts of the world and makes every effort to defend Quebec nationalism as a special case, one that is markedly different from the nationalism of ethnic affirmation movements. However, it would be surprising if such arguments were to shortcircuit the tendency in Washington to analyze the Quebec situation from the perspective of the broader problem of increasing secessionist claims. And from this perspective, arguments about the peaceful and uniquely democratic character of the sovereignty quest in Quebec appear to be counterproductive.

These are seen as necessary but insufficient criteria for recognition in recent assessments in the United States of the relevance of granting international recognition to new states in the post–Cold War context. Halperin and Scheffer, for instance, write about the good conduct of the selfdetermination movement and the risk of instability following secession, and include them in this category of necessary but insufficient criteria.[47] Conversely, violent conduct by the ruling government and the potential for instability resulting from resistance or action to block secession are considered far more critical when they are not seen as sufficient grounds for recognition in and of themselves.[48] For instance, a history of repression or discrimination by the central government against the minority claiming independence not only legitimizes the secessionist option, but also justifies recognition, because it renders an internal solution to the conflict impossible.[49] But even that has not yet been sufficient to grant recognition to Kosovar independentists.

Thus, the fact that Quebec's sovereignty debate and referendums are taking place in a democratic climate that is respectful of human rights and in an institutional framework that already allows the people of Quebec a certain degree of selfdetermination probably makes Quebec's secessionist movement unique. This also makes Quebec's case one of those typical claims for autonomy which should, according to the Americans, be solved within the existing state. This being said, however, it would be an error to think that the United States would never consider recognizing a sovereign Quebec.

An American policy of unconditional support for the status quo is practically unthinkable in this case. In general, such a policy has the advantage of sending a very clear message to autonomist movements, but the disadvantage of restricting the ability of the United States and the international community to influence the final political outcome of a specific situation.[50] In the case of Kosovo, for example, the Americans were seen as both saying that secession was not an option for them and insisting that the parties negotiate without preconditions, i.e., ruling out any option. Considering the closeness of Canada-U.S. relations and the proximity of the two countries, Washington would probably first react to a Quebec UDI by laying out—more or less clearly—its guidelines regarding claims to selfdetermination. However, this would still leave plenty of room for a realist assessment of the situation. Some observers have suggested that the United States, after a victorious referendum for the sovereigntist side, might consider sending signals encouraging Canada and Quebec to negotiate a solution that avoids secession. Washington could make overtures to Quebec and request that a federal offer be considered and at the same time make it clear to Ottawa that recognition of Quebec remained an option if the rest of Canada was not ready to meet some of Quebec's demands.[51] Such behaviour would be consistent with the expected role of the international community contained in the Supreme Court opinion on Quebec's secession: ultimately foreign states should put the necessary pressure on the parties in order to make sure that they negotiate in good faith.

In the face of American resistance, sovereigntist strategists have always been strongly tempted to get round the problem by relying once again on Paris instead of developing a real American strategy. Having become convinced that the United States "will not be inclined to recognize a Quebec that declares itself sovereign, unless they cannot do otherwise,"[52] Jacques Parizeau formulated the strange hypothesis that, jealous of their regional predominance, the Americans would react to the possibility of an act of recognition by France by surprising it and proceeding before it.[53] This hypothesis is no doubt based on an overestimation of French support for the sovereigntist cause, overlooking one of the fundamental lessons of recent history about the recognition of new states, that is, the act of recognition is now a collective action that obeys a regional logic. In other words, France will not act on its own but in concert with other European powers, and Europe will only act in conformity with American preeminence in regional matters. But what is more worrying about this hypothesis is that it provides a rationalization for the sovereigntist strategy's quasineglect of the American political front. Thus, in his book, Jacques Parizeau clearly dismisses the American political class and advocates a minimalist commitment towards Washington.[54]

Mexico
Quebec has operated a full-fledged delegation in Mexico City since 1980. In addition, Québec City maintains regular contact with Mexican officials through the Quebec-Mexico Working Group, which was set up in 1980 to allow Quebec to take part in the Canada-Mexico Cooperation Agreement and

to defend its interests in areas under its jurisdiction, especially education and culture. In other words, Quebec did not wait for NAFTA to take an interest in Mexico, even though the institutional mechanisms linking the two have taken on a vitality that they lacked prior to 1994. Furthermore, Mexico's admission into the North American free trade zone spurred the Quebec government to take more economic initiatives with this new partner, but also broadened Quebec's Mexican agenda to include cultural, educational, scientific, environmental, and other issues. In short, Quebec came to see Mexico as more than just an economic partner, and as what could be called a geopolitical partner as well.

Unlike the United States, the Mexican federal government seems to have been relatively open to representatives from Quebec. Quebec government ministers, who have visited Mexico with increasing frequency since the early nineties, have met with people such as the Mexican minister of external affairs and members of the Senatorial Committee on External Affairs.[55] In addition, efforts by Quebec's minister of international relations in recent years to enhance the formalism and legal status of agreements on tuition fees have also proven successful. The new agreement negotiated was signed by the Mexican Secretariat of Public Education, the National Council on Science and Technology, and the Secretariat of External Affairs.[56]

Nevertheless, Mexico's diplomacy remains extremely conservative with regard to the principles of sovereignty and noninterference. Moreover, as a federal state, it has certain centrifugal forces of its own to deal with. The Mexican government has therefore been cautious in its relations with Quebec, both to avoid offending the Canadian government and out of respect for the principle of the unity of Canadian representation. Mexico's Secretariat of External Relations has made it clear that it recognizes the Canadian embassy as the sole official channel of communication between Mexican authorities and Canadian provinces and carefully ensures that Quebec's links with Mexico fall squarely within the framework of Canada-Mexico diplomatic relations.[57]

Agreements between Quebec and Mexico also remain limited in scope. Apart from the agreement on student exchanges, two other deals were signed with the Secretariat of Agricultural and Hydraulic Resources. In 1993, Quebec hoped that the intensified relations fostered by the implementation of NAFTA would lead Mexican authorities to sign agreements to help strengthen the framework for trade mobility by covering issues such as taxation and legal cooperation.[58] However, these initiatives went nowhere.

Finally, as regards Mexico's federated states, Quebec does maintain some links with states like Queretaro, Zacatecas, Guanajuato, and the Federal District. All have signed cooperation agreements with Quebec, especially in the areas of science and technology. But it is clear that Quebec does not consider them to be important players from a political perspective. In the action plan setting out the main orientations of Quebec's policy toward Mexico, the

Mexican states are not even mentioned.[59] To sum up then, the channels of political communication that Quebec has managed to develop with Mexico may fall short of the province's ambitions, but are nonetheless quite remarkable in light of Mexico's diplomatic conservatism.

This conservatism, however, will probably turn out to be a dominant factor in determining Mexico's attitude toward a Quebec UDI. For historical reasons linked primarily to American interventionism in Latin America, Mexico has elevated the principle of nonintervention to the realm of dogma, so much so that it considers recognizing a foreign government as interference—what Mexicans refer to as the Estrada Doctrine.[60] Of course, recognizing a government and a state are two different things, but Mexico's attitude regarding the former makes it unthinkable for the country to pave the way to international recognition of a new Quebec state. Mexico will only confirm Quebec sovereignty as a fait accompli which has already been recognized by the major powers, and probably even by Canada itself. As a result, all that Quebec's current government can expect from NAFTA's third partner is zealous application of the principle of noninterference and abstention from any form of official recognition of Quebec during the postreferendum transition period when Quebec will be seeking international support.

However, as a member of NAFTA, Mexico can play a much more critical role. This issue will now be examined.

The New North American Framework

Governments in Québec City and the majority of Quebecers have always been strong supporters of free trade agreements—first CUSTA, then NAFTA. Unlike Ontario, they have never openly protested against the new legal arrangements created by these two deals. Yet the new continental trade zone leaves the provinces and states with very few options when it comes to defending their own interests. Although the possibility of a ratification formula involving the provinces was raised and backed by Quebec during CUSTA negotiations, it never got past the suggestion stage. So not only did the provinces have no part in the agreement, they also ended up being directly governed by the new law created by NAFTA. In other words, they are the object and not the subject of this law.[61] They play no official role in NAFTA institutions or dispute resolution mechanisms.[62] And although they have the right to appear as interested parties before a special binational group set up to resolve disputes over compensatory rights and dumping, that right is a product of U.S. legislation, for the agreement leaves this issue to domestic law. Moreover, the provinces are subject to the new law to the extent that NAFTA imposes constraints on provincial powers that overlay the Canadian constitution.[63] This has led Vilaysoun Loungnarath to predict that "provincial paradiplomatic activity in international economic relations will be increasingly marginalized in the future."[64]

It is interesting to note that not only has Quebec accepted this new state of affairs, but that the indépendantiste Parti Québécois government has also insisted that the Quebec National Assembly pass a bill to implement the agreement. Centralist Ontario, on the other hand, threatened to challenge the legality of the agreement before the Supreme Court on the grounds that it was an intrusion into provincial jurisdiction.

This ardent commitment to NAFTA is not unrelated to the question of sovereignty. In fact, the sovereigntists present the treaty as a safety net that would guarantee Quebec free access to its natural markets following sovereignty. Therefore, the matter of Quebec's support for NAFTA has already been used by actors inside and outside Canada to influence the outcome of the current political situation.[65] Throughout the last prereferendum debate, the Quebec government strove to convince voters that a sovereign Quebec and a new, divided Canada would more or less automatically succeed the former Canada as members of NAFTA.[66] In doing so, it clearly attempted to convince Quebec voters that independence would not alter the terms of Quebec's economic participation within the North American economic space. However, the reality is that a sovereign Quebec will not succeed Canada as part of NAFTA, and will be obliged to follow the procedure for joining the agreement that is outlined in article 2204.

Not only do the experts agree unanimously on this position,[67] but it is also openly held by the American and Mexican administrations.[68] The Mexicans were the first to make their position public. Immediately following the PQ's 1994 election victory, the Mexican Ambassador to Canada said that Quebec would be subject to the customary membership procedure and would not be considered as a successor state.[69] As for the United States, it is useful to recall the words of Warren Christopher during the last days of the 1995 referendum campaign:

> I think it's probably useful for me to say that we have very carefully cultivated our ties with Canada, and they have been very responsive in relation with all those ties and I think we shouldn't take for granted that a different kind of organization would just obviously have the same kind of ties.[70]

This means that Quebec's entry into NAFTA would have to be approved by the United States Congress, and thus would be subject to the whims of the internal dynamics of American politics. Furthermore, Quebec's membership would also be subject to negotiations during which the United States would likely ask for concessions in such important and politically sensitive areas as culture, agriculture, and the automobile industry. In Mexico, the economic pressure to take prompt action on Quebec's application will be much less strong. Moreover, Mexico may well decide that other aspiring NAFTA candidates should have priority or that Quebec's admission into

NAFTA would pave the way for other NAFTA hopefuls, something they are not yet ready for.

There is a paradox here. Quebec, which played such a critical role in Canada with its strong support for the creation of a North American free trade zone, could find itself temporarily sidelined from the zone while English Canada, which was far less supportive, remains a member.

Conclusion

The changes that have occurred in the international world order since the end of the Cold War have not been particularly favourable for Quebec's expression of a distinct political identity abroad. In conclusion, it should be pointed out that the reason for Quebec's current problems in getting people to accept its conception of its international role is largely due to the interstate logic that is increasingly asserting itself as the exclusive mode of international relations in its immediate external environment. Moreover, this interstate logic is becoming more and more conservative.

Since the beginning of this decade, Quebec has seen itself become increasingly dependent on one region—North America—which has never been very open to the idea of Quebec as either a paradiplomatic or protodiplomatic actor. This regionalization, which is largely desired by Quebecers, is not accompanied—as in the case of Europe for example—by an affirmation movement from federated states and other subnational units. In other words, on this side of the Atlantic, growing regional interdependence did not give rise to the kind of transgovernmentalism envisaged by many people, allowed subnational governments to play a greater role abroad. On the contrary, the new North American space is constructed, politically and legally, on the basis of a profoundly interstate logic that leaves little room for the expression of internal particularisms.

This affirmation of the interstate principle can also be observed in the case of the Francophonie. As the francophone organization grows and is politicized, it is becoming less and less the voice of a community of French-speaking peoples and more and more a statecontrolled diplomatic forum like any other.[71] Moreover, the mechanisms invented in the 1970s to allow Frenchspeaking communities in Canada and Belgium to participate fairly directly were not reproduced elsewhere.

More generally, the established interstate order has toughened its position in the post–Cold War period because it feels threatened. It may seem paradoxical to see, in a world shaken by the after-effects of the dismantling of multiethnic countries, repeated calls for the territorial status quo, but nothing could be more natural.[72] Faced with the fear of the unknown and without contingency models, it is only normal that the international community prefers to solidify the existing order. Therefore, the significance given to Quebec's demands today, when ethnic revivalism and secession claims are emerging nearly everywhere in the world, is very different from that of the 1960s to the 1980s.

Does this new context mean that the external resources that have until now allowed Quebec to fuel its needs for external recognition are becoming scarce? While the answer to this question should probably be yes, it should also be noted that there has never been any really favourable context for the development of Quebec's presence on the international scene. Moreover, this context has changed over the past few years and will continue to change in the future. Might this context then make it more difficult to legitimize the Quebec sovereigntist project? The answer is both yes and no. Yes, to the extent that anticipation of the process of accession to sovereignty is made more complex by an international community that is not very inclined to recognize it, thus dampening some people's enthusiasm. No, if confronted with reduced scope for paradiplomatic action, other people in Quebec are led to believe that sovereignty is the only way to ensure Quebec an acceptable level of participation in the community of nations.

NOTES

1. This doctrine was set out by the then Minister of Education, Paul-Gérin Lajoie. See his 1965 speech to Montreal's consular corps reproduced in *Le Québec dans le monde: Textes et documents I* (Sainte-Foy: Association Québec dans le monde, 1990) pp. 101–6.

2. For a discussion on para- and protodiplomacy, see Ivo D. Duchacek, *The Territorial Dimension of Politics: Within, Among and Across Nations* (Boulder, CO: Westview Press, 1986) pp. 246–48. This meaning of "protodiplomacy" is not to be confused with the one proposed by James Der Derian, i.e. revolutionary diplomacy. See his *On Diplomacy: A Genealogy of Western Estrangement* (Cambridge, MA: Basil Blackwell, 1987).

3. For a complete overview, see Louis Balthazar, Louis Bélanger, Gordon Mace et al., *Trente ans de politique extérieure du Québec, 1960-1990* (Québec: CQRI/Les éditions du Septentrion, 1993).

4. See Earl H. Fry, *State and Provincial Governments As International Actors* (Toronto: Centre for International Studies, Occasional Paper no. 1996-3, 1996), pp. 12–13.

5. See the contributions in *Études internationales* 25/3 (September 1994).

6. "Ontario Changing Trade Strategy: Closing of 17 Foreign Offices Will Lead to Closer Ties with Private Sector," *Globe and Mail*, 24 April 1993.

7. Luc Bernier, *De Paris à Washington. La politique internationale du Québec* (Ste-Foy: Presses de l'université du Québec, 1996), p. 46.

8. See Douglas M. Brown and James Groen, "Attitudes et comportement des gouvernements provinciaux du Canada à l'endroit des Etats-Unis," *Études internationals* 25/3 (September 1994), p. 514.

9. For exact figures and sources, see Louis Bélanger, "L'espace international de l'État québécois dans l'après-guerre froide: vers une compression?" in *L'espace québécois*, eds. Alain G. Gagnon and Alain Noël (Montréal: Québec/Amérique, 1995), pp. 90–92.

10. See Louis Bélanger, "Les enjeux actuels de la participation du Québec à la francophonie multilatérale: de la paradiplomatie à la protodiplomatie," *Politique et sociétés* 16/1, pp. 39–59.

11. See Gouvernement du Québec, Le Québec dans le monde ou le défi de l'interdépendance: Énoncé de politique de relations internationals (Québec: Ministère des Relations internationales, 1985).

12. Bernard Landry, *Les relations internationales du Québec: refléter notre réalité*, notes for an address by Bernard Landry, Deputy Premier, Minister of International Affairs, Immigration and Cultural Communities, Minister responsible for la Francophonie, Montréal, 14 December 1994, p. 4.

13. Gouvernement du Québec, Le monde pour horizon. Le Québec et l'interdépendance: éléments d'une politique d'affaires internationales (Québec: Ministère des Affaires internationales, 1991), p. 11.

14. *Ibid.*

15. See, for example, the various attempts to extend to the regional governments and administrations the obligations contracted by central governments during the Uruguay Round.

16. See, for example, Panayotis Soldatos, "Cascading Subnational Paradiplomacy in an Interdependant and Transnational World" in *States and Provinces in the International Economy*, eds. Douglas M. Brown and Earl Fry (Berkeley: Institute of Governmental Studies Press, 1993), pp. 45–64.

17. See the contributions in Hans J. Michelman and Panayotis Soldatos, eds., *Federalism and International Relations: The Role of Subnational Units* (Oxford: Clarendon Press, 1990), pp. 98–99.

18. David K. Dyment, *The Reluctant Traveller: Understanding the International Activities of a Non-protodiplomatic Component Government: The Case of The Ontario Government from 1945 to 1995* (paper presented at the annual meeting of the Canadian Political Science Association, St. Catharines, Brock University, 2 June 1996) pp. 7–12; Ministère des Relations internationales, <<Crédits 96–97: Le Québec maintient six Délégations générales à l'étranger>>, *Communiqué de presse*, Québec, le 28 mars 1996.

19. This argument was developed by Bélanger.

20. In 1980, René Lévesque's PQ government was refused this mandate by a sixty percent majority.

21. National Assembly, Bill 1. An Act respecting the future of Québec, First session, Thirty-fifth legislature, Québec Official Publisher, 1995, section 26.

22. See Supreme Court of Canada, *Reference re Secession of Quebec*, 20 August 1998, sec. 103.

23. Reproduced in Jacques-Yvan Morin, Francis Rigaldies and Daniel Turp, *Droit international public: Notes et documents. Tome II: Documents d'intérêt canadien et québécois* (Montréal: Éditions Thémis, 1992), p. 519. Our translation.

24. Secrétariat de la Conférence, Actes de la quatrième Conférence des chefs d'États et de gouvernements des pays ayant en commun l'usage du français, Paris, La documentation française, 1992, pp. 282–283.

25. *Rapport général*, 6e Conférence ministérielle de la Francophonie, Cotonou, 29 and 30 November 1995, 4.2 (Rapport final du comité de réflexion pour le renforcement de la Francophonie), adresse W3:<<http://www.francophonie.org./instances/6ecmf/p1s1.htm#p1s1a4>>.

26. Michel Venne, "La Francophonie gardienne de la paix? Le Canada pousse pour que le sommet francophone appuie la prévention des conflits," *Le Devoir*, 28 November 1995, p. A2 and "La Francophonie se dotera d'un porte-parole unique," *Le Devoir*, 14 November 1995, p. A5.

27. Gouvernement du Québec, *Le Monde pour horizon*.

28. Réal Pelletier, "La Francophonie vit ses premières tensions. L'esprit de la fête prend le pas sur les divergences Ottawa-Québec," *La Presse*, 4 December 1995, reproduced in National Assembly, *L'Argus*, 4 December 1995, p. A16, A17.

29. Lia Lévesque, " Réforme de la Francophonie: Québec rejette la position de la France," *Le Devoir*, 30 November and 1 December 1996, p. A11.

30. See Claude Morin, *L'Art de l'impossible. La diplomatie québécoise depuis 1960* (Montréal: Boréal, 1987), pp. 373–74.

31. "Between maintaining the status quo and pure and simple secession of Quebec, taking up the constitutional dialogue again may facilitate the search for a middle road towards a renewed federalism that is highly decentralized and reflects the tremendous diversity of Canada as a whole," [translation] Sénat, 2 *Rapport du sénat no. 203 sous la présidence de M. Jacques Larché : "le fédéralisme à la croisée des chemins—le Québec à l'heure de la souveraineté?"*, 1994–1995: quoted in Isabelle Roy, *Entre la noningérence et la nonindifférence: les relations entre la France et le Québec depuis 1976*, Individual research report, Paris, École nationale d'administration, 1996.

32. Manon Tessier, "Chronique des relations extérieures du Canada et du Québec," *Études internationales* 26/2 (June 1995), p. 400.

33. It is true that this scenario corroborates statements made by French politicians, including Jacques Chirac, when he was a candidate in the second presidential elections. See Tessier, "Chronique des relations extérieures", p. 400.

34. See Jacques Parizeau, *Pour un Québec souverain* (Montréal: VLB éditeur, 1997), pp. 318–20.

35. Conseil exécutif national du Parti Québécois, *Le Québec dans un monde nouveau* (Montréal: VLB éditeur, 1993), p. 76.

36. External Affairs Canada, *Federal-Provincial Relations: Operational Framework* (Ottawa: January 1989), pp. 26–29.

37. Gouvernement du Québec, *Recueil des ententes internationales du Québec 1990–1992* (Québec: Publications du Québec, 1993).

38. Michel Venne, "Pas de guerre des drapeaux à Washington," *Le Devoir*, 19 and 20 November 1944, p. A-8.

39. Michel Venne, "Parizeau ne veut pas embarrasser Washington: il se rendra a New York plutôt que dans la capitale," *Le Devoir*, 24 November 1994, pp. A-1 and A-8.

40. The following paragraphs draw heavily on the previous article "The United States and the Formative Years of an Independent Quebec's Foreign Policy," *American Review of Canadian Studies* 27/1 (Spring 1997), pp. 11–25.

41. See Joseph T. Jockel, *Washington and "An Act Respecting the Sovereignty of Québec"* (Washington: Center for Strategic & International Studies [Decision Quebec Series, Study 1], 1995) and Charles F. Doran, " Les relations canado-américaines dans une ère d'incertitude," *Études internationales* 27/2 (June 1996), pp. 281–285.

42. Many writings maintain that in matters of foreign policy, the U.S. government reasons more by analogies than in keeping with the elements peculiar to each situation. See in particular Yuen Foong Khong, *Analogies at War* (Princeton: Princeton University Press, 1992).

43 In 1993, at his confirmation hearings before the Senate Foreign Relations Committee, Warren Christopher identified this as one of the primary issues the Clinton Administration would have to deal with: "If we don't find some way that the different ethnic groups can live together in a country, how many countries will we have? We'll have 5,000 countries rather than the hundred plus we now have." Quoted in David Binder, "Trouble Spots: As Ethnic Wars Multiply, U.S. Strives for a Policy," *The New York Times*, 7 February 1993, p. 1.

44. See, for example, Joseph S. Nye Jr., "The Self-determination Trap," *The Washington Post*, 15 December 1992, p. A-23. Nye's opinion is interesting because right after this article was published he has been appointed director of the intelligence council and assistant secretary of defense in the new Clinton administration. He returned to academic life in 1995 but still has close ties with the government.

45. Morton H. Halperin and David J. Scheffer, with Patricia L. Small, *Self-Determination in the New World Order* (Washington, DC: Carnegie Endowment for International Peace, 1992), p. 74.

46. What Kamal Shehadi calls the demonstration effect: "It is frequently argued that a successful bid for selfdetermination in one state will encourage other states to do the same. For this demonstration effect to work, the same causes of, and the same conditions for, self-determination need not exist. Politicians learn selectively from historical and contemporary events." *Ethnic Self-determination and the Breakup of States*, London IISS and Brassey's, Adelphi Paper No. 283, December 1993, p. 54.

47. See Halperin and Scheffer, *Self-Determination*, pp. 78–80.

48. According to Max Kampelman, regarding conduct of the ruling government, the 1970 UN Declaration on Friendly Relations has already legalized this principle. In

Max M. Kampelman, "Secession and the Right to Self-determination: An Urgent Need to Harmonize Principle with Pragmatism," *The Washington Quarterly* 16/3 (Summer 1993), p. 8.

49. Here, Halperin and Scheffer take Québec as a counter-example: "The claim of a self-determination movement facing repression may be more legitimate than the claim of a movement that is not. For example, a Quebec that has substantial political and cultural autonomy may have a lesser claim to independence than Iraq Kurds who are denied both." Halperin and Scheffer, *Self-Determination,* pp. 76–77.

50. *Ibid.,* pp. 2, 71, and 72.

51. Amitai Etzioni, who favours an intransigent U.S. policy in the face of secessionist claims, concludes that in Canada's case, "The merits of enhancing Ottawa's responsiveness and allowing for some redefinition of the central government's role far outweigh the benefits of dismembering the union." In "The Evils of Self-determination," *Foreign Policy* 89 (Winter 1992/1993), pp. 21–35. See also Jockel, *Washington,* p. 24.

52. Parizeau, *Pour un Québec souverian,* p. 285.

53. *Ibid.,* pp. 49, 285–86 and 341.

54. *Ibid.,* p. 287.

55. See Tessier, "Chronique des relations extérieures."

56. *Accord dans le domaine de la formation universitaire entre le Gouvernement du Québec et le Gouvernement des États-Unis du Mexique,* 13 October 1994.

57. Maria Isabel Studer and Jean-François Prud'homme, " Quebec-Mexico Relationships: A New Partner," in *Quebec Under Free Trade: Making Public Policy in North America,* ed. Guy Lachapelle (Sainte-Foy: Presses de l'université du Québec, 1995), p. 112.

58. Ministère des Affaires internationales, *Plan d'action Québec-Mexique,* Québec City, 1993.

59. *Ibid.*

60. Studer and Prud'homme, "Quebec-Mexico Relations," p. 112.

61. Vilaysoun Loungnarath, "L'incidence de l'accord du libre-échange Canada-États-Unis sur le développement de la paradiplomatie provinciale," *La revue juridique Thémis* 26/3.

62. *Ibid.,* p. 313.

63. *Ibid.,* pp. 318–20.

64. *Ibid.,* p. 322.

65. See Earl Fry, "Quebec's Sovereignty Movement And Its Implication For the American Economy," *Canada Watch* 5/1, Centre for Public Law and Public Policy and Robarts Centre for Canadian Studies, York University (September/October 1996), p. 17; Christopher Sands, "The American National Interest in Quebec and Canada," *Canada Watch 5/1,* p. 19; Jockel, *Washington,* pp. 14, 15, and 24.

66. See in particular the widely distributed government documentation: Gouvernement du Québec *Guide de participation aux Commissions sur l'avenir du Québec,* 1995, pp. 11–12; Gouvernement du Québec, *Le commerce avec un Québec souverain: les États-Unis favorisent la continuité,* Québec, Secrétariat à la Restructuration, May 1995; Gouvernement du Québec, *Projet de loi sur l'avenir du Québec,* 1995, p. 15 (sec. 15). The government also made much of a study by Rogers and Wells according to which the United States would apply to the membership of an independent Québec in NAFTA the rule of "presumption of succession" without clearly specifying that this rule would apply only during the transitional period between

accession to sovereignty and Québec's formal admission, following negotiations, as a party to the Agreement. See David W. Bernstein and William Silverman, *Advisory Memorandum Regarding the Effect of Independence of Quebec Upon Treaties and Agreements with the United States of America* (New York: Rogers and Wells, March 7, 1995).

67. See Bernstein and Silverman, *Advisory Memorandum*, pp. 8–11 and Ivan Bernier, *La dimension juridique des relations commerciales d'un Québec souverain*, a study prepared for the Institut national de la recherche scientifique, 1995, pp. 46–47.

68. On the eve of the last referendum, a White House spokesperson said with regard to the admission of an independent Québec to NAFTA: "It is impossible to answer this question with certainty before the referendum, but membership would not be automatic" (adaptation). Quoted in Marie Tisson, "Clinton s'affiche clairement pour un Canada Uni," *La Presse*, 26 October 1995, p. B4. See also comments by one of President Clinton's economic advisors reported in Canadian Press, "Un Québec souverain accéderait à l'ALÉNA par les mécanismes prévus," *Le Devoir*, 26 March 1995, p. B3.

69. Studer and Prud'homme, *"Quebec-Mexico Relations,"* p. 122.

70. U.S. State Department, *Transcript*, 8 October 1995.

71. Today, the Agence de la Francophonie has forty-nine full members, of whom three are participating governments (the French community of Belgium, Canada-New Brunswick, and Canada-Quebec).

72. See James Mayall, "Non-intervention, Self-determination and the New World Order," *International Affairs* 67/3 (1991), pp. 421–29; Gidon Gottlieb, "Nations Without State," *Foreign Affairs* 73/3 (May/June 1994), pp. 100–12.

Entre la discorde
et l'indifférence
le Québec, le Nouveau-Brunswick et la
Francophonie internationale

CHEDLY BELKHODJA

Département de science politique
Université de Moncton

Nombreux travaux ont fait part des notes discordantes entre le gouverne-ment fédéral et le Québec en ce qui concerne la place acquise par cette province au sein de la Francophonie internationale[1]. En revanche, on connaît peu de chose quant à la teneur des relations entre les deux gou-vernements canadiens, membres participants de l'Agence de la Francopho-nie, le Québec et le Nouveau-Brunswick. Depuis 1970, le Québec a obtenu le statut particulier de gouvernement participant au sein de l'Agence de la Fran-cophonie, statut octroyé au Nouveau-Brunswick en 1977. La participation d'acteurs non souverains au sein de cette organisation internationale con-stitue un caractère original mais aussi une source de tension pour un État fédéral comme le Canada.

La présente étude se propose de cerner les rapports entre le Québec et la province du Nouveau-Brunswick dans le contexte de leur engagement au sein de la Francophonie institutionnelle[2]. Par des routes différentes, ces deux provinces francophones ont su définir un champ d'action international. Depuis les années soixante, le Québec a été fort présent dans le processus de consolidation de la Francophonie naissante. Dans la gestion de ce dossier, le pouvoir provincial a toujours privilégié une approche spécifique considérant sa personnalité unique en tant que foyer principal de la langue française en

Amérique du nord et sa légitimité d'agir sans la médiation du gouvernement central. Pour sa part, le Nouveau-Brunswick a adopté une attitude plus réservée à proximité de la position du Canada en tant qu'acteur de la francophonie canadienne.

Dans le contexte politique canadien, la méfiance entre le Québec et les provinces minoritaires francophones l'a souvent emporté, provoquant des conjonctures difficiles. Il est juste d'affirmer que le Québec s'est parfois senti agacé par la présence du Nouveau-Brunswick dans les instances de la Francophonie. Faut-il pour autant considérer, comme certains décideurs québécois l'ont pensé et dit, cette province comme étant à la solde de la thèse du gouvernement fédéral cherchant à banaliser la présence du Québec sur la scène internationale francophone? Dans cette recherche, nous cherchons à mieux saisir le rapport Québec/Nouveau-Brunswick tout en souhaitant nous dégager de cette lecture trop "nationale" et "politisée" des rapports entre les provinces canadiennes et le monde de la Francophonie. En souhaitant tenir compte des bouleversements globaux qui ont affecté les relations internationales, ne pourrait-on pas plutôt poser l'hypothèse de l'indifférence entre deux acteurs qui cherchent à se déplacer de façon autonome dans un nouvel espace d'opportunités de tout genre qu'est la Francophonie. Dans ce contexte, le Nouveau-Brunswick semble avoir une longueur d'avance par rapport au Québec dans le sens où il n'a pas de projet d'affirmation nationale.

Cette analyse reste exploratoire car le matériel étudié provient de sources principalement secondaires. Néanmoins quelques entrevues avec des personnes clefs de la scène politique de la francophonie ont permis de préciser certaines questions quant aux rapports entre les deux provinces. Dans un premier temps, il s'agit de présenter et de définir la place des provinces canadiennes comme acteurs sous-nationaux de la scène internationale. Ensuite, le parcours des deux provinces sera présenté de façon à voir les grandes différences entre le Québec et le Nouveau-Brunswick. Enfin, afin de répondre à notre hypothèse de travail concernant l'indifférence dans les relations entre le Québec et le Nouveau-Brunswick concernant la Francophonie.

La place des provinces canadiennes sur la scène internationale

Même si peu remarqué, plusieurs provinces canadiennes ont développé des relations extérieures. Il est intéressant de noter que les analyses de politique provinciale tendent à négliger cette dimension se limitant au rôle strictement national des provinces. Deux aspects portent à croire que la place des provinces canadiennes dans l'espace international est sujette à croître rapidement dans les années à venir. D'une part, le cadre particulier du fédéralisme canadien a toujours laissé un espace à conquérir aux unités fédérées. D'autre part, les bouleversements globaux comme la mondialisation ont pour effet d'internationaliser le rôle des provinces en tant qu'acteurs de la scène internationale.

Le fédéralisme

À la différence d'un État unitaire, le cadre fédéral offre un tableau différent en ce qui a trait aux relations extérieures. Les unités fédérées telles les provinces, les états ou les cantons sont amenées à développer des rapports avec l'environnement externe. Cette pratique peut parfois provoquer des tensions nationales concernant l'équilibre entre le pouvoir central, gardien du principe sacro-saint du monopole de la souveraineté nationale, et les unités fédérées[3]. Sur le plan juridique, la Constitution canadienne (AANB de 1867 et Loi constitutionnelle de 1982) n'évoque pas le rôle des provinces considérant que le fédéral assure la représentation de la souveraineté nationale. Selon Kim Richard Nossal: "As a consequence, the Constitution Acts, 1867-1982, remain as silent today as the original act was in 1867".[4] En fait, l'absence d'une règle écrite permet une pratique de coopération entre les deux paliers de pouvoir. On évoque alors le pragmatisme canadien qui doit refléter les traits particuliers d'un nouvel État en processus de construction nationale. C'est dans cette optique que s'instaure un partage de compétences entre le fédéral et les provinces, entre ce que les spécialistes de politique étrangère ont défini comme les domaines de *High* et de *Low Politics*[5]. Le gouvernement fédéral, l'unique porte parole de la fédération canadienne, détient le monopole de pouvoir de décision en politique étrangère et exerce le commandement des forces armées du pays. De leur côté, les provinces développent des relations moins symboliques mais tout aussi importantes dans plusieurs champs concomitants. Elles défendent particulièrement leurs intérêts dans les secteurs économique et environnemental[6]. Dans un contexte économique plus décentralisé, les provinces s'engagent volontairement aux côtés du fédéral dans la recherche de nouvelles opportunités économiques. On pense par exemple aux voyages d'affaires de l'Équipe Canada (Team Canada) en Asie du Sud-est, en Chine et au Mexique.

La mondialisation

Depuis les années soixante-dix, le monde des États s'est vu confronter à des logiques globales, notamment la crise du pétrole de 1973. Cette interdépendance croissante a annoncé une modification importante des relations internationales où l'acteur étatique est devenu plus conscient d'un processus de changement global. Comme l'explique James Rosenau, le paysage international de l'après-guerre froide ne se limite plus à la seule dimension étatique et doit dorénavant co-exister avec un univers multi-centrique, c'est à dire un monde où gravite une panoplie d'acteurs, soit les forces transnationales, les firmes multinationales, les villes, les régions[7].

De nos jours, réagir devant la mondialisation est devenu un passe-temps courant. Le débat intellectuel autour de cet enjeu est très présent dans nos sociétés, réduisant souvent la question à une opposition de visions : d'une part les partisans optimistes de l'ouverture des frontières et des marchés, d'autre part, les prédicateurs apocalyptiques affolés par les conséquences d'une érosion de l'espace territorial[8].

Il est difficile de dégager une définition de la mondialisation car celle-ci n'est qu'une dynamique en cours. De nos jours, définir la mondialisation, c'est en fait tenir compte d'un profond bouleversement dans les habitudes du cadre national à plusieurs niveaux. Premièrement, au niveau économique, on remarque un processus d'accélération des échanges qui modifie la nature de l'économie capitaliste classique, se transformant d'une économie structurée autour des échanges commerciaux entre pays à une économie mondialisée caractérisée par l'importance des flux financiers[9]. Deuxièmement, au niveau technologique, la mondialisation facilite la mise en place d'un univers sans frontières, se passant de la notion de temps[10]. Enfin, au niveau politique, plusieurs observateurs soulignent le dépassement de l'État-nation, cadre historique dorénavant confronté à l'émergence de nouvelles formes de solidarités transnationales et d'acteurs de toute sorte[11].

Dans notre cas, est-ce-que les provinces canadiennes ont la capacité de s'ajuster à ce nouveau contexte international? Selon Louis Bélanger: "les conditions d'exercice d'une province peuvent être affectées par les transformations actuelles de la scène internationale[12]". Une chose est certaine, le rapprochement entre le local, le national et le global bouleverse le cadre classique de l'activité économique des provinces. Dans le village global, les provinces sont en mesure de participer activement car l'impératif territorial perd de son importance au profit de relations transnationales. Comme d'autres provinces, le Québec et le Nouveau-Brunswick investissent beaucoup dans de nouvelles activités qui tendent à déborder le cadre géographique. Depuis le début des années 1990, le Nouveau-Brunswick, par exemple, a misé beaucoup sur les secteurs des nouvelles technologies et du tourisme. Comme nous le verrons, le Québec se lance également dans "l'univers des réseaux" mais se distingue par maintenir intact le projet de reconnaissance de la souveraineté nationale. Cette logique territoriale de la diplomatie québécoise ne colle plus à la réalité de la mondialisation.

De façon générale, en ce qui concerne le domaine des relations internationales, les provinces canadiennes ne cherchent pas à prendre le dessus sur le gouvernement central en préférant plutôt développer des liens économiques avec l'étranger, principalement les états américains frontaliers[13]. Le cas particulier de la Francophonie va dans un sens à l'encontre de ce principe en raison de la volonté politique d'une province déterminée à se propulser sur la scène internationale par le biais de ce nouveau forum.

Les provinces canadiennes et la Francophonie internationale

La Francophonie institutionnelle est une grande famille en expansion, constituée de cinquante-deux membres et environ 400 millions d'individus ayant en commun le français comme langue de partage. Cette organisation émerge à la fin des années soixante, lorsque plusieurs États africains se décident de consolider leurs aspirations post-coloniales au sein d'une organisation internationale. À noter que la Francophonie prend racine en Afrique même, la France préférant se tenir à l'écart en raison du passé colonial et d'un désaccord quant à la dimension multilatérale souhaitée par les pays du sud. Contrairement au Commonwealth qui rassemble les anciens dominions britanniques, dès sa naissance, la Francophonie apparaît tel un espace à construire. Plusieurs aspects de cette organisation sont novateurs: d'une part, la nouvelle organisation se réunit autour du principe unificateur de la langue française, d'autre part, elle va permettre à des acteurs non souverains sur le plan du droit international de participer aux travaux de l'organisme. En 1970 (Niamey II), le Québec a obtenu le statut de gouvernement participant, statut qui a été accordé au Nouveau-Brunswick en 1977. D'autres provinces comme l'Ontario et le Manitoba ont également eu la possibilité de s'impliquer dans l'organisation sans pour autant aspirer à un statut comparable. Le parcours des deux provinces "canadiennes" participantes doit être brièvement présenté car il met en présence des trajectoires particulières.

Le Québec : la quête d'un État souverain

Depuis la Révolution tranquille en 1960, il existe une constance dans la politique québécoise qui consiste à valoriser le projet de la construction nationale. Dès lors, la scène internationale est devenu un espace privilégié afin de définir une personnalité distincte de celle du Canada. Micheal Keating distingue trois fondements dans l'institutionnalisation d'un espace extérieur pour l'État québécois[14]. Premièrement, plus que tout autre province au pays, le Québec a le désir de s'affirmer souverain à l'extérieur de ses frontières. Un important dispositif diplomatique sous-tend le projet international du Québec, dont notamment une représentation à l'extérieur des frontières et de nombreuses ententes signées avec des États souverains. En 1988, afin de s'ajuster au nouvel ordre international, le gouvernement québécois a créé le Ministère des Affaires internationales. Deuxièmement, dans le cadre de la politique du libre-échange et de la globalisation des marchés, le Québec a accordé une dimension de plus en plus importante aux échanges et investissements économiques à l'étranger, principalement avec les États-Unis, 6e partenaire commercial qui absorbe plus de quatre-vingt pourcent des exportations du Québec. Enfin, la promotion de la spécificité culturelle québécoise à l'étranger a fait partie d'un projet à la fois économique et identitaire de défense de l'univers francophone considéré sous la menace du marché américain.

Dans le cadre de son engagement dans la Francophonie, le Québec développe rapidement une position d'autonomie estimant que la province représente la spécificité francophone en Amérique du Nord. Depuis l'allocution du ministre de l'Éducation Paul Guérin-Lajoie, en 1965, aux divers énoncés de principe du Ministère des affaires internationales, la Francophonie apparaît pour le peuple québécois tel un espace vital et essentiel où la province doit prendre des initiatives:

L'appartenance du Québec à la francophonie relève d'une nécessité vitale. Notre situation géographique nord-américaine risque constamment de mettre en péril notre spécificité culturelle qui a survécu et s'est développée depuis plus de quatre cents ans.[15]

D'après Louis Bélanger, la Francophonie constitue une voix d'accès vers l'universel: "En raison de sa valeur symbolique, la participation du Québec à la francophonie est indissociable de l'évolution des modes d'articulation de l'identité québécoise. Elle permet d'inscrire l'affirmation identitaire québécoise dans une perspective plutôt universaliste que particulariste."[16] Dans la façon de mener le dossier, la province prend les devants et décide d'agir seule en interprétant la Constitution canadienne qui lui permet de lier des ententes internationales dans certains domaines de compétence, notamment l'éducation et la culture. En 1968, au Gabon, la province reçoit une invitation officielle et directe à participer à une conférence réunissant des ministres francophones de l'éducation. Dans le contexte international de l'époque, le Québec s'inscrit dans la mouvance de la décolonisation, ce qui lui permet de nouer des liens fraternels avec les anciennes colonies françaises d'Afrique et la France. Par conséquent, la quête d'un statut souverain apparaît légitime car elle s'inscrit dans un discours nationaliste émancipé et légitime. Il faut également noter que la réalité canadienne est peu connue en Afrique et que la France se fait le porte-parole de la cause de la souveraineté sur le continent. À ce chapitre, comme nous le verrons plus loin, il est intéressant de constater que la lecture changera radicalement après la fin de la guerre froide.

La Francophonie multilatérale devient rapidement un enjeu de discorde entre le gouvernement fédéral et le Québec. Ce qui gène Ottawa, c'est que le Québec agit de façon quasi-souveraine dans ses relations extérieures. La logique territoriale du gouvernement québécois modifie sensiblement les pratiques du passé caractérisées par des relations entre les francophones au sein de diverses associations issues d'un réseau traditionnel. Devant la montée d'un mouvement nationaliste québécois revendicateur, Ottawa décide de réagir afin de réduire la visibilité québécoise au sein du monde francophone. Dans la politique fédérale, deux critères sont nettement valorisés. Premièrement, en s'inscrivant dans la lignée du rapport de la Commission Laurendeau-Dunton et de la Loi sur les langues officielles de 1969, le Canada en tant que pays bilingue cherche à donner une voix à l'autre réalité francophone, soit celles des minorités francophones établies dans plusieurs provinces. Les grands rassemblements de la Francophonie sont donc des lieux propices où dévoiler l'expérience canadienne. Deuxièmement, afin de se dégager de l'enclave américaine, le gouvernement libéral cherche à accroître les rapports multilatéraux en politique étrangère. La Francophonie comme le Commonwealth, l'OTAN et l'ONU sont donc des forums internationaux où le Canada doit jouer un rôle de taille[17].

La réaction du Québec sera vive. On accuse le fédéral de faire de la Francophonie un enjeu national et, par conséquent, de réduire, voir banaliser la visibilité québécoise. Dans cette perspective, le gouvernement québécois voit d'un mauvais œil la participation "orchestrée" des provinces, comme celle du Nouveau-Brunswick.

Le Nouveau-Brunswick : un pragmatisme à saveur fédéraliste

Le Nouveau-Brunswick présente une autre réalité francophone constituée dans un milieu minoritaire. Avant les années soixante, les gouvernements qui ont succédé au pouvoir n'ont pas véritablement considéré le fait francophone. Ce qui existe néanmoins est la vitalité d'un réseau associatif francophone en retrait de la politique reposant sur des institutions traditionnelles telles la Société Nationale de l'Acadie (SNA) fondée en 1881. À l'extérieur des frontières, le peuple acadien est reconnu et représenté par des associations comme le Conseil de la vie française en Amérique et l'Ordre de Jacques Cartier[18]. En 1960, l'arrivée au pouvoir d'un premier ministre acadien n'a pas bouleversé le paysage politique mais a annoncé la reconnaissance politique de la communauté acadienne au niveau provincial et un désir d'institutionnaliser des rapports déjà existants entre cette communauté et le monde francophone, particulièrement la France. Plusieurs étapes marquent l'évolution des rapports entre le Nouveau-Brunswick et le monde de la Francophonie. Il ne s'agit pas ici de faire l'étude descriptive du parcours mais plutôt de retenir trois aspects, à nos yeux, déterminants[19].

D'abord, en ce qui concerne les relations avec le monde francophone, le contexte néo-brunswickois présente une situation assez différente de celle du Québec, caractérisée par une dualité ou dédoublement de la "personnalité internationale". Au Québec, même si le gouvernement Lesage (1960–1966) éprouve quelques difficultés à réduire la visibilité des acteurs traditionnels, le processus de construction nationale s'est fait sous la seule autorité de l'État et non du monde des associations. Comme nous l'avons mentionné, pendant longtemps, la communauté acadienne se trouve représentée par un réseau associatif structuré et non par le gouvernement provincial. C'est au nom du Peuple acadien que les premiers rapprochements s'établissent avec l'étranger, par le biais d'un réseau, notamment le Conseil de la vie française en Amérique qui sert de courroie de transmission. Durant les années soixante, le gouvernement Robichaud cherchait à réduire la portée symbolique du rôle d'une association telle la SNA à l'étranger, légitimée par ses relations bilatérales étroites avec la France[20]. À plusieurs reprises, le premier ministre doit croiser le fer avec cette association, considérant que la SNA abuse de son pouvoir de porte parole de l'Acadie[21]. Cette situation a évolué rapidement avec la volonté de Fredericton de normaliser les relations franco-acadiennes et de s'activer au niveau de la francophonie internationale.

Deuxièmement, le gouvernement provincial adopte un pragmatisme politique dicté par des impératifs à la fois externe et interne. En janvier 1969, en vacances en Tanzanie, Louis Robichaud a accepté de présider la délégation canadienne à la conférence des ministres de l'éducation francophones au Congo-Kinshasa[22]. Fédéraliste convaincu, Louis Robichaud répond à l'appel de Trudeau: "Si je pouvais rendre des services aux grands principes de la francophonie à l'intérieur du Canada, j'allais servir même si je servais d'outil ... mais j'étais celui qui maniait l'outil."[23] Les actions pragmatiques et ponctuelles de Robichaud reposent sur trois principes : assurer sa juridiction dans les domaines relevant de l'autorité gouvernementale, accepter le principe de banaliser la place internationale du Québec et développer les structures gouvernementales de sa province. Le facteur Québec est omniprésent et, selon Roger Ouellette et Philippe Doucet, Robichaud: "espérait que les relations culturelles internationales du Nouveau-Brunswick amenuiseraient quelque peu l'éclat des relations France-Québec.[24]" Comme le rappelle le sous-ministre de l'éducation, Armand St-Onge, présent à ces réunions, Robichaud considère que sa province a toutes les raisons légitimes de siéger à ces conférences internationales traitant de l'éducation. D'une part, le Nouveau-Brunswick est la seule province canadienne bilingue ayant reconnue les deux langues officielles au pays. D'autre part, le premier ministre croit en ces moments de rassemblement entre les peuples, qui visent à réduire les inégalités et les injustices[25]. En revanche, ce qui énerve le Nouveau-Brunswick et les autres provinces minoritaires est le manque de direction accordée par le fédéral aux provinces qui trouvent la situation parfois frustrante: "Nous sommes fatiguées d'être traitées telles des marionnettes. Nous sommes fatiguées d'aller à ces conférences pour l'unique raison que le Québec y soit. Nous y allons pas seulement en tant que fédéralistes mais parce qu'il y a du travail intéressant à accomplir.[26]". Durant les années soixante-dix Richard Hatfield s'est retranché également derrière Ottawa qui a invité fortement le Nouveau-Brunswick à se faire reconnaître en tant que gouvernement participant au sein de l'Agence de la Francophonie[27]. La demande néo-brunswickoise s'est fait sans grand tapage médiatique, ce qui a laissé supposer une stratégie politique timide afin de ne pas éveiller à la fois la susceptibilité de la majorité anglophone et des organismes acadiens. Depuis l'époque Robichaud, Fredericton a en effet souvent utilisé l'argument de la réaction anglophone au progrès de la cause acadienne "backlash". De nos entretiens, ce qui se dégage est plutôt une sorte d'indifférence de la population anglophone peu informée du projet.

Enfin, à partir de 1987, Fredericton a développé une stratégie plus précise quant à son action internationale. La province commence à considérer l'intérêt à élargir son champ de compétences au sein de la Francophonie, qui passe dans un premier temps par l'amélioration de l'appareil francophone au sein de la fonction publique. Premier geste de taille, le nouveau gouvernement dirigé par le libéral Frank McKenna créé le Ministère des affaires intergouvernementales, chargé de gérer le dossier de la Francophonie auparavant rattaché au bureau du premier ministre[28]. La lecture des rapports annuels permet de définir une ligne de conduite plus claire par rapport à la Francophonie. En se référant à l'article 3.3. de la Charte de l'ACCT, la province intervient de plein droit dans les secteurs considérés prioritaires, notamment l'éducation, la formation technique et professionnelle et les nouvelles technologies. Cet aspect se précise nettement à partir de 1995, lorsque que le gouvernement provincial développe une stratégie précise quant à sa participation au sommet de Cotonou en 1995:

> La tenue en décembre 1995, à Cotonou au Bénin, du Sommet des Chefs d'États et de gouvernements ayant le français en partage aura été l'un des événements majeurs de l'année dans les relations internationales du Nouveau-Brunswick. La province y a participé activement en fonction de trois priorités: les inforoutes, l'enseignement professionnel et technique ainsi que l'économie.[29]

Ce qui ressort cependant est la valorisation de la dimension économique au détriment du lien identitaire. Dans le discours du trône de 1988, le premier ministre Mckenna reconnaît: "l'importance de développer des liens économiques avec les pays du sommet de la Francophonie.[30]"

Depuis le début des années quatre-vingt-dix, l'espace de la francophonie constitue alors un lieu privilégié afin de conclure des affaires. Le gouvernement y voit des circonstances favorables afin de s'inscrire dans l'univers de la globalisation et des réseaux transnationaux. Bernard Thériault, ministre des affaires intergouvernementales et autochtones: "Notre participation à la Francophonie, qui s'inscrit dans le prolongement de la politique étrangère du Canada sur la scène internationale représente une occasion unique pour le Nouveau-Brunswick de se faire connaître, tant sur le plan économique que culturel et social, en démontrant notre savoir-faire et notre dynamisme "[31].

En novembre 1997, au sommet de Hanoï premier ministre par intérim, Raymond Frenette (Hanoi) va dans le même sens: "(...) l'idée même de pouvoir accueillir le sommet de la Francophonie en terre l'Acadie constitue une reconnaissance à l'égard de son dynamisme et de sa vitalité. Au-delà des mots, l'Acadie d'aujourd'hui vit au signe de l'ouverture, de partage et des échanges.[32]"

D'une approche pragmatique, limitée au secteur de l'éducation, le Nouveau-Brunswick a su se démarquer en développant une action internationale dans des secteurs de pointe tels les nouvelles technologies. un moyen de se dégager de la position fédéraliste. De définir un champ d'action au point de ne plus se sentir pris de l'engrenage national et paraître comme étant à la solde du fédéral.

Tensions à indifférences

Entre les provinces canadiennes, il existe généralement un fédéralisme de collaboration reposant sur des intérêts communs à atteindre. Depuis les années soixante, les provinces se sont rencontrées régulièrement dans le cadre des réunions des premiers ministres provinciaux et plusieurs ont signé des ententes de coopération, dont le Nouveau-Brunswick et le Québec en 1969. Les relations entre le Québec et le Nouveau-Brunswick concernant leur engagement au sein de la Francophonie ont néanmoins connu des moments de friction le plus souvent provoqués par la politique du gouvernement fédéral. Dans cette dernière section, il s'agit de faire un tour d'horizon des quelques accrochages entre les deux provinces et, ensuite, de considérer l'incidence que peut avoir des bouleversements globaux dans le rapport entre les deux acteurs provinciaux.

Dès son arrivée au pouvoir en 1968, le premier ministre Trudeau a souhaité voir les provinces francophones minoritaires jouer un rôle aux cotés du gouvernement fédéral. En 1969, le fait que le gouvernement Robichaud a présidé la délégation canadienne a apparu tel un compromis acceptable pour le Québec qui a obtenu la vice-présidence, se sentant pas pour autant tenu de suivre les consignes d'Ottawa. Ce qui s'est produit lors de ces rencontres, à savoir des histoires de querelles de drapeaux et de rendez-vous manqués, peut paraître de l'ordre de l'insignifiant. Selon Robichaud, il faut y voir cependant la détérioration des rapports entre les deux paliers de pouvoir. Rapidement, Québec voit le rôle des autres provinces tel un moyen de marginaliser sa place prépondérante au sein de l'Agence de Coopération Culturelle et Technique (ACCT) et tend par conséquent à déconsidérer le Nouveau-Brunswick. Selon Armand St-Onge:

> Le Québec nous a toujours vu, dès ces premières conférences et tout au long de ces conférences auxquelles j'ai assisté, comme des encadreurs, des agents du fédéral. Cela nous a pas empêcher de se parler amicalement, mais disons, dans la pensée officielle du Québec, nous étions des gens qui encadraient, des espions du fédéral. Ils ne se gênaient pas pour nous le dire: "vous êtes ici comme des petits accompagnateurs".[33]

En 1977, au lendemain de la victoire du Parti québécois aux élections provinciales de 1976, un durcissement des rapports entre le Québec et le gouvernement fédéral a placé le Nouveau-Brunswick dans une situation difficile. Le Nouveau-Brunswick a obtenu le même statut de gouvernement participant à la Francophonie, ce qui provoque une réaction du Québec qui y voyait principalement encore une manigance politique de Trudeau. Il est intéressant de noter la façon dont laquelle le Québec va reconnaître l'adhésion de la province acadienne toute en marginalisant la place du gouvernement Hatfield. Dans le contexte de la Francophonie, il apparaît évident que le Québec ne cherche pas à légitimer le gouvernement "anglophone" de Fredericton de sorte à garder un rôle unique au sein de l'organisation. Le Québec prétend être le seul gouvernement francophone et rappelle aussi que son cheminement au sein de la Francophonie s'est fait par une "haute lutte" dans un contexte difficile d'hostilité de la part des autorités fédérales[34]. Il y a tout de même dans la presse québécoise et dans le discours officiel le désir de reconnaître le parcours du peuple acadien allant jusqu'à garantir sa protection. Le ministre québécois des affaires intergouvernementales, Claude Morin accueille favorablement le "gouvernement participant de l'Acadie": "(...) il paraissait en effet important d'établir une distinction entre le Nouveau-Brunswick et l'Acadie, tout en montrant qu'à la vérité l'arrivée des Acadiens dans l'ACCT était directement reliée à l'action extérieure du Québec.[35]" En fait, l'accent mis sur la notion de peuple et communauté acadiens permet au Québec de diluer la notion de souveraineté étatique attachée au statut de gouvernement participant. Au Nouveau-Brunswick, la Société des Acadiens et Acadiennes du Nouveau-Brunswick (SAANB) et encore plus vigoureusement le Parti nationaliste acadien (PA) tiennent un discours proche de la thèse québécoise, considérant la place du Québec au sein de la Francophonie plus légitime que le gouvernement de Fredericton. On accuse surtout le gouvernement Hatfield de ne pas tenir compte des revendications de la communauté acadienne et le gouvernement fédéral de se servir de la communauté acadienne dans leur opposition au nationalisme québécois[36].

L'attitude québécoise envers le Nouveau-Brunswick peu paraître ambivalente dans le sens où Québec utilise les deux registres afin de se donner un espace politique: d'une part, il vise à agir en tant qu'État souverain lorsqu'il s'agit des rapports avec l'étranger, mais d'autre part, devant les minorités francophones nationales, il exploite certains mythes traditionnels, par exemple, la nation canadienne française protectrice des minorités francophones à travers le pays. Dans le cadre de la Francophonie, le Québec se perçoit plus légitime que le gouvernement fédéral et tente alors de rassembler les minorités francophones du pays.

Ce qui ressort assez clairement de ces épisodes, c'est que les rapports entre les deux provinces évoluent au détriment du contexte politique national et de la conjoncture partisane en place. Pendant le règne des libéraux à Ottawa et des péquistes à Québec, la tension était forte. Elle a diminué considérablement entre Brian Mulroney et Robert Bourassa. Durant les années quatre-vingt, le triangle Ottawa-Québec-Fredericton a connu en effet une période d'accalmie facilitant l'accommodation. En 1985, lors de la tenue du premier Sommet de la Francophonie réunissant les Chefs d'États des pays francophones, le gouvernement Mulroney a opté pour une stratégie de conciliation, appliquant la même règle au Québec et au Nouveau-Brunswick. Les deux provinces agissaient en tant que participants actifs dans les secteurs leur revenant, soit la coopération culturelle et le développement international. Depuis le retour du Parti québécois au pouvoir, en 1994, la diplomatie québécoise s'est rapprochée "de la doctrine traditionnelle développée au cours des années 1960 à 1980"[37]. Par conséquent, il est logique de remarquer une détérioration des rapports entre Ottawa et Québec.

Le contexte externe offre un tout autre aperçu de l'état des relations entre les deux provinces. En considérant l'évolution de la scène internationale, trois éléments peuvent influencer l'action des provinces canadiennes. Ce qui nous paraît intéressant est le fait que ces mutations sont en train de modifier sensiblement la lecture auparavant favorable à l'endroit de la diplomatie québécoise.

Le premier, plus spécifique à l'évolution de la Francophonie, est la volonté de politiser l'organisation pour en faire un forum international plus crédible. Au dernier sommet à Hanoi, l'agence a cautionné un vaste processus de politisation souhaité par le premier secrétaire élu, le diplomate égyptien Boutros-Boutros Ghali. À l'image du Commonwealth, La Francophonie doit, par exemple, se pencher sur les enjeux tels les processus de transition démocratiques et la protection des droits de la personne. Une conséquence importante de ce nouveau virage est la possibilité de voir les acteurs non étatiques être marginalisés au profit d'un retour des États. C'est d'ailleurs la grande crainte du Québec car les questions strictement politiques mettent au devant de la scène les États nationaux et non les provinces[38]. Pour sa part, le Nouveau-Brunswick ne se sent pas véritablement concerné par ce débat préférant développer l'optique du marché dans son action internationale.

Le deuxième, depuis la fin de la guerre froide, la Francophonie a suivi de près l'évolution de la scène internationale, notamment ce que plusieurs observateurs avaient qualifié dans un premier temps de réveil démocratique à l'échelle planétaire visible par les processus de démocratisation en Amérique Latine, la fin du bloc communiste et l'abolition de l'apartheid en Afrique du sud. Cette interprétation rationnelle d'un processus d'émancipation a laissé rapidement place à un réveil plus douloureux caractérisé par la résurgence des expressions ethnique, religieuse et nationaliste. Devant cette ethnicisation du monde, nombreux membres de la Francophonie, auparavant favorables aux revendications nationalistes du Québec, sont nettement plus réservés quant à la place accordée à l'État provincial. La modification des lunettes conceptuelles en relations internationales peut donc nuire au Québec surtout dans un contexte international en proie à un amalgame rapide autour de la fragmentation. Comme le souligne Louis Bélanger, le Québec doit rappeler la spécificité de son nationalisme: "C'est la désagrégation d'une certaine structure cognitive présente au sein de fonctionnement des relations internationales et qui pourrait "sécuriser" un comportement atypique comme celui du Québec qui soulève le plus grand défi.[39]"

Enfin, la mondialisation définit un nouveau contexte politique plus favorable aux unités non centrales. Le Nouveau-Brunswick représente ce que Micheal Keating appelle des collectivités sous-nationales: "qui n'ont pas de base territoriale déterminée et dont les structures institutionnelles ne correspondent pas à une structuration étatique[40]". Il faudrait aller plus loin et distinguer entre des unités qui projettent une volonté d'affirmation nationale et des acteurs peu portés par cet enjeu.

Conclusion

Dans cette recherche, nous avons cherché à mieux cerner les rapports entre le Nouveau-Brunswick et le Québec dans le contexte de leur participation à la Francophonie. Ce qui se dégage de notre étude, c'est que la vision fondamentalement opposée entre les deux gouvernements participants lorsque le Québec cherche à obtenir une légitimité nationale sur la scène internationale. Dès le début des années soixante-dix, Ottawa a réagi à la situation nouvelle d'une province plus nationaliste qui cherche à profiter de sa visibilité dans l'espace francophone afin de consolider le projet politique de la souveraineté. Encore aujourd'hui, l'affirmation d'une personnalité internationale québécoise déplaît au fédéral. Dans un sens, le Québec est prisonnier de cette logique nationaliste qui caractérise plutôt l'attitude d'un État-nation et non celle d'une province. Pour sa part, le Nouveau-Brunswick a opté pour une approche pragmatique, au départ peu structurée, mais qui au fil des années s'est consolidée et s'est définie surtout autour des considérations économiques. Depuis les années quatre-vingt-dix, la province s'inscrit dans la mondialisation, développant ainsi une expertise auprès des États francophones. Par conséquent, le Nouveau-Brunswick semble s'éloigner de ce débat national mais doit en faire les frais lorsque les choses vont mal.

NOTES

1. Se référer aux travaux de Paul Painchaud (sous la dir.), *Le Canada et le Québec sur la scène internationale*, Montréal, Presses de l'Université Laval, 1977; Louis Balthazar, Louis Bélanger, Gordon Mace et coll., *Trente ans de politique extérieure du Québec, 1960–1990*, Québec, Centre québécois de relations internationales/Édition du Septentrion, 1993.

2. Dans cette recherche, on se limite à la Francophonie institutionnelle réunissant des États et des gouvernements participants aux diverses instances de l'organisation, soit les Sommets des Chefs d'États et de Gouvernement, l'Agence de la Coopération Technique et Culturelle (ACCT), la Conférence des Ministres de l'Éducation (Confemen), et la Conférence des Ministres de la Jeunesse et des Sports (Confeges).

3. William H. Riker, *Federalism: Origin, Operation, Significance*, Boston, Little Brown, 1964.

4. Kim Richard Nossal, "Anything But Provincial: The Provinces and Foreign Affairs", dans Christopher Dunn, *Provinces: Canadian Provincial Politics*, Peterborough, Broadview Press, 1996, p. 505.

5. Voir Ivo D. Duchacek, "Perforated Sovereignties: Towards a Typology of New Actors in International Relations", dans H.J. Michelmann et Panayotis Soldatos, *Federalism and International Relations: The Role of Subnational Units*, Oxford, Clarendon Press, 1990, p. 1–33.

6. Kim Richard Nossal, *op.cit.*, p. 507–510.

7. James Rosenau, *Turbulence in World Politics: A Theory of Change and Continuity*, Princeton, Princeton University Press, 1990.

8. Nombreux ouvrages ont abordé la question de façon polémique. Certains considèrent la mondialisation telle un processus favorable à l'accroissement logique des échanges économiques et à l'émergence d'une société internationale cosmopolite. D'autres y voient les malheurs d'une croissance effrénée, de la perte du sentiment national, voire de la disparition des États-nations. Pour un aperçu de ce débat intellectuel, se référer aux analyses suivantes: Guy SORMAN, *Le monde est ma tribu*, 1997; Serge LATOUCHE, *La mégamachine*, 1995; Ignacio RAMONET, *Géopolitique du chaos*, 1997; Paul VIRILIO, *Cybermonde: la politique du pire*, 1997.

9. Susan Strange, *The Retreat of the State: The Diffusion of Power in the World Economy*, Cambridge, Cambridge University Press, 1996.

10. Zaki Laïdi, "Espace et vitesse à l'heure de la mondialisation, *Politique étrangère*, printemps 1996, p. 179–190.

11. Bertrand Badie et Marie-Claire Smouts, *Le retournement du monde: Sociologie de la scène internationale*, Paris, Presses de la Fondation nationale des sciences politiques, 1992.

12. Louis Bélanger, "L'espace international de l'État québécois dans l'après-guerre froide : vers une compression? ", dans Alain Gagnon et Alain Noël, *L'espace québécois*, Québec/Amérique, 1995, p. 71.

13. Ivo Duchacek, *op.cit.*

14. Micheal Keating, *Nations Against the State. The New Politics of Nationalism in Quebec, Catalonia and Scotland*, New York, St-Martin's Press, 1996, p. 103.

15. Ministère des Affaires internationales du Québec, *Le Québec dans la francophonie: les priorités.* adresse: <<http://www.mri.gouv.qc.ca/dans_le_monde/francophonie/francophonie_quebec_fr.html>>

16. Louis Bélanger, "Les enjeux actuels de la participation du Québec à la Francophonie multilatérale: de la paradiplomatie à la protodiplomatie", *Politique et Sociétés*, vol. 16, no. 1, 1997, p. 39–59.

17. Janice Gross Stein, "Living with Uncertainty: Canada and the Architecture of the New World Order", *International Journal*, XLVIII, été 1992, p. 614-629.

18. Marcel Martel, *Le Deuil d'un pays imaginé: rêves, luttes et déroute de Canada français*, Ottawa, Presses de l'Université d'Ottawa, 1997.

19. Pour une analyse historique de l'engagement du Nouveau-Brunswick au sein de la Francophonie, consulter: Michel Saint-Louis et Roger Ouellette, "L'Acadie et le Nouveau-Brunswick sur la scène internationale: de l'improvisation à la plannification, *Égalité*, 1989, p. 53–71.

20. On se rappelle de la fameuse visite de quatre représentants acadiens à Paris, officiellement invités par le général de Gaulle à l'Élysée.

21. Dans un entretien, Robert Pichette rappelle l'affaire d'un don important de livres par la France à l'Acadie. Dans l'esprit du programme de Chances égales pour tous, le gouvernement Robichaud entend gérer ce don plutôt que de le laisser entre les mains de la SNA. Entretien avec Robert Pichette, le 9 septembre 1998. Se référer également à l'ouvrage de Robert Pichette, *L'Acadie par bonheur retrouvée*, Moncton, Éditions d'Acadie, 1996.

22. Consulter la thèse de doctorat de Thomas Allen Levy, *Some Aspects of the Role of the Canadian Provinces in External Affairs : A Study in Canadian Federalism,* thèse de doctorat (science politique), Durham, Duke University, 1974.

23. Entretien avec Louis-J. Robichaud, le 29 août 1998.

24. Philippe Doucet et Roger Ouellette, "L'évolution de la structures des agences gouvernementales au Nouveau-Brunswick: 1960–90", *Administration publique du Canada*, 36, 1, printemps 1993, p. 28.

25. Entretien avec Armand St-Onge, le 25 août 1998.

26. Notre traduction, Thomas Allen Levy, *op.cit.,* p. 443.

27. "N.B. Gets Ottawa's Blessing To Seek Government Status", *Telegraph Journal*, 15 décembre 1997.

28. Philippe Doucet et Roger Ouellette, "L'évolution de la structures des agences gouvernementales au Nouveau-Brunswick: 1960–90", *Administration publique du Canada*, 36, 1, printemps 1993, p. 24–37.

29. Ministère des Affaires intergouvenementales et Autochtones, *Rapport annuel*, Frederciton, 1996. Document disponible à l'adresse internet <<http://inter.gov.nb.ca/iga/rapan97/partie19697.htm>>

30. Cité dans Michel St-Louis et Roger Ouellette, *op.cit.,* p. 65.

31. Ministère des Affaires Intergouvernementales et Autochtones, *Communiqué: Participation du N.-B. au Sommet de Hanoï*, Fredericton, le 6 novembre 1997. Document disponible à l'adresse internet <<http://inter.gov.nb.ca/cnb/newsf/iga/7f1795ig.htm>>

32. Raymond Frenette, discours prononcé à Hanoï lors du septième Sommet de la Francophonie, le 16 novembre 1997 <<http://www.sommet97.org/communique/frenette.htm>>

33. Entretien avec Armand St-Onge, le 25 août 1998.

34. Lise Bissonnette, "L'Acadie deviendrait gouvernement participant", *Le Devoir*, 7 décembre 1977.

35. Claude Morin, *L'art de l'impossible. La diplomatie québécoise depuis 1960*, Montréal, Boréal, 1987. p. 246.

36. Robert Poirier, "La SANB demande la non-reconnaissance du gouvernement du Nouveau-Brunswick", *L'Évangéline*, le 13 décembre 1977; "Le Parti Acadien est indigné par les événements d'Abidjan", *L'Évangéline*, 17 décembre 1977.

37. Louis Bélanger, *op.cit.*, 1995, p. 96.

38. Tout récemment le problème s'est posé concernant la visite officielle au Canada du Secrétaire générale de la Francophonie, Boutros Boutros-Ghali. Le prétexte utilisé par Ottawa, c'est que le Secrétaire général de l'Agence de la Francophonie est reçu au titre analogue de chef d'État. Globe and Mail, 9 septembre 1998.

39. *Ibid.*, p. 76.

40. Cité dans Serge Latouche, "Le Canada et le Québec à l'heure de la globalisation et de l'incertitude" dans Alain G. Gagnon et Alain Noël, *op.cit.*, p. 62.

Contributors

LOUIS BÉLANGER is an assistant professor in the Department of Political Science at Université Laval. His latest book, co-edited with Gordon Mace, is entitled *The Americas in Transition: The Contours of Regionalism* (Lynn Rienner Publ., forth). Professor Bélanger is also co-editor of the academic *Journal Études Internationales*.

CHEDLY BELKHODJA is assistant professor in the Department of Political Science at the Université de Moncton. His main topic of research is populism, political parties, and new forms of political mobilization. He is also interested in the place of Canada and the provinces in *la Francophonie*.

RAYMOND B. BLAKE, formerly the director of the Centre for Canadian Studies at Mount Allison University, is now the director of the Saskatchewan Institute of Public Policy at the University of Regina. He has a volume forthcoming from the CIIA/Irwin Publishing series on Canadian fisheries policy.

MICHAEL BONSER is a Master's student in the Department of Political Science at Acadia University. He has worked in Ottawa as an assistant to an MP. Most recently he worked with the Bangladesh Institute of Human Rights.

P.E. BRYDEN is head of the Department of History at Mount Allison University. She specializes in 20th-century Canadian public policy history, and is author of *Planners and Politicians: Liberal Politics and Social Policy, 1957-1963* (McGill-Queen's University Press, 1997).

KEN COATES is the dean of arts and a member of the Department of History and Political Science, University of New Brunswick at Saint John. He has written primarily in the field of Northern Canadian history, native-newcomer relations, and indigenous rights in world history. His most recent publication, with P.G. Mc Hugh, is *Living Relationships: The Treaty of Waitangi in the New Millennium* (Wellington: Victoria University Press, 1998).

MARSHALL CONLEY, professor of political science, Acadia University teaches courses on human rights, international organization, peace studies and Canadian foreign policy. He is the author of over 100 publications and professional papers.

GEORGE J. DE BENEDETTI is professor of economics at Mount Allison University.

LOUIS A. DELVOIE is a retired Canadian diplomat. He is now Skelton-Clark fellow and adjunct professor in the Department of Political Studies at Queen's University.

PETER DESBARATS is a journalist and retired academic living in London, Ontario. From 1981 to 1997 he was dean of the Graduate School of Journalism at the University of Western Ontario. He served as one of three commissioners of the Commission of Inquiry into the Deployment of Canadian Forces to Somalia and is the author of *Somalia Cover-Up—A Commissioner's Journal.*

DAVID B. DEWITT is professor of political science and, since 1988, has served as director of the Centre for International and Security Studies, York University, Toronto, Canada. He is author, editor and contributing author of numerous books and articles dealing with Canadian foreign, security, and defence policy, regional security and conflict management, security approaches in the Asia Pacific, security policies in the Middle East, arms control, and international security.

J.L. GRANATSTEIN taught history at York University for thirty years. He is now director and CEO of the Canadian War Museum in Ottawa, and he writes on Canadian national history, including foreign and defence policy.

FRANCES W. KAYE is a professor at the University of Nebraska-Lincoln. She was a Fulbright professor at the Universities of Calgary and Montreal and has published numerous articles and books on the cultural history of the Great Plains and Prairies.

DEAN F. OLIVER is senior historian at the Canadian War Museum. He also lectures at The Norman Paterson School of International Affairs and in the Department of Political Science, Carleton University. He is the foreign affairs and defence policy contributor to *The Canadian Annual Review of Politics and Public Affairs.*

DENIS STAIRS is McCullogh Professor of Political Science at Dalhousie University. A former president of the Canadian Political Science Association, he has served as Dalhousie's vice-president (academic and research). He specializes in Canadian foreign and defence policy, Canada-U.S. relations, and related subjects.

MICHAEL TUCKER is professor and head of the Department of Political Science at Mount Allison University. He has written extensively on Canadian foreign policy and Canadian arms control and disarmament policy.

Québec, Canada
2000